MW01194440

Trump's Triumph

Trump's Triumph

AMERICA'S GREATEST COMEBACK

NEWT GINGRICH

CENTER
STREET®

NEW YORK   NASHVILLE

Copyright © 2025 by Newt Gingrich

Cover design by Studio Gearbox.
Cover photography © Chip Somodevilla / Getty Images.
Cover copyright © 2025 by Hachette Book Group, Inc.

Hachette Book Group supports the right to free expression and the value of copyright. The purpose of copyright is to encourage writers and artists to produce the creative works that enrich our culture. The scanning, uploading, and distribution of this book without permission is a theft of the author's intellectual property. If you would like permission to use material from the book (other than for review purposes), please contact permissions@hbgusa.com. Thank you for your support of the author's rights.

Center Street
Hachette Book Group
1290 Avenue of the Americas, New York, NY 10104
centerstreet.com
@CenterStreet

First Edition: June 2025

Center Street is a division of Hachette Book Group, Inc. The Center Street name and logo are registered trademarks of Hachette Book Group, Inc.

The publisher is not responsible for websites (or their content) that are not owned by the publisher.

Center Street books may be purchased in bulk for business, educational, or promotional use. For information, please contact your local bookseller or the Hachette Book Group Special Markets Department at special.markets@hbgusa.com.

Library of Congress Cataloging-in-Publication Data has been applied for.

ISBN: 978-1-5460-0879-8 (hardcover), 978-1-5460-0958-0 (signed edition), 978-1-5460-0959-7 (B&N signed edition), 978-1-5460-0881-1 (ebook)

Printed in the United States of America

LSC

Printing 1, 2025

This book is dedicated to President Donald J. Trump.
His vision, courage, and love of country will redefine
Washington and usher in a new Golden Age for America.

Contents

Trump's Triumph

ONE

Triumph

No candidate for president of the United States has run the personal and political gauntlet that President Donald J. Trump endured from 2015 to his reelection on November 5, 2024.

Andrew Jackson was an aggressive change-oriented crusader who felt he had the presidency stolen from him in 1824. Jackson campaigned for four solid years to defeat incumbent president John Quincy Adams. Even Jackson never faced the scale and intensity of institutional opposition that has assailed President Trump every step of the way.

This victory over all opposition made the 2024 election a moment of triumph for President Trump and all his supporters. The consequences of his success are huge.

Just imagine how different things would be if Vice President Kamala Harris had won and the decay of the previous four years had been validated. Or imagine if a conventional, pre-Trump, establishment Republican had been nominated by the GOP. In either case, we would have had a president committed to working within the framework of the left-wing bureaucratic system. This system has been growing since President Franklin Delano Roosevelt's election in 1932. It then accelerated dramatically under President Lyndon Johnson's Great Society from 1964 to 1968 and again under President Barack Obama from 2009 to 2017.

President Trump rejected this system from the start, even as a candidate in 2015. Early on he decisively sided with the legacies of Barry Goldwater, Ronald Reagan, and, frankly, myself. We were for fundamental change within the GOP and had taken on the Gerald Ford–Bush family–Mitt Romney accommodationist wing of the Republican Party. President Trump's willingness to reject the old order led to the rise of the Never Trumpers and the bitter anti-Trump wing of the GOP and Washington establishment—many of whom are no longer in office.

After President Trump's first term, the GOP's old order and the establishment Democrats understood that a second Trump administration would mean the end of their world. They were fighting for their ideological and political lives. This is why it made perfect sense for Liz Cheney, the heiress of the GOP establishment, to campaign enthusiastically with Harris in the closing days of the 2024 campaign. They were on the same side, representing the same interests. And they opposed President Trump with the same fervor and intensity.

So, in many ways, President Trump's reelection saved America from a future of government domination, economic decay, aberrant social policies, and other domestic and foreign threats that could eliminate our freedom.

President Trump's reelection was the triumph of a man and a movement. Each needed the other if America was to be saved. Without President Trump, no movement would have been possible. Without millions of Americans wearing Make America Great

Again hats, attending rallies, donating to the campaign, putting up yard signs, and standing by their movement champion, President Trump could not have won.

For nine years—starting when then-businessman Trump and his wife, Melania, came down the long escalator at Trump Tower—the establishment did everything it could to destroy him. He was the first real threat to its political dominance in modern times. This victory felt like a triumph far greater than the popular vote margin or the electoral college. It was the scale of the effort to destroy President Trump that made his resilience and ultimate victory so amazing.

Consider the scale and endless effort of the federal government and its establishment allies to destroy the president chosen by the American people. First, there was the FBI intelligence community–enabled Russia hoax of 2016 (initially funded by the Hillary Clinton campaign). Then came the lurid, dishonest rumors about Russian recordings of the new president's personal behavior by then–FBI director James Comey.[1] Then came the jailing of Trump's first national security adviser on totally phony charges. Recall the Robert Mueller investigation, which produced nothing but empty headlines after two years of investigations. We saw two impeachments in the Democrat-controlled House, which were rejected by the Senate. Move on to the massive outpouring of money and information games in the 2020 election. We then saw the kangaroo court January 6 Committee led by Cheney.

Throughout all this, countless lawsuits were designed to drain President Trump's money, absorb his time, discredit him with the American people, and potentially put him in jail. Finally, there were two assassination attempts—one of which President Trump survived only through providential intervention.

The establishment and its followers used every deceitful and disgusting tool available to crush and drive him out of public life. They feared him as a mortal threat to their careers and self-identities.

Consider the extraordinary and unprecedented lengths the Washington political machine went in its desperate effort to block a Trump victory. After the presidential debate on June 27, 2024, it became clear President Joe Biden could not be propped up enough to win the election. The political bosses of the Democratic Party, namely former Speaker Nancy Pelosi and Obama, moved to dump Biden from the ticket. This action was stunningly unprecedented. The final blow apparently was a July 10, 2024, letter from actor and Democratic Party activist George Clooney. Clooney had hosted the largest Democratic fundraiser in history just a month earlier for President Biden. He argued that President Biden's performance against President Trump in the debate was so bad Biden could not possibly win the general election. He argued time was undermining his good friend President Biden as he grew more fragile and more prone to being inarticulate and cognitively challenged.

The Clooney letter may have been the final straw. Ten days later, on July 21, 2024, President Biden announced he was withdrawing from the race. However, President Biden went a stage beyond stepping down. He also guaranteed Harris would be his replacement as the Democratic nominee. Toward the end of his withdrawal statement, he said:

> My very first decision as the party nominee in 2020 was to pick Kamala Harris as my vice president. And it's been

the best decision I've made. Today I want to offer my full support and endorsement for Kamala to be the nominee of our party this year. Democrats—it's time to come together and beat Trump.

This additional step was remarkable because it completely overrode the closing sentiments of Clooney's letter. He wrote:

We Democrats have a very exciting bench. We don't anoint leaders or fall sway to a cult of personality; we vote for a president. We can easily foresee a group of several strong Democrats stepping forward to stand and tell us why they're best qualified to lead this country and take on some of the deeply concerning trends we're seeing from the revenge tour that Donald Trump calls a presidential campaign.

President Biden essentially nullified the fantasy of a mini-primary and mini-nomination process. With his endorsement coming straight out of his withdrawal statement, he had virtually guaranteed that Vice President Harris would become the Democratic nominee. The combined shock of the president's withdrawal and the vice president's effective coronation meant that within a few days she would have enough delegates to become the nominee. None of the governors or senators who might have challenged her had a chance to get in the race once President Biden anointed her as his successor.

This sudden shift from Biden to Harris had two consequences that were not obvious that day. First, the vice president would have no genuine legitimacy. President Biden acquired 3,905 delegates in 56 contests (all others got 44 delegates). He received 14,465,529 votes in the primary.

For a Democratic Party that had been lecturing Americans for three years on the importance of democracy, President Biden's legitimacy should have been beyond question.

By contrast, Vice President Harris participated in no contests, won no votes, and persuaded no delegates to her side. When you look back at her 2019 presidential primary campaign, she withdrew before voters in any states cast a single ballot. In short, she was remarkably unsuited to be the Democratic nominee.

However, the second challenge for Vice President Harris may have been even more harmful to her candidacy. She had no opportunity to practice as a candidate. She had not developed an effective set of answers to inevitable questions about the changes in her positions—or the extremism of her views during her 2019 campaign. She simply had no in-depth experience of interacting with the news media and answering random questions.

During the campaign, it was clear candidate Harris could not cope with complicated questions on nearly any topic. She had not thought through how to explain herself or minimize the damage caused by some of her policy positions on energy production, the Southern border, gender politics, and other divisive issues.

However, Harris's weaknesses only became obvious as the election neared. In late July 2024, Democrats and their propaganda media allies had propped up Vice President Harris enough to achieve the largest flood of donations in American history. More than $1 billion poured into her campaign. The media wanted us to believe she was unstoppable.

This sudden cycle of events was totally jarring and confusing to President Trump and his campaign. It was like riding a roller coaster blindfolded.

I had warned for months that if the Democrats' lawfare strategy to stop Trump by jailing him failed, the next threat would be physical. Someone would try to kill him. I first warned Sean Hannity about this in mid-summer. It seemed inevitable to me that the left's desperate mania would push someone into the kind of rationale that led John Wilkes Booth to assassinate President Abraham Lincoln. Allen Guelzo, one of the greatest living Lincoln scholars, had told me that the anti-Lincoln media among the slave states and the modern anti-Trump rhetoric were eerily similar. Both represented oligarchies in danger of losing their power—and with it their identities. Both saw themselves threatened with extinction if their opponents prevailed. I was following the historic parallel of a movement leader who was a mortal threat to an entrenched system.

All this came terrifyingly close to reality on July 13, 2024, just three days after Clooney's letter calling on President Biden to step aside.

At a campaign rally in Butler, Pennsylvania, President Trump was saved from death by a providential intervention. I said so that evening, and I truly believe it. There is no other practical explanation to my mind. President Trump turned to look at a chart about illegal immigration on a giant screen and turned back at the exact moment the bullet passed. His chance movement turned what would have been a fatal head wound into a bloodied ear.

Americans watched on live television as President Trump fell to the ground and insisted on standing back up. He walked off the platform with blood streaming down his face and his fist in the air. All the while, he chanted, "Fight, fight, fight." It was one of the most iconic moments in American presidential campaign history.

I was already in Milwaukee, Wisconsin, for the Republican National Convention. Two days later, the convention began. President Trump announced Senator J. D. Vance as his vice presidential nominee. Vance's book *Hillbilly Elegy* was a bestseller and Callista and I had seen the film adaptation. He married a classmate at Yale Law School, Usha Chilukuri, in a joint Christian and Hindu wedding. They have three children. His nomination was generally well received.

When President Trump walked into the convention center, it was an electrifying moment. He had a bandage over his ear. Everyone in the building was desperately concerned that he survive, continue to lead the Make America Great Again movement, and ultimately fix the country.

Callista and I were there for all four nights—including the President's acceptance speech Thursday night. It had been preceded by Hulk Hogan in a tribute to the sporting component of the Trump coalition.

We went back to Virginia after the convention, and everything seemed to be working. The President and his team had done a remarkable job winning the Republican nomination and unifying the Republican Party across the country. The convention had worked, and Republicans were cheerfully marching to victory.

Then came Biden's July 21, 2024, announcement. I will never forget it. I was sitting down to watch TV and Callista said to me, "By the way, Biden just dropped out." I was stunned. I found it almost impossible to believe. A few minutes later, we learned that he had announced his support for Harris.

It was a stunning turnaround of events. President Trump and his team knew how to beat President Biden. They were confident they could execute the campaign and achieve a comfortable victory in November. They were relaxing after surviving an assassination attempt and managing a successful convention.

Suddenly, every assumption about the fall campaign was out the window. They had to think through a new strategy and re-examine all their planning.

It was immediately clear that the American people would be more open to a Harris candidacy than they had been to a Biden reelection effort. Democrats who had been anxiety-ridden about President Biden's inability to do the job suddenly had new hope.

The propaganda media reinforced the confusion. Reporters, anchors, and pundits emphasized the wave of support for Harris's candidacy and the number of groups she would be able to reach that had lost faith in President Biden.

For several weeks, the Trump team grappled with how to operate in this new environment—and cope with a massive onslaught of opposition money.

Most of us were convinced that Trump would eventually beat Harris. We thought the country was truly tired of the economic disaster the Biden-Harris team had created. From polling, we knew Americans rejected the radical social values for which the Democrats stood and worried about the administration's incompetence on the world stage in an increasingly dangerous planet.

However, we also knew we had to endure a temporary surge of all-out propaganda. The media built her up with softball interviews and photo ops. The so-called experts and pollsters showed how much stronger she was than President Biden.

These early post-Biden weeks were probably the most disorienting weeks of the entire campaign for the Trump team—and for the candidate himself. He had to develop a new analysis and a new language to take on a younger female candidate. Ironically, she was trying to be the candidate of change while having served four years as vice president.

I was confident President Trump would eventually figure out exactly how to describe and define Harris—just as he had 15 Republican candidates in 2016, Hillary Clinton, and ultimately President Biden.

Ultimately, with the Biden-Harris shell game, Trump became the only presidential candidate to face two major opponents in one election cycle.

Thus, the sprint to the election began.

Kamala's Collapse

The campaign between President Donald J. Trump and Vice President Kamala Harris was surprisingly short and amazingly expensive.

The opening phase was a relatively unfocused Trump campaign effort to find the right language and examples to define Harris. Meanwhile, she was running around the country repeating simple mantras and attracting supporters who were energized by her replacement of President Joe Biden as the Democratic standard bearer.

A major feature of Vice President Harris's early campaign was the emergence of her appeal to the so-called Divine 9, a nationwide organization of nine Black sororities and fraternities. One example of their involvement was a July 25 Zoom fundraiser that brought together 4,000 sorority and fraternity members from around the country and raised an initial $151,000.[1] Ironically, the Democrats' problems with young Black males may have been exacerbated by the emphasis on Harris's sorority background. Black males who did not go to college or belong to fraternities were alienated from the Democratic Party—and hurt by its economic failures. The more Harris campaigned among the college elite, the more she convinced working class Blacks that they should show their independence and vote for President Trump.

The vice president's opening weeks of campaigning were positive and given unbelievably positive coverage. The propaganda media did everything it could to humanize her. Throughout the campaign, it was relentlessly driven home that Harris was raised in a middle-class neighborhood and brought up by a single mom.

Then she confronted her first big decision: whom to pick as her vice presidential running mate. From a general election perspective, there was an obvious choice in Pennsylvania governor Josh Shapiro. After years as the state's attorney general, Shapiro won a big victory for governor against a flawed Republican candidate (who believed in no exceptions for abortion and was seen as an extremist by most Pennsylvanians).

The Keystone State was also going to be the most important swing state. It was hard to see how Harris could win the electoral college if she failed to carry Pennsylvania. This challenge was made more difficult by her 2020 campaign pledge to ban all fracking. Western Pennsylvania has two of the four largest natural gas fields in the entire world. They are worth billions of dollars and thousands of jobs in the state. Her original anti-fracking position made Harris a hard sell in the Pittsburgh area. Shapiro would have helped alleviate that challenge.

In the end, she could not pick Shapiro for two powerful reasons.

First, he is Jewish and vocal elements of the Democratic Party are increasingly pro-Palestinian and anti-Semitic. The rabid mobs of pro-Palestine activists on university campuses (and the faculty who support them) are virtually all Democrats. Furthermore, Muslim communities in Michigan and Minnesota have been increasingly supportive of the Democratic Party and opposed to pro-Israel positions.

About two-thirds of American Jews historically aligned with the Democratic Party. From Franklin Delano Roosevelt's liberalism to President Harry S. Truman's recognition of the State of Israel, there are deep historic bonds between American Jews and the Democratic Party.

However, the current anti-Israel and anti-Semitic sentiments are strong. It is possible a Shapiro nomination for vice president might have been booed on the floor of the Democratic National Convention. It might even have led to a protest candidate being nominated against him.

The second problem with a Shapiro vice presidential candidacy was he wanted real power and a clear grant of authority. It would have taken far too long to outline a power sharing arrangement between Harris and Shapiro. This was reportedly a nonstarter. With Shapiro unacceptable, Harris turned to Minnesota governor Tim Walz. He fit her ideology and personality.

From the standpoint of the Trump team, the selection of Walz was a great help. As governor, Walz presided over a large part of Minneapolis being burned by looters and rioters in 2020. He had a discriminatory and anti-religious COVID-19 lockdown policy. Bars were granted higher occupancies than churches. The Mall of America was granted a partial exemption from lockdown for so-called retail therapy while places of worship were closed.

Walz also had extreme positions on abortion and transgender rights. His policy of putting tampons in middle school boys bathrooms got him the nickname "Tampon Tim."[2]

As governor, Walz supported the largest tax increases in Minnesota history. For the first time, Minnesota's per capita income fell below the national average. Walz had grown increasingly unpopular everywhere in rural and small-town Minnesota. He survived because of huge majorities from the increasingly liberal and radical voters in the Twin Cities.

In addition to his policy extremism, Governor Walz had a habit of exaggerating his own record. Casual hyperbole—and even outright lying—seemed to be a consistent part of his political personality. Phony stories, which had been accepted as fact for years, fell apart under the kind of scrutiny a presidential campaign attracts.[3, 4, 5]

After getting through a relatively successful, celebrity- and music-infused Democratic National Convention, the first major news media outing of the new Harris-Walz ticket did not help the cause.

Harris and Walz joined CNN for an exclusive interview. Even when CNN's Dana Bash asked sympathetic questions, Harris offered deer in the headlights responses. Also, no one on the Harris campaign team had enough television experience to realize Walz was seated in the foreground of the shot. He looked much more important than Harris. Her constant refrain of "I grew up in a middle-class household" soon became a joke and was mocked by her opponents.

Harris's household mantra was soon matched by Walz, who in the vice presidential debate with Senator Vance admitted, "I'm a knucklehead at times." While admitting your faults at times has a certain charm, it is hardly a good advertisement for becoming second in line to the presidency and a potential commander in chief.

Vice President Harris had two huge problems in trying to campaign outside carefully controlled and scripted settings. She could not believably provide a coherent set of explanations. It eventually got to the point that even her supporters in the media were demanding that she cut out the fluff and answer questions.

The second problem plaguing Vice President Harris was that she simply could not cope with free flowing interviews. It put her in constant danger of making fatal mistakes. This came crashing down when she went on *The View* in early October. Harris had spent a month trying to convince voters she was the candidate of change and that she would fix everything on day one. Of course, people knew that Harris's day one had been January 20, 2021, when she started her work with the Biden administration.

When Sunny Hostin asked Harris if she would have done anything differently than President Biden during the previous four years, Harris responded, "There is not a thing that comes to mind."[6]

The clip of Harris confessing that she would have done everything President Biden had done was gold for President Trump and the Republican campaign. It became the centerpiece of an endless number of TV ads.

It's unclear if Harris didn't want to publicly speak against President Biden or if she simply didn't have any answers.

Harris's one shining moment on TV was her only debate with President Trump on September 10, 2024. She did better than people expected. She did not decisively do better than Trump, but her ability to be coherent was a surprise victory that energized Democrats. Harris seemed to have studied, and she had some pretty good lines to use against Trump. She never seemed to carry this preparation into future events, but for one night she seemed to be on her game.

With the two ABC moderators totally on her side, the debate was really three-on-one. David Muir and Linsey Davis were blatantly pro-Harris and anti-Trump—and Americans noticed. This helped her performance during the debate, but for millions of voters it was further proof of media bias. In many ways, this strengthened Trump.

Many of Trump's advisers (including me) urged him to be more passive, patient, and calm. We feared that a full-blown Trump debate approach would overwhelm Harris. She would become the sympathetic figure, and he would seem like a bully. With the singular exception of Vice President Harris baiting President Trump about the size of his crowds, Trump did an admirable job of staying on message.

It is important to understand that the two candidates were playing different games. You had to measure their success against their goals. Vice President Harris wanted to win a personality contest in which she was more acceptable than Trump. President Trump was focused on winning an argument about policy and performance.

As happened in many Trump debate media post mortems, the initial analysis by so-called experts assumed he underperformed. However, within a week it was clear his authenticity and focus on Biden and Harris's failures meant more to voters than Harris's clever but ephemeral verbal gymnastics. The same pattern showed up in the vice presidential debate. Senator Vance was precise and focused on drawing the contrast of performance and policy between the first Trump administration and the Biden-Harris administration. The bias from the CBS moderators was even more egregious than in the ABC debate. Margaret Brennan and Norah O'Donnell seemed to work overtime to represent the worst versions of one-sided liberalism and media arrogance.

The biggest surprise of the vice presidential debate was the degree to which Vance and Walz agreed with different policy statements—and expressed comity and empathy for their lives and achievements. For Trump, this was a net plus. It moved Vance toward the middle and made him more likable. For Harris, it was a loss. Her campaign strategy required making the Trump ticket look totally unacceptable. Yet, Walz cheerfully chatted with Senator Vance and couldn't bring himself to be negative about his new friend.

With the debates behind them, the campaigns began moving into the closing five-week grind. The Harris team apparently concluded it could not win the policy and performance argument about the economy or about transgenderism. The campaign decided its only hope was to define Trump as an extremist who could not be trusted to govern without trying to create a dictatorship.

This was not a new theme. It was a reversion to President Biden's failed campaign strategy, which he elaborately expressed in a foreboding speech from the National Constitution Center in Philadelphia on September 1, 2022. It was also a parallel to the Democrats' lawfare project, which guided the January 6 Committee and the raid of Mar-a-Lago, and coordinated indictments and lawsuits in Washington, New York, and Atlanta. This included the series of criminal charges by the U.S. Department of Justice launched by Jack Smith, a lawyer who had once been unanimously rebuked by the U.S. Supreme Court for perverting the law to destroy Republican governor Robert McDonnell.

To the shock of the Democrats and their propaganda media allies, the stream of indictments did not hurt President Trump. In fact, the left's persecution of President Trump guaranteed his nomination, made it virtually unthinkable among most Republicans to oppose him, and increased his stature.

On August 24, 2023, the Fulton County Sheriff's Office brought President Trump in for a mug shot. Everyone on the left was excited and confident that this was the beginning of the end. Instead, the mug shot was immediately iconic. Almost immediately, it was reprinted by his supporters as a symbol of toughness and defiance to the government establishment. Trump began to appeal to communities of Americans who felt they, too, were persecuted by law enforcement and crooked attorneys. Trump's supporters became further enraged and even more deeply convinced that the entire lawfare strategy was a profoundly unfair violation of the Constitution.

In fact, virtually every time President Trump stepped into a courtroom, he grew in stature and his left-wing lawfare opponents shrank. Given this history, it is hard to figure out why Harris and her consultants thought doubling down on calling Trump a fascist and a dictator, and comparing him to Hitler would work. His supporters came to believe that he was being persecuted because he stood between them and a truly frightening vindictive system that was destroying the rule of law in favor of the rule of power.

So, while Vice President Harris's closing arguments were in a political language that only made sense to the hard left, the Trump team developed a totally different approach. President Trump and Senator Vance focused on the performance difference between the Trump years and the Biden-Harris years. They talked about the economy (especially inflation), energy, the border, and keeping the world stable and peaceful. The Democrats were involved in an abstract argument about Trump threatening democracy and the Constitution (which most normal Americans did not believe). The Republican team focused on issues that impacted Americans directly.

In the end, it was clear the Trump team had the better strategy and the dramatically better candidate. There were days when Vice President Harris did only one campaign event, while President Trump routinely went out for three, four, or more events. Harris was afraid she would make major mistakes if she participated in long interviews. She wouldn't go on Joe Rogan's podcast (with the biggest audience in the podcast world) because she knew he would ask her questions about flip-flops on policy and other embarrassing things. She simply would not be able to handle them. Harris also knew that she did not have the mental stamina to do a three-hour podcast. She offered to do it for an hour and was turned down by Rogan, who said three hours or nothing. After she turned it down, Senator Vance was happy to take the freed-up interview time.

By contrast, President Trump was totally comfortable with long-form interviews. He had been practicing with hour-long sessions with Sean Hannity since 2015. Rogan's interview of Trump attracted an estimated 33 million listeners in the first few days. When you consider that MSNBC's nightly audience at that time was about 700,000, it's clear how much President Trump was helped by his ability to make the legacy and alternative media rounds. The president's son Barron also helped by suggesting podcasts that were listened to by younger voters. While Vice President Harris's ability to communicate with the American people was drastically limited by her weaknesses as a communicator,

President Trump's remarkable command of issues, and his joy as an entertainer-educator, gave him a huge advantage. In fact, Trump's ability to get many hours of earned media was key to overcoming Harris's four-to-one fundraising advantage.

As the final weeks began to build, the difference between the Trump and Harris efforts became more obvious. President Trump was simply a better candidate. He could campaign longer, draw bigger crowds, and had a better grasp of the issues. The Trump team was clearly a better team. The Harris campaign was limited by the tension between the original Biden reelection team, the Harris team, and the Obama alumni who came to help. The Trump team, with Susie Wiles's leadership and Chris LaCivita's relentless implementation, was faster and more aggressive than its competition.

The Trump team, starting with President Trump, also had an aggressive and comprehensive sense of what would work. Trump had nine years of campaigning compared to her two months. It was simply an experience gap she could not bridge. One of the first examples of this difference between the two teams came on September 21, 2024, when Harris skipped the Alfred E. Smith Memorial Foundation Dinner. The Al Smith Dinner is the biggest Catholic charitable event in New York. In 2024, it raised more than $10 million for Catholic charities. Ever since John F. Kennedy and Richard Nixon spoke together at the 1960 dinner, it has been a tradition for the parties' nominees to attend and speak. They are supposed to be polite—but also make fun of their opponents and themselves in humorous ways. President Trump outshined Hillary Clinton in the 2016 dinner.

Vice President Harris had a clear reason to attend the Al Smith Dinner. Catholics are a quarter or more of the vote in every one of the swing states. The Al Smith Dinner would be nationally televised and would especially resonate in Catholic communities. Furthermore, there was a growing sense that the Democratic Party was a secular party and was anti-Catholic. My wife, Callista, as former U.S. ambassador to the Holy See, reinforced this view in a series of direct columns.

Despite this clear political calculus, Harris announced she would skip the dinner. Cardinal Timothy Dolan, the archbishop of the Archdiocese of New York and host of the dinner, was surprised. He said, "We're not used to this. We don't know how to handle it. This hasn't happened in 40 years, since Walter Mondale turned down the invitation. And remember, he lost 49 out of 50 states. I don't want to say there's a direct connection there."

As the campaign progressed for the next three weeks, Harris's issue with faithful voters grew. Then, she sent a disastrously offensive video to the dinner. It was a sign of the left's isolation that no one in Harris's inner circle realized that a video based on an old *Saturday Night Live* skit making fun of Catholic school girls would be offensive to the audience at the Al Smith Dinner. When Callista and I saw it, we couldn't believe it.

Six days later, Harris guaranteed her failure with most Catholics, and indeed from most people of faith in general, when she announced that she opposed any conscience exception from government mandated medical procedures. As one Catholic bishop said to me after the election, Harris's victory would have killed all Catholic health care. Roughly 1,100 Catholic hospitals simply would not be able to operate in accordance with Catholic doctrine. Harris was clearly seen as a mortal threat to religious Americans' way of life. This almost certainly helped President Trump carry the seven swing states and improved his support among Latino Americans.

The next big break for President Trump was classic. It was yet another reminder that money doesn't beat a system-wide press of earned media. In October, Trump worked the drive-through window at a Pennsylvania McDonald's. He learned how to make french fries (all captured on camera, of course) and then worked the window handing out food to astonished customers.

Since 87 percent of Americans visit a McDonald's at least once a year—and some 40 million Americans have worked at a McDonald's (including Jeff Bezos)—the symbolism of the everyday down-home candidate was overwhelming. The entire event was fun, and people everywhere got a kick out of watching Trump work the drive-through. It was also clear he was having fun. This was something you couldn't quite imagine Harris doing. The original idea had been to highlight that Vice President Harris had been unable to prove that she had ever worked at McDonald's, as she claimed. But the event took on a life of its own and dominated weekend campaign coverage.

Callista and I attended the next great Trump event—the rally at Madison Square Garden. As a native New Yorker, Trump had long wanted to do an event at the iconic arena. He had already held more campaign events in New York than any Republican presidential candidate in modern times. The Garden was filled with at least 20,000 people, and tens of thousands more outside. The event was also a remarkable introduction to the new Trump Coalition, which is potentially going to replace the Roosevelt Coalition after its 90-year run. My favorite moment was when Hulk Hogan was followed by Dr Phil. I couldn't imagine a bigger jump in style and appearance than those two.

Listening to Robert F. Kennedy Jr. rip apart the modern Democratic Party as alien to the party to which his father and uncle had belonged in the 1960s was also an amazing moment. Kennedy was followed by Tulsi Gabbard, who had been a Democrat. As a military veteran, she made the case against endless wars and the Biden administration's tragic mishandling of the withdrawal from Afghanistan. I felt like I was watching history as Liz Cheney campaigned with Vice President Harris and Gabbard campaigned with President Trump. First Lady Melania Trump was gorgeous as usual and gave a fine talk and introduced her husband. Then, President Trump gave a solid and rousing summary of what the campaign was all about.

Callista and I left feeling buoyant. We then learned that the propaganda media had ignored all the historic aspects of this emerging coalition and was appalled by one clumsy comedian's stupid joke about Puerto Rico. During the media uproar, *The Daily Show* host Jon Stewart hit back at critics of the comedic performance saying, "There's something wrong with me. I find that guy very funny. I'm sorry, I don't know what to tell you."[7] Of course, the country, and most Puerto Rican Americans, ignored the desperate effort by the media to create conflict where none existed. As a result, it had no impact on the campaign except to further divert the Harris campaign and the Democrats from the cost of living issues that really mattered.

The lack of common sense and concern for people's feelings really hurt the Harris campaign when they held a rally in the Ellipse in front of the White House two days after the Madison Square Garden event. They attracted an estimated 75,000 supporters, which made sense since the rally was in the heart of their support. Washington bureaucrats, lobbyists, and left-wing think tank workers all came rushing to the Harris rally. However, in what would turn into a huge strategic mistake, the

Harris campaign either forgot about—or were intentionally ignoring—the couple in the White House directly behind the rally. President Biden and Jill Biden did not get over being bullied out of the race, despite having won the primaries and the delegates. They were further alienated by the Harris campaign decision to run as a change candidate and indirectly repudiate her four years as his vice president.

In fact, President Biden had indicated his unhappiness on October 4, 2024, when for the first time in his presidency he showed up in the press room and made clear that it had been a Biden-Harris administration—and that she bore shared responsibility for everything that had happened. As President Biden said, "I'm in constant contact with her. She's aware we all, we're singing from the same song sheet." That appearance directly undercut the Harris campaign's major change-agent, fresh ideas theme. I am convinced at some point, the Bidens decided it would be a pretty good legacy to be the only person to beat Donald Trump. Now that his vice president was humiliating him by having 75,000 people in front of his home—and not inviting him to be on stage—President Biden found a new way to undercut her campaign.

During a Voto Latino get-out-the-vote call, he said that he thought Trump's supporters were "garbage." At that point, the political press shifted to covering Biden's comment, which was interpreted as an attack on all Trump supporters parallel to Hillary Clinton's "basket of deplorables" comment in 2016. Virtually nothing of Harris's closing message got covered as the media shifted to Biden, then to Biden's effort to reinterpret it, then to various Democrats' reactions (Governor Shapiro was clear that he would never use that language for fellow Americans).

This was the moment that President Trump and his team showed just how good they really are. The next day on the way to a rally in Green Bay, Wisconsin, someone on the plane suggested that Trump ride in a garbage truck to bring more attention to Biden's nasty comment. They were able to find a new, clean garbage truck and put Trump signs on it before the plane landed. Ever the showman, President Trump promptly put on a reflective vest. Then, with the national press corps watching, he climbed into the truck and got a campaign full of pictures.

The real Trump instinct for dominating the news and having fun then kicked in, and he walked into the rally wearing the garbage collector vest. He told the crowd that someone had said the vest made him look thinner, and he was considering wearing it for the rest of the campaign.

Finally, having dominated the last three weeks of the campaign, President Trump finished out the ninth year of campaigning. On the Monday before the election, he had rallies in Raleigh, North Carolina, and Reading and Pittsburgh, Pennsylvania, and ended with a rally in Grand Rapids, Michigan. Tired but satisfied, he headed home.

It was time for the American people to speak.

Callista and I were in West Palm Beach at the campaign rally on election night. We were chatting with then-senator Marco Rubio near the stage when President Trump and his team came out to speak.

The moment it was announced that President Donald Trump had defeated Vice President Kamala Harris, the room erupted with excitement. It was an exhilarating moment of vindication for nine hard years of work—and innumerable false, vicious attacks.

This had been a near decade-long fight to take on the left-wing establishment and insist on profound changes in Washington. We endured the Russia hoax and the Mueller investigation. We survived the public health establishment lying to and misinforming the American people about the disastrous COVID-19 pandemic. We watched two impeachment attempts, and a deeply disputed, rigged 2020 election.

Then we joined President Trump's effort to gain decisive control of the Republican Party and arouse a new working-class GOP. It attracted new voters to the GOP in unexpectedly large numbers. After the election, there was a sigh of relief that all his hard work and courage had paid off with victory. It was the satisfying culmination to a nine-year campaign. Against all the odds—and the full weight of the left-wing establishment—our team won.

And yet there was something deeper and more profound about the way people were reacting to the defeat of Harris. At first, I attributed this sense of catharsis to normal political feelings about defeating Harris's atrocious four years of bad government.

However, in a long dinner conversation in Rome, Italy, with Liz Lev, one of the brightest historians I know, my views were changed. I gained a much deeper and more profound cultural sense of what was at stake in the 2024 election.

Lev is a history professor who also serves as a tour guide to Rome for people who want a sophisticated introduction to the Eternal City. Her voluminous knowledge ranges from the founding of the Roman Republic up through the Middle Ages and the Renaissance. She thinks as deeply about the tides of history as anyone I know. Her personal relief at the defeat of Harris forced me to think about the cultural nature of what we are living through. Lev said a Harris victory would have shattered the country at a deep cultural level. It would have meant Americans' core beliefs about work and effort were no longer relevant.

She noted that President Trump worked tirelessly hard. Despite every obstacle and attack, he kept going. Trump had earned the presidency the old-fashioned way—he had worked for it. In the meantime, Harris violated every rule of merit and earning your way. Everything was handed to her. Lev said Harris's nomination was the very essence of privilege.

It was clear that Harris did not know much, did not study, and was just plain lazy. It was also clear that she had risen in California, and then nationally, through a series of political connections. This started with former San Francisco mayor Willie Brown and was reinforced by Barack Obama supporting Harris in California.

Then, Harris somehow magically set aside the incumbent president and became the Democratic nominee without winning a single vote—or proving in any way that she was the right candidate.

Finally, she ran a campaign that reflected her laziness, ignorance, and incompetence. The Democratic Party bosses who destroyed Biden could have put anyone on the ticket, and we would have been told to vote for them.

Lev's sense was that the 2024 election was the ultimate test of whether the alliance between left-wing ideologues and taxpayer-funded machines could dominate the whole country as it dominates Chicago, Baltimore, San Francisco, and other great cities.

If Harris won, it would have meant the American people had given up on hard work and merit. It would have meant Americans were willing to accept whatever candidate the machine selected— no matter how incompetent, incapable, or undeserving.

Lev's insight that this was a cultural more than a political decision was exactly right. People who were afraid, indeed in many cases terrified, by the prospect of a Harris victory were being motivated by more than ideology or partisanship. Harris personified Democratic machine politics. Her only claim to be president was that it was her turn.

It is easy to forget how bad her campaign was. She could not name a single decision in four years in which she disagreed with President Biden, yet she wanted to be the candidate of change. She could not do freewheeling press conferences or long podcast interviews because she could not operate coherently without a script.

It is a frightening tribute to the establishment media's power. The media successfully protected President Biden from scrutiny over his cognitive problems for more than half his term. Then it was able to invent a supposedly competent, popular candidate Harris.

In the shortest presidential campaign in modern times (107 days), Harris managed to raise $1.5 billion. This is about $100 million a week for 15 weeks. Remarkably, the campaign spent slightly more than that. Harris's team spent twice as much as President Trump's in the closing days of the campaign. It also had the enormous benefit of continuously biased media coverage.

Despite all the advantages of the establishment news media, the huge money pouring in, and the still significant labor union and special interest group machines, Harris lost. She may have been the worst candidate in modern times.

The idea that someone who was ideologically out of step with most Americans—and utterly incompetent—could win against someone who took endless questions, openly campaigned, and earned the support of millions of Americans created a real sense of anxiety.

Millions of Americans understood that a Harris victory would mean the end of the American system of hard work and merit. It would re-establish a party-run, oligarchical system. Boss-picked mediocrities could overrule popular candidates.

The entire country was in danger of becoming a place like Chicago. President Trump and his supporters pulled us back from that abyss—for now.

THREE

The Trump Mandate

One of the hardest things for the propaganda media to come to grips with was the reality that candidate and then President Donald Trump's appeal to millions of Americans came from issues and policies rather than personality and charisma.

Of course, President Trump is charismatic and has a strong personality. He is clearly the most charismatic politician of his generation. He also has a strong and interesting enough personality to keep many tens of thousands of people waiting for hours to see him in a rally. He has mastered the 90-minute speech. He makes it part politics, part vaudeville, part personality, and part magic. After all, enlisting the Village People and making *Y.M.C.A.* the No. 1 song after more than 40 years through force of personality is hardly the work of a dull person.

However, the branding began at the beginning of his first campaign in 2015. Trump is a businessman and an amazingly good marketer. He had 13 years of experience starring in *The Apprentice*. He owned and operated the Miss Universe contest, along with golf courses, hotels, condominiums, and office buildings. Businessman Trump long ago learned the power of branding and how to reach lots of people at the lowest possible cost.

What made candidate Trump unique was that he knew the brand could not be Trump. That would be too narrow, personal, and small. It would not engage the deepest emotions of the American people. He knew he needed emotional engagement if he was to defeat 15 other Republican candidates and Secretary Hillary Clinton (who had spent a lifetime becoming the dominant Democrat in the country).

Candidate Trump understood what President Ronald Reagan observed in his 1989 Farewell Address. Reagan said:

> I won a nickname, "The Great Communicator." But I never thought it was my style or the words I used that made a difference: it was the content. I wasn't a great communicator, but I communicated great things, and they didn't spring full bloom from my brow, they came from the heart of a great nation—from our experience, our wisdom, and our belief in the principles that have guided us for two centuries. They called it the Reagan revolution. Well, I'll accept that, but for me it always seemed more like the great rediscovery, a rediscovery of our values and our common sense.

Candidate Trump instinctively knew he had to have a "great thing" to communicate. He concluded that it was to "make America great again." When as a marketer he translated that into MAGA, MAGA hats, MAGA T-shirts, MAGA bumper stickers, and MAGA signs, suddenly a big idea was born. Candidate Trump became the leader of a movement far bigger than himself.

In those four words, he captured two big ideas that would defeat the establishment and the left. First, the establishment and the left had failed and were increasingly repudiated by many Americans. Second, an action verb, "make," combined with the most patriotic and powerful word in our national vocabulary, "America," and followed by a positive and exciting future, "great again," captured the interest of the American people. There is no way to know how strong or how far "Trumpism" would have gone. We now have absolute proof of how powerful and how resilient MAGA has been and still is.

Part of Trump's genius is his ability to use huge rallies as focus groups. The media never realized that he listens as much as he speaks at these events. He learns which phrases and issues work and which fall flat. He tried ideas out and he kept the winners.

In 2015, early in his first campaign, candidate Trump intuited from the crowds that illegal immigration and crimes committed by illegal immigrants were big issues. Every time he raised them, audiences reacted emotionally and loudly. I first learned about the power of illegal immigration as an issue—and the effective way Trump communicated it—in August 2015. Vince Haley told me about C-SPAN's coverage of a rally in Phoenix. Trump asked a father whose son had been killed by an illegal immigrant to come up on stage and share his personal anguish with the crowd. It was an electrifying moment. Something was happening without parallel in recent American history. Americans were emotionally identifying their deepest fears and hopes with one person—and they were going to make that person president.

The media never understood the issue-importance of Trump's rally speeches. He was educating the country into a dramatically different interpretation of reality—and a new set of issues. No other current politician could have pulled it off. In some ways, Trump was campaigning the way Presidents Abraham Lincoln, Franklin Delano Roosevelt, and Ronald Reagan had done. He was not just asking people for their vote. He was asking them to join him in a new and profoundly different way of thinking about the world. He has continued this in various forms since the campaign. Through the campaign and before taking office, President Trump released 47 issue videos on his social media accounts to help educate the public.

This process of letting the American people tell the candidate what they cared about was captured perfectly in Reagan's first campaign for governor of California. He had hired a prestigious Republican political consulting firm in California. As an actor, the consultants wanted to brief him on state issues so people would think he was capable of being governor. They gave him a large shoebox filled with 4-by-6-inch cards. Each one described a specific issue on voters' minds and gave talking points for each. As a professional actor, Reagan memorized them easily. Then he went to his first town hall meeting. The first question was what was he going to do about the radical student protests at Berkeley. It wasn't in the box. At the second town hall, the first question was again about the radicals at Berkeley. It still wasn't in the box. The supposed experts reassured Reagan that the Berkeley riots weren't a real issue. Reagan replied that if the voters thought it was an issue, it was an issue. Indeed, it ended up being a major topic in the campaign. Reagan's ability to let the people rather than the so-called experts define his campaign was a key factor in the rise of Trump.

One of the most fascinating aspects of President Trump's nine-year journey to lead America was his ability to force the steady drift away from the establishment-left worldview and toward a different, bold vision of America. Trump's vision is based on fundamentally different values and proscribes a dramatically different role for America in the world.

Two important institutions provided intellectual and political ammunition for the development of this approach to solving America's problems—and creating a new framework for American politics. One is the America First Policy Institute. The second is America's New Majority Project, which we run at Gingrich 360. The two efforts were separate, but they complemented each other.

The America First Policy Institute grew out of the effort by Brooke Rollins and Linda McMahon to gather the Trump team from the first term. Faced with the loss in 2020, they decided the ideas were bigger than the election. Some institution had to continue developing them to Make America Great Again. They gathered more than 400 former Trump administration policy makers. For four years, they worked on ideas and developed positive proposals.

The America First Policy Institute was a major factor in developing the hundreds of executive orders Trump signed in his early days in office. They thought through policies to genuinely and deeply replace the establishment and the deep state. While President Trump was campaigning, the America First Policy Institute was thinking and planning to make his second term in office dramatically faster and more impactful. However, the America First Policy Institute team also engaged at a practical level through its political arm, America First Works. Ashley Hayek started with 19 key counties that would help carry the seven swing states. She then expanded their targeting as more volunteers and resources became available. Ultimately, America First Works visited 5.7 million doors seeking to turn out low propensity voters.

It was no accident that McMahon, who chaired the America First Policy Institute, became the cochair of the transition in charge of policy. She then went on to be named secretary of education. It was also no accident that Rollins, the driving force behind the America First Policy Institute, served in the first Trump White House and was then named secretary of agriculture. (As a leader in 4-H, an agricultural economics major at Texas A&M, and a rancher, she had a solid background for helping rural America.)

The research and policy development at the America First Policy Institute and the Trump campaign was often informed by polling and focus groups developed by America's New Majority Project. This project was founded in 2018 by the late Bernie Marcus. The purpose was to find issues so powerful and popular they could break out from the balanced political forces that had been defining American politics since 2000.

At America's New Majority Project, we specialized in strategic polling designed to create a new set of choices, issues, and policies. The aim was to find issues that attract a large majority of Americans. It grew out of the Reagan principle of finding 70 percent to 80 percent issues and standing next to them. Your opponent either agrees with you and stands in your shadow or disagrees with you and is isolated. This concept of large strategic choices paid off for Reagan in 1984. Vice President Walter Mondale said in his acceptance speech to be the Democratic nominee, "I will raise your taxes." It created such a wide gap in public opinion that Reagan went on to win 49 states and a popular vote landslide.

Two things became obvious in our work at America's New Majority Project. First, there was a greater opportunity on issues among Latinos and African Americans than traditional Republicans thought. Second, the biggest, most decisive gaps were cultural. The elite media and establishment left simply could not acknowledge or react to them. The left's semi-religious belief in radical values made it impossible to understand the revulsion most Americans had for them.

John McLaughlin, one of the Trump campaigns' two major pollsters, summarized the impact of our work this way:

> America's New Majority Project played a truly unique and important role this past election. While most candidate and party sponsored polls focus on the horse race aspects of the campaign, America's New Majority Project from April 2023 to September 2024 sponsored 27 national polls that gauged public opinion support among 27,000 registered voters, probing where they stood on critical issues including: economic issues, immigration, health care, tax cuts, freedom, national security, crime, Social Security and Medicare, education, election integrity. This research became a voter opinion resource for candidates for the House, Senate and even president. Candidates and their advisors could focus upon important policy questions that their own limited campaign resources would not be able to answer. In fact, much of this research seems to have set a strong foundation for the

popular Republican Party platform that promoted a return to common sense.

The America's New Majority Project advanced the learning done by Gingrich 360 between 2019 and 2023 that included the national polls and piggybacking questions upon 11 other national polls. Furthermore, Gingrich 360 conducted qualitative focus group research in a variety of over 30 voter focus groups that probed in depth attitudes among swing voter groups of African Americans, Hispanics, Chinese, Korean, Filipino, Hindu and other voter segments.

The synergistic interaction between America First Policy Institute's substantive work and America's New Majority Project's guide to how the American people felt created a zone of opportunity that President Trump emphasized in perhaps the most revolutionary Inaugural Address in American history.

The cultural issues are the ones that seem to most confuse and anger the elites. However, consider a survey by the Napolitan News Service of some of these key issues:

Just 16 percent believe it is appropriate to teach that members of a particular race or sex bear responsibility for actions committed in the past by other members of the same race or sex.

Just 12 percent believe it appropriate to teach that meritocracy or traits such as hard work are racist or sexist.

Only 13 percent believe teaching that members of certain groups are inherently racist and seek to oppress others is appropriate.

Seventeen percent believe it is appropriate to teach that the U.S. is fundamentally racist or sexist.

Twelve percent believe it is appropriate to teach that a person's moral character is determined by their race or sex.

Just 11 percent think teaching that one race or sex is inherently superior is appropriate.

Instead, voters strongly support attitudes associated with America's noble founding ideals of freedom, equality, and self-governance.

Eighty-eight percent believe it is appropriate to teach that everyone should be treated equally, regardless of gender, race, social orientation, or age.

Eighty-seven percent believe it's best for companies to hire the best person for the job rather than to hire people who match the gender, racial, and ethnic profile of their community.

This summary of the American people's beliefs makes it easy to understand the power of President Trump's Inaugural Address—and the deep dilemma the Democrats face. They are trapped between the American people and the almost religious fervor of their woke left flank. If Democrats try to accommodate the vast majority of Americans, they risk alienating their hard left and creating a civil war in their party. If they accept the minority views of their hard left, they risk being repudiated by the American people.

This is a major policy divide that may well enable the Republicans to grow their majority in 2025 and 2026 as people see the vast difference between the two parties. With a less revolutionary president, many of these issues would not surface—because they so clearly outrage the left. With President Trump, they will become defining areas of American politics and government to the great advantage of Republicans.

From all the polling data—and the election outcome for the House, Senate, and president—it is clear there is a real mandate for action. The driving force of President Trump ensures that mandate is going to be implemented.

FOUR

Governing vs. Campaigning

Despite their remarkable success, President Donald Trump and his team must stay focused on one fact of politics: governing is much harder than campaigning.

I tell this to candidates all the time. Whether you win the presidency, a congressional seat, a governorship, or any other elected position, the campaign is not the job. Momentum from a campaign victory will not make it easier to get things done in office. Winning an election only gets you a ticket to the dance of governing. You must work even harder—and be much more strategic—if you want to be successful governing.

THE WORLD IS BIGGER THAN YOU

There are three practical reasons governing is harder than winning a political campaign.

First, the world is much bigger than you. Problems that you never dreamed possible will come up. You must figure out how to solve them without getting derailed from your main objectives.

President John F. Kennedy was a sailor and former U.S. Navy patrol torpedo boat captain. He was grateful as president when Admiral Hyman Rickover, the father of the nuclear navy, gave him a plaque with the "Breton Fisherman's Prayer" by Winfred Ernest Garrison written on it: "O God, thy sea is so great and my boat is so small."

Surrounded by the power and majesty of the White House, it is easy for presidents and vice presidents to conclude they have real power. Similarly, people who are called "the Senator" by their staff—and virtually everyone else—can come to believe they have been vested with uncommon capabilities. Members of the House live in a cloistered existence with police guarding the buildings, staff seeking to please them, and interest groups currying their favor. These trappings of power can be intoxicating and deeply misleading.

President Harry Truman captured part of this reality when he said about newly elected President Dwight Eisenhower: "Poor Ike, when he was a general, he gave an order and it was carried out. Now he's going to sit in that big office and he'll give an order and not a damn thing is going to happen." President Truman knew how challenging it was to get anything done. He recognized Israel as a state on May 14, 1948, only 11 minutes after it was created. In doing so, he was taking on virtually the entire senior U.S. Department of State, including Secretary of State General George Marshall, whom Truman had appointed. Marshall had said about Truman recognizing Israel immediately, "If I were to vote in the next election, I would vote against the president." The senior American diplomats at the United Nations tried to stall a U.N. resolution endorsing Israel in direct opposition to President

Truman's position. President Truman had to impose his will against enormous internal pressure.

Later, in 1950, President Truman found General Douglas MacArthur so impossible to manage that he fired him as commander during the Korean War. The challenges of managing subordinates in a giant government often causes enormous trouble for presidents. Truman had several scandals involving White House staff (corruption was a major Republican theme in the 1952 election).

President Eisenhower also found himself with a White House scandal. In 1958, White House chief of staff Sherman Adams (former governor of New Hampshire) was forced to resign over accepting improper gifts.

Of course, President Richard Nixon won an enormous popular vote victory for reelection in 1972 (he earned 60.7 percent of the vote). Nixon completely underestimated the danger of a second-rate burglary by a handful of overzealous (and fairly dumb) subordinates. His efforts to contain the investigation into the burglary at the Watergate ultimately cost him the presidency 21 months after his historic victory.

President Ronald Reagan took months to respond to what became known as the Iran-Contra scandal. This was in part because he sincerely did not believe he had ever agreed to trade weapons for hostages. His junior national security staff, particularly Lieutenant Colonel Oliver North, had acted on their own. They worked outside normal channels to try to get help to Nicaragua without congressional approval. Ultimately, Reagan had to make a painful address to the nation accepting responsibility. The American people accepted his apology, and he went on to effectively win a third term with George H. W. Bush as the candidate.

In the fall of 1996, President Bill Clinton and I were planning major bipartisan reforms for Medicare and Social Security. This era was brilliantly recorded in Steven Gillon's book *The Pact: Bill Clinton, Newt Gingrich, and the Rivalry That Defined a Generation.* The Monica Lewinsky scandal exploded and destroyed the opportunity. Clearly, neither of us saw it coming—and yet it changed everything. Neither one of us could have possibly ignored or downplayed it without facing severe political consequences.

When President George W. Bush took office, he wanted to focus on domestic issues. The terrorist attacks of September 11, 2001, changed everything. Bush was forced to instead manage three wars—against Afghanistan, which had housed Al Qaeda for the planning of the attack; Saddam Hussein in Iraq, who the Bush-Cheney team were desperate to replace before he could acquire weapons of mass destruction; and radical Islamists on a worldwide basis. President Bush found his administration gradually losing popular support and having to focus its management capabilities on war issues instead of the domestic challenges he had hoped to solve. Similarly, when Hurricane Katrina hit southern Louisiana and Mississippi on August 29, 2005, no one foresaw how big the disaster would become. When 1,392 lives were lost and $125 billion in damage was inflicted, the confidence in the management capabilities of the Bush team collapsed. The executive branch must execute to retain popular support. The following year, Republicans lost control of the House for the first time in 12 years and Nancy Pelosi became Speaker. Still exhausted by the endless wars and the disaster with Katrina, the Bush administration was further overwhelmed by the 2007–2008 financial crisis. It led to the deepest recession since the Great Depression.

In 2008, President Obama won handily against a strong, truly remarkable Republican candidate in Senator John McCain. The Republican Party had simply lost favor through mismanagement and lack of an effective response to the wars, the hurricane, and then the financial crisis. President Bush was not prepared for any of these crises, and his team simply could not cope with them. However, President Obama was equally unprepared for the Russian invasion of Crimea, Syria ignoring his "red line" over the use of chemical weapons, the tenacity of the Taliban in Afghanistan, and anger generated by his racist comments in a series of police controversies.

During his first term, President Trump was totally surprised by the outbreak of COVID-19 (as was virtually everyone on the planet), and it shaped his final year in office.

When President Biden entered office, he had no idea that the Afghanistan withdrawal would be so disastrously executed and become a national humiliation. He had no clue that Vladimir Putin would invade Ukraine. Biden had no expectation that Hamas would launch the largest massacre of Jews since the Holocaust on October 7, 2023. Here at home, President Biden and his advisers could not realize that their policies would lead to an explosion of inflation—and that higher prices would drive Americans into deep hostility to his program.

Furthermore, there is no reason to believe President Biden had any understanding that accepting an open border would lead to a wave of illegal immigrants—and that vicious crimes committed by some of those immigrants would be blamed on him and his administration. Finally, there seemed to be no normal Americans in the White House who could explain the political costs of anti-religious dictates, extremist transgender policies, or appointees who seemed just plain nuts (recall the Office of Nuclear Energy appointee who was arrested for stealing women's luggage at airports while on government paid trips).

I list these examples to serve as a warning to all current and future leaders. You must be aware of the larger world. You must carefully assess challenges and changes. Figure out if they can be handled within your current planning and structure or whether they require significant changes and potentially redirection of management resources. These stories take us back to the plaque on President Kennedy's desk. The ocean *is* enormous. Even presidents have small boats compared to the forces of history that surround them.

By contrast, a campaign is a motorboat. You know victory is your goal. You know your competitor. You design a strategy for victory. You allocate resources and the candidate's schedule to achieve the victory. While it is intense and focused, a campaign is contained and simple compared to governing.

DIFFICULT BY DESIGN

Governing is supposed to be hard. The U.S. Constitution was designed to make getting things done incredibly difficult. The Founding Fathers intentionally created hurdles to prevent any single candidate or political party from having full control of the country at any given time. People running for executive offices, such as president and governor, are often shocked when they are elected and face a complicated Congress or legislature that is hard to deal with.

House and Senate members find it frustrating to negotiate with an executive branch and each other simultaneously. Further, the House and Senate are remarkably different institutions. They have different cultures, traditions, centers of power, and interests. Adding to this, the executive and legislative branches may come to an agreement on a law and then have it rejected by the U.S. Supreme Court as unconstitutional. Then it's back to the drawing board with new parameters.

This sense of frustration is further compounded by federal and state constitutions that have various (important) limitations on government. The whole system is made more complicated for federal officials because the 10th Amendment of the Constitution guarantees that "powers not delegated to the United States by the Constitution, nor prohibited by it to the States, are reserved to the States respectively, or to the people." Finally, state officials find themselves limited by the federal government on one side and their own, often lengthy, state constitution on the other.

This difficulty is so fascinating because it is all by design. The Founding Fathers studied the history of many attempts at successful self-government—including Athens, Rome, the Venetian Republic, and the Dutch Republic—and the growth of law and limited government in Britain. They understood there was an inherent danger in having a government strong enough to protect Americans from foreign aggression. This was a major concern shortly after the American Revolution. Britain, France, and Spain all were seen as potential predators seeking to divide and conquer the American states. The Founders wanted a government strong enough to protect Americans without being strong enough to dominate and control them.

In short, they wanted to avoid tyranny. They knew the tendency was for free societies to quickly degenerate into a dictatorship. The Greek city-states collapsed into bitter, bloody civil wars. The ensuing dictatorships were a sobering reminder of the danger of the mob—and of a government that could be taken over and turned against its own citizens. The decay of the Roman Republic through corruption and a decline of civic virtue ended the most recognized system of limited government prior to the American Revolution.

The Founding Fathers were deeply influenced by the French judge Montesquieu's 1748 political treatise *The Spirit of Laws*. He argued that dividing power into three different branches would guarantee liberty because the three would balance each other. Montesquieu was more widely cited than any other source, except the Holy Bible, in political writing leading up to the American Revolution. He deeply influenced James Madison and other key authors of the Constitution.

In effect, the Founding Fathers sought to protect freedom by inventing a machine so complex and divided against itself that no dictator could force it to work quickly. The result was a system of government so complicated that even today we can barely get it to work voluntarily. When I was Speaker, we were able to get a remarkable number of reforms adopted into law. We constantly reminded ourselves that House Republicans could make noise on our own—but we could only enact our ideas into law if we got the Senate's approval and the president's signature.

President Clinton and I got an amazing amount done because we started with recognition of our dependence on one another. We did not have to like each other or agree ideologically. We had to work from a basis that we needed each other and had to talk things out to get something done. That included 35 days of face-to-face negotiations to agree on the only four balanced budgets in the last century.

The House Republicans were also helped enormously by having two Republican Senate majority leaders to work with—first Bob Dole and then Trent Lott. Both men served in the House before going to the Senate. They understood the need to work together to get things done.

Presidents and their staffs get tired of working with members of Congress. Over time, virtually every president has found it more pleasant to focus on their peers in foreign countries. Prime ministers share the same "top of the system" attitude and worldview as American presidents, so there's a congeniality among peers. From the perspective of the White House staff, members of Congress seem arrogant, self-centered, pushy, and demanding. This is mostly true. Members of the House and Senate put their careers and reputations on the line by entering the public arena. They put in a lot of their own money—and spend a lot of time begging supporters for money. They endure hostile, sometimes idiotic press coverage. They must defeat opponents who use every possible attack to try to defeat them. When they finally win, they feel like they have accomplished something. They also have an enormous surge of adrenalin, because elections are always near-death experiences. When the people vote, you win or lose. It is an anxiety-ridden and sobering experience.

Because of this high personal cost in time, money, energy, and reputation, members of Congress are eager to get things done. Achievements justify what they went through to get to Washington. Then they discover everyone else had the same experience.

They each have a little power, but none of them have a lot of power. Even legislative leaders normally have less power than the media suggests.

The House is like a collection of 435 high school class presidents. Everyone thinks they matter. Everyone has ideas. Everyone is in a hurry to get his or her thing done. They must learn to work with each other and bargain to get what they want. The Senate is even more complicated. The Senate is like a collection of 100 potential future American presidents. Each Senator has six years between elections. They can be remarkably independent. Furthermore, the Senate Rules give individual members enormous power if they are willing to use it.

This sense of earned power and status is deeply offended when 26-year-old executive branch staff members treat members of Congress as though they don't matter. Members of Congress understand that the president and vice president have earned unique power and authority by winning an election involving all the American people. However, they deeply resent presidential staff behaving as though *they* had won the election. Since members of Congress deal with executive branch staffs far more often than they deal with presidents and vice presidents, there is constant frustration and tension.

Faced with the difficulties of courting and working with the legislative branch, presidents often fall back on executive orders to get things done quickly or do things that might take a long time or even be impossible to achieve through Congress. Executive orders are useful—especially in the opening days of an administration or in response to sudden challenges (hurricanes, war, pandemics, etc.). President Trump demonstrated this at the start of his second term. His executive orders halting illegal immigration, calling federal employees back to their offices, ending left-wing DEI initiatives, and renaming the Gulf of America and Mount McKinley were perfect examples of effective executive orders. However, many executive orders have great weaknesses.

Mainly, the general public doesn't notice or understand them. You are generally not building a reservoir of public support and commitment if something can be accomplished (or demolished) with the stroke of a pen. What one president dictates, the next president can undo just as easily. Note the revolving door of President Trump's executive orders being replaced within days by President Biden's executive orders (only to be replaced again by President Trump's second-term executive orders).

Permanent change requires passing laws—and in rare cases constitutional amendments. In the most famous constitutional amendment case, President Abraham Lincoln feared the law abolishing slavery could be overturned in the future. He concluded that he had to pass a constitutional amendment so freedom for African Americans would be protected in perpetuity. The culminating fight of his struggle to abolish slavery began two years earlier with the Emancipation Proclamation. It may surprise people today, but getting the votes necessary for a constitutional amendment—even one to abolish slavery—was hard. It took a great deal of Lincoln's time, persuasive powers, and political shrewdness. His years in the Illinois legislature served him well as a training ground for this fight.

Passing major legislation is almost as hard as changing the Constitution. By definition, a bill big enough to be historic will attract opponents and advocates in great numbers. Virtually all major legislation requires bipartisan support. With the current narrowly divided House and Senate, this is certainly true. When

I was a junior member, we had to get nearly one-third of House Democrats to vote with us to pass President Reagan's three-year tax cut. It was the key to the economic prosperity and growth that became known as Reaganomics.

During my time as Speaker, we appealed to the American people on welfare reform and got enough support that House Democrats split evenly, 101 to 101 on final passage. This was the most conservative social reform of our lifetime. It required work to receive federal welfare funds and changed welfare offices into employment centers. Real grassroots pressure from their home districts got 101 Democrats to support it.

This is the key to effective bipartisan action: sustained popular support. Through all the distractions, unexpected events, and inevitable failures, you must maintain popular support. The hard problems of reality can overcome rhetoric, communications experts, and oratory. You must continuously check in with the American people and ensure you are doing what *they want*.

YOU MUST HAVE POPULAR SUPPORT

President Lincoln captured the key reality of a free society during his famous debates with Democrat Stephen Douglas:

> In this and like communities, public sentiment is every-thing. With public sentiment, nothing can fail; without it nothing can succeed. Consequently he who moulds pub-lic sentiment, goes deeper than he who enacts statutes or pronounces decisions. He makes statutes and decisions possible or impossible to be executed.[1]

President Lincoln's constant focus on learning from and communicating with the American people was key to him sustaining four years of brutal civil war. It is an education in how to lead a free society.

President Reagan communicated the same belief in the power of the people when he said in his 1989 Farewell Address:

> Our Constitution is a document in which "We the People" tell the government what it is allowed to do. "We the People" are free. This belief has been the underlying basis for everything I've tried to do these past eight years...I've had my share of victories in the Congress, but what few people noticed is that I never won anything you didn't win for me. They never saw my troops, they never saw Reagan's regiments, the American people. You won every battle with every call you made and letter you wrote demanding action.

President Reagan learned a great deal about the power of focusing on and unlocking people while working at General Electric. Thomas Evans's brilliant book *The Education of Ronald Reagan* outlines what Reagan learned at General Electric during his eight years as a spokesperson for the company from 1954 to 1962. Reagan worked with Lemuel Boulware, the senior GE executive in charge of employee relations. General Electric was heavily unionized. For a long time, it had an adversarial relationship with the unions. Boulware was asked to change the pattern of labor conflict. He emphasized dealing with the employees as you would customers. He emphasized educating them on the practicalities of

General Electric's economic situation and organized study programs for employees and their wives.

Reagan learned from Boulware a concept called "moving the M." The M is the majority of people. If you can move the majority, then the leadership has to follow. President Reagan transformed this model into the simple phrase, "I shone the light on the American people, and they turned up the heat on Congress." Similarly, Prime Minister Margaret Thatcher boiled all this down to "first you win the argument, then you win the vote."

The most successful American politician of the 20th century, President Franklin Delano Roosevelt, learned this lesson the hard way. He had won a big election victory in 1932 and a remarkable increase in his party's strength in the House and Senate in 1934. In 1936, he won a stunning victory with 60.8 percent of the vote and an electoral college landslide of 523 to 8 (the Kansas Republican Alf Landon carried only Maine and Vermont). President Roosevelt's streak of winning three consecutive elections led him to overestimate the power of his popularity and underestimate the power of the American people and the potential opposition of Congress.

Filled with hubris, in February 1937, President Roosevelt announced a program to pack the Supreme Court and overwhelm the conservative justices who had been blocking much of his program. To President Roosevelt's shock and dismay, the same people who had voted for him turned on him. His popularity cratered as people felt he had gone too far. Democrats in Congress rebelled and refused to pass the court packing plan. The economy, which had begun to recover, fell back into a recession. In 1938, the Republicans made substantial gains in the House and Senate.

Roosevelt was so shaken by his failure to understand the limits of his popularity—and his failure to appreciate how strongly the American people and their representatives in Congress would react—he grew dramatically more cautious. It explains much of his slow response to the rise of the Axis powers and the emergence of war in Europe and the Pacific. He was afraid of being repudiated again and reacted much more timidly than he might have had he not gotten so out of step with the American people.

In a more modern example, President George H. W. Bush learned this lesson when he failed to listen to his base, which had been galvanized by his "read my lips, no new taxes" pledge at the 1988 Republican National Convention. Bush's staff was captured by the inside-the-beltway's belief in higher taxes. They apparently had no idea how much selling out on taxes would cripple his reelection effort.

So, effective leaders must listen carefully to the American people. When we developed the Contract with America, we consciously relied on this principle. Everything in the Contract had 60 percent public approval or better. The biggest issues—balancing the budget, welfare reform, congressional reform—were all in the 80 percent or higher range. We successfully negotiated reform after reform with a Democratic president for four years. This was because we constantly had the American people supporting the issues we were trying to pass. We listened first and then communicated. We learned the model from Lincoln, Reagan, and Thatcher.

President Trump's emergence in 2015–2016 came largely because he understood a deep feeling of anger that at least half the American people felt. Americans were tired of dealing with an establishment they felt despised and failed them. As candidate, and then president, Trump developed a series of issues that grew out of the hearts and minds of the American people. Trump did not invent anger over illegal immigration; he responded to it.

In 2024, President Trump did not invent the crises of higher prices and inflation. He recognized the American people were hurting and became their spokesperson. President Trump's development of the remarkable bold proposals for rethinking the entire federal government—and America's role in the world—will require paying even more attention to the American people.

What do the American people hear about these bold changes? How do they process them as they apply to their lives? What questions do they need answered so they can enthusiastically pressure their members of Congress to support the changes? Bringing the same sensitivity to the opinions of the American people to the White House that President Trump brought to the campaign will be key to his second term's success—and success in the 2026 election.

Keeping all these realities in mind while trying to focus the team, adapt to changes, and achieve goals is an exhausting and challenging process. Few presidents and members of the House and Senate really succeed. Those few who do are worth studying. Of course, those who fail are also worth studying, because failure is the greatest teacher. Sometimes there are useful, obvious lessons about what to avoid.

Regardless, governing is intentionally hard to do. Trump and his team must work tirelessly to achieve big goals.

FIVE

Make America Affordable Again

P erhaps the most immediate and imperative challenge President Donald Trump and Republicans face is getting our economy back on the right track. They must work to significantly lower inflation, not simply slow the rate of it on paper. This means developing an actionable plan to make everyday costs of gasoline, housing, groceries, electricity, lumber, and other commodities much more affordable.

Since inflation is a measure of change to the Consumer Price Index (which tracks the price of key goods), it is easy to assume lowering inflation and lowering prices are the same. They are not. One of the biggest communication blunders of the Biden-Harris administration was to constantly tout slowing monthly inflation rates while costs for people at home continued to rise or remain high. People saw a serious disconnect between what Washington was telling them and what they were seeing at the grocery store, at the gas station, and in their monthly bills.

Despite White House talking points, prices soared under President Biden. David Winston and Myra Miller of the Winston

Group developed what they call the "presidential inflation rate" shortly after Biden took office. As the Winston Group explained, this metric "measures a president's progress in handling inflation over time, from their inauguration month to the month of the most recent CPI report."

Typically, the U.S. Department of Labor's Bureau of Labor Statistics measures monthly and 12-month changes to the CPI. This can be misleading. If real prices remain high and plateau for an extended period, the monthly and annual inflation rates might still appear small. In Biden's case, the Winston Group used the CPI in January 2021 as a benchmark. It then went month to month comparing the updated price index to the 2021 figure. This provided a more practical view of inflation's impact over the entire Biden administration. According to the Winston Group, "The percent difference between the two index points gives us Biden's 'Presidential Inflation Rate,' the overall increase in the level of inflation at this point in his term."

The Winston Group's data presents a much different picture from what the Biden administration described. The official inflation rate and Biden's presidential inflation rate tracked within a few tenths of a percent for the first year of his administration but steeply diverged starting in March 2022. By June 2023, the official inflation rate was 3 percent, but the Winston Group's data shows actual prices had risen 16.3 percent since Biden took office. As I'm writing this, the Winston's Group's latest data from late 2024 shows official inflation at 2.6 percent—but Biden's presidential inflation rate at 20.7 percent.

Only Presidents Jimmy Carter and Ronald Reagan had higher presidential inflation rates. President Carter's presidential inflation rate was a debilitating 45 percent. This was the era of gas lines and Carter's malaise. President Reagan followed Carter in office and immediately began working to energize the economy. As a result, Reagan's presidential inflation rate was 21 percent. Prices were still high, but it's remarkable that Reagan was able to slow Carter's inflationary effect by more than half. For further comparison, President Trump's 7.2 percent presidential inflation rate is the lowest of the last eight presidents.

Notably, only Presidents Reagan and Trump were able to trigger deflationary effects (actual price decline) for some products in their tenure. In both cases, average gasoline prices fell dramatically. President Reagan was able to bring average gasoline prices down by 3.8 percent over the course of his two-term presidency. President Trump brought average gas prices down by 6.6 percent in his first term.

In addition to lowering real costs for Americans, President Trump and Republicans must work to reduce the cost of government, increase take-home pay, lower taxes, and put America on a path to cut the national debt and balance the federal budget by 2034 at the latest. This is the only way we are going to truly secure the American dream for future generations of Americans.

BRINGING DOWN PRICES

Solving the inflation and cost-of-living challenge must be the first step. In the spirit of making the biggest gains first, the administration should work to dramatically lower costs for domestic oil and gas production to reduce the price of gasoline and electricity. Gasoline and electricity generation costs drive up the price of every good and service in the economy. Every business needs gasoline to ship goods and electricity to run facilities. Even small, service-based businesses must keep the lights on to operate. There is energy overhead in everything. If energy prices drop, Americans will feel it. As the incoming executive, President Trump's lowest hanging fruit for lowering prices across the board is to revoke a series of Biden-era regulations, which drove up the costs and timelines of production for oil and natural gas and made selling overseas more difficult.

During President Trump's first term, he led a massive deregulation effort that dramatically reduced costs for industries and citizens alike. The petroleum industry was no exception. Oil and gas producers made large investments to increase domestic production thanks to Trump's deregulation and pro-energy policies from 2016 to 2020. As a result, American oil and gas production is still operating at record levels despite President Biden and Democrats' attacks on the industry.

As the U.S. Energy Information Administration reported on March 11, 2024:

> The United States produced more crude oil than any nation at any time, according to our International Energy Statistics, for the past six years in a row. Crude oil production in the United States, including condensate, averaged 12.9 million barrels per day (b/d) in 2023, breaking the previous U.S. and global record of 12.3 million b/d, set in 2019. Average monthly U.S. crude oil production established a monthly record high in December 2023 at more than 13.3 million b/d.[1]

When President Biden entered office, one of his first real efforts was to undo everything President Trump had done to bring down energy costs and make America energy independent. As E&E News by Politico reported on November 11, 2024:

> The Biden administration raised federal royalty rates from 12.5 percent to 16.66 percent, increased statewide bonding for oil and gas leases twentyfold, instituted more expensive limits on methane emissions, and last week finalized a first-ever fee on excess methane emissions.[2]

In January 2024, President Biden also halted almost all liquified natural gas (LNG) export approvals from the United States—also pausing five planned export terminals in what is now the Gulf of America. This was done in the name of studying the potential climate impacts of LNG and the ships on which it is transported. Because natural gas must be chilled to minus 260 degrees to become liquid, and the ships on which it is carried require fuel, Cornell University professor Robert Howarth asserted in a paper that LNG has a larger carbon footprint than even traditional coal. Dozens of anti-energy zealots seized on the paper as evidence that we must fully abandon all traditional energy sources, regardless of cost or consequences.

This is unproven, biased academic hogwash. As *Scientific American* reported on February 6, 2024, Howarth's paper is yet to be peer reviewed and fails to explain how U.S. power sector carbon emissions dropped by a third from 2005 to 2022 as the sector moved from coal to natural gas.[3] Six months after Biden's LNG ban, a federal judge halted the president's pause, but the half-year quagmire damaged the LNG market, robbed the industry of a major revenue source, and slowed plans to build five major facilities. This all cost the industry money and

Americans jobs. It did nothing to curb demand for oil and gas, so the prices increased.

To the surprise of no one, Biden's efforts to attack domestic energy did not slow production, they just made it much more expensive. (Although some argue this was by design to drive Americans away from gas-powered vehicles.) Throughout President Trump's first term, the national average price of gasoline reached a peak of $2.72 per gallon in 2018, according to Statista. By the end of his term, gasoline cost $2.17 per gallon. When President Biden took office, gasoline shot to $3.01 per gallon and peaked at $3.95 per gallon in 2022 (an 82 percent increase in two years).[4] In late 2024, the national average price of gas was $3.06 per gallon, ranging from $2.56 per gallon in Oklahoma to as high as $4.57 per gallon in Hawaii, according to AAA.[5]

So, from President Trump's perspective, it is not enough to simply make policy that aims to increase oil and gas production. The new Trump administration's focus must be to make production cheaper to reduce prices. With Biden-era limitations still in place, there are no incentives for oil and gas producers to increase production and drive down the price of their product. Further, Americans already use most of the domestic oil we produce. The only way to drive the price of gasoline down is to make producing it cheaper. This starts with striking Biden's expensive, unnecessary regulations. Then President Trump could accelerate LNG exports (which could allow oil companies to endure lower domestic prices) and reopen exploration on federal land so that companies can plan for the future. Reducing the price of fuel and electricity production would drive down costs across the board. It is a key step in solving the inflation problem.

MAKING GOVERNMENT CHEAPER

A second major step toward reinvigorating the economy will be bringing down the cost of government. This effort will be driven largely by Elon Musk as he leads the Department of Government Efficiency (DOGE). This is perhaps one of President Trump's boldest ideas—and it is certainly the most terrifying to the Washington, D.C., establishment. Musk has said he plans to cut $2 trillion from federal spending. If successful, he could begin to reverse the expensive big government Washington bureaucratic culture that has been growing since Franklin Delano Roosevelt's New Deal.

According to Musk, the DOGE will start by studying and carving away at approximately $500 billion in annual costs that are not authorized or directed by Congress. These are actions the White House could take on its own without running into difficulties with the Impoundment Control Act of 1974, which bars the executive branch from withholding funds—or simply not spending—money authorized and appropriated by Congress. As Musk mentioned in an op-ed for the *Wall Street Journal* with Vivek Ramaswamy, these costs include hundreds of millions of dollars that fund public broadcasting, grants for international aid programs, and establishment-favored nonprofit groups such as Planned Parenthood.[6]

The DOGE team could also follow years of existing advice from the Government Accountability Office and work to curb improper payments made by the Centers of Medicare and Medicaid Services. These include overpayments, underpayments, and payments that should never have been made. The two programs reportedly make more than $100 billion of these improper payments annually. Closing this financial hemorrhage would save an additional $1 trillion over a decade. As the GAO reported on April 16, 2024, this is particularly important following a general increase in Medicare and Medicaid spending, which was exacerbated by the COVID-19 pandemic.

As the GAO reported:

In the current fiscal environment, addressing improper payments and providing sufficient oversight of program spending, more generally, is particularly important. Federal spending for Medicare and Medicaid has grown by almost 80 percent over the past decade and growth in these and other health programs is projected to continue.[7]

There are also a host of Biden-era executive actions that could be revoked to save money. The Committee for a Responsible Federal Budget wrote on November 25, 2024, that reversing a series of Biden actions could save up to $1.4 trillion over nine years.[8] Biden's series of college loan debt cancellation schemes, which the U.S. Supreme Court may ultimately find unconstitutional, could save anywhere from $15 billion to $550 billion, according to the committee. Reversing Biden's efforts to increase SNAP payments, limit vehicle carbon emissions, and rewrite provisions related to public housing, Social Security Disability, and Internal Revenue Service enforcement could net another $390 billion. The committee also pointed to a handful of other health care–related executive orders in Medicare and Medicaid that could be reversed for savings estimated from $345 billion to $385 billion. Of course, Musk and the DOGE team have their work cut out for them. As Eric Boehm wrote for *Reason*, it will take about $8 trillion in cuts over 10 years to simply slow the growth of the $36 trillion national debt.[9] Interest payments alone are ballooning the debt at an alarming rate.

As a final example, the DOGE could investigate the possibility of reshaping how and where federal employees work. While most federal civilian employees already work outside of the Washington, D.C., metropolitan area, there is money to be saved by relocating some Washington-based federal agencies outside the national capital. This could provide several possible benefits. First, since federal salaries are based on the cost of living in the area in which people work, moving federal agencies to less-expensive states will immediately provide savings on personnel. A December 2024 poll by the Napolitan Institute found that 60 percent of Americans favor this idea (and 20 percent favor it strongly). This has the added effect of spreading federal jobs throughout the country to support states outside of the Beltway. Critics argue this may lessen cooperation between federal agencies, but the Napolitan Institute found 63 percent would find it beneficial.

This idea has the added effect of having the federal government sell surplus property left behind when agencies are relocated. In fact, there are already many millions of dollars' worth of surplus property in the General Service Administration's logbooks. Many of these buildings are more than 50 years old and require a great deal of upkeep. According to the Federal News Network, the Washington-based Public Buildings Reform Board found that the GSA already has a multi-billion dollar maintenance backlog.[10] So, billions of dollars could be carved from federal spending by auctioning unused or under-used property. This would provide revenue coming into federal coffers from the auction and erase billions of dollars of maintenance and upkeep costs.

Musk should push for shedding federal property even if agencies aren't moved from Washington. In March 2024, the Public Buildings Reform Board reported to Congress that most federal agency headquarters were mostly empty. As Federal News Network reported:

> The board, in its report, said commercial real estate experts use this data extensively to establish use patterns.
>
> PBRB's data analysis finds the federal headquarters buildings operated at 12 percent of their estimated capacity, on average, between January and September 2023.
>
> At a maximum, the U.S. Agency for International Development saw 26 percent occupancy of its headquarters building during this period.
>
> Meanwhile, data shows the headquarters for the U.S. Agency for Global Media reached, on average, 2 percent of its building capacity.

In some cases, this lack of occupancy was due to federal workers still operating under COVID-19 remote work rules. President Trump worked to solve this by signing an executive order forcing full-time federal employees to return to the office. Those who refused were offered an eight-month buyout as a "deferred resignation." The American people support this idea. Napolitan Institute found that 57 percent of Americans support requiring federal workers to return to the office. For federal employees who refuse to return to work, 53 percent of the American people say they should be fired. This is a no-brainer. Remote federal employees should be ordered back to the office. Those who don't should be invited to find new jobs. Then, if agency buildings are still under-utilized, agency staffs should be collapsed into shared buildings and the extra buildings should be auctioned. As the PBRB reported to Congress, the "status quo of nearly empty federal buildings is not financially or politically sustainable."

The DOGE, despite being an official government department, will only be able to do so much. Congress must step up to the plate and follow the mandate the American people gave them. While the Republican majority is slim following the 2024 election, the GOP still has an opportunity to create a popular, bipartisan effort to shrink the cost of government and balance the federal budget.

In September 2024, I went to the U.S. Capitol to celebrate the 30th anniversary of the Contract with America. While I was there, I was struck by how many of us were involved in that effort—and how much we accomplished. I ran into Joe Scarborough, who now hosts MSNBC's *Morning Joe* but also served with me as a House Republican in Congress. He pointed out something remarkable to me. He said the Contract with America Republicans were the only American elected officials in the last 100 years to pass four consecutive balanced budgets. That is remarkable. I bring this up for two reasons.

First, when we were trying to balance the federal budget in the mid-90s, virtually everyone in the Washington and media establishments told us it was impossible. We narrowly lost the vote to pass a balanced budget amendment to the U.S. Constitution. Since the vote was so close, we House Republicans decided to just balance the budget anyway. Of course, when we were successful, the establishment media credited President Clinton for balancing the budget, due to his 1993 tax hikes. This was balderdash.

As Stephen Moore wrote for the Cato Institute in 1998:

And 1993—the year of the giant Clinton tax hike—was not the turning point in the deficit wars, either. In fact, in 1995, two years after that tax hike, the budget baseline submitted by the president's own Office of Management and Budget and the nonpartisan Congressional Budget Office predicted $200 billion deficits for as far as the eye could see. The figure shows the Clinton deficit baseline. What changed this bleak outlook?

Newt Gingrich and company—for all their faults—have received virtually no credit for balancing the budget. Yet today's surplus is, in part, a byproduct of the GOP's single-minded crusade to end 30 years of red ink. Arguably, Gingrich's finest hour as Speaker came in March 1995 when he rallied the entire Republican House caucus behind the idea of eliminating the deficit within seven years.

Skeptics said it could not be done in seven years. The GOP did it in four.[11]

Musk and Republicans at large are being given the same treatment by the Washington establishment. Just as the Republican House GOP did, they should ignore the nay-sayers and keep working.

Second, success breeds success. We set out to balance the budget in seven years—and we did it in four. As the DOGE, the White House, and congressional Republicans start peeling back layers of the federal budget, they will find more areas that can be made leaner and more efficient. As the saying goes, the best way to eat an elephant is one bite at a time. So, the best advice I have for the Trump administration's Office of Management and

Budget and Republicans in Congress is: Don't listen to the establishment. The bureaucrats in Washington are just trying to protect themselves—and the media is just trying to help their friends in the bureaucracy.

DRIVING ECONOMIC GROWTH

While Republicans cut spending, they must also enact provisions to drive economic growth. The quickest way to do this will be to resume work from President Trump's first term. The Tax Cuts and Jobs Act of 2017 was the most extensive reform of American tax law in 30 years. It reduced the corporate tax rate from 35 percent to 21 percent to make America more attractive to big companies. It doubled the standard deduction for everyday Americans and their families to $6,350 and $12,700 respectively. It also doubled the child tax credit from $1,000 to $2,000 and introduced a host of other pro-growth tax cuts designed to maximize take-home pay, increase business investment in America, and spur economic growth.

It was based on the style of supply-side economics practiced and advocated for by economists Art Laffer, Larry Kudlow, and others during the Reagan administration. Laffer argued that there is a maximum marginal tax rate that will generate the maximum possible tax revenues in an economy. Raising the marginal tax rate beyond this ideal point leads to a slowdown in economic activity and ultimately yields fewer tax revenues. Therefore, lowering a high marginal tax rate to a certain point can spur economic growth enough to match—or overcome—any shortage with new tax revenues.

Tax cuts inherently spur an initial dip in tax revenues, which opponents of supply-side economics often highlight. However, as economic growth revs up, tax revenues increase. This is exactly what we saw with President Reagan's tax cuts in the 1980s (however, economic growth was hamstrung by monetary tightening by the U.S. Federal Reserve). It is also the pattern we saw when we pushed President Clinton to cut taxes in 1997. Our 1997 tax cut legislation lowered the capital gains tax from 28 percent to 20 percent, invented the child tax credit (then $500 per child), created tax credits for higher education, established Roth IRAs, and made a host of other cuts. As Heritage Foundation reported:

> In 1995, the first year for which these data are available, just over $8 billion in venture capital was invested. Venture capital is especially critical to a vibrant economy because high-risk/high-return investment permits promising new businesses to blossom, rapidly spreading new technologies and new ideas into the marketplace and across the economy. Such investments, when successful, generate returns to investors that are subject primarily to the tax on capital gains. By 1998, the first full year in which the lower capital gains rates were in effect, venture capital activity reached almost $28 billion, more than a three-fold increase over 1995 levels, and by 1999, it had doubled yet again.[12]

When venture capital investment increases six-fold over four years, tax revenues naturally go up—along with take-home pay, employment, and middle class growth. We know this works because we have done it. President Trump and Republicans should push to make the core provisions of the Tax Cuts and Jobs Act (TCJA) of 2017 permanent and expand the law with new tax cuts to help Americans keep more of their money. Several important parts of the law are set to expire by the end of 2025. The marginal tax rates for individuals would increase back to pre-2017 levels. Standard deductions for individual and joint filers—and the $2,000 child tax credit—would be cut in half. Together, this will mean taxes will go up for every taxpayer in America, from the lowest earning taxpayers to the wealthiest and everyone in between. On the campaign trail, President Biden (and later Vice President Kamala Harris) repeatedly claimed the TCJA only cut taxes for the wealthy. However, on December 22, 2022, five years after the bill became law, House Budget Committee ranking member Jason Smith (MO-8) pointed out that the law had saved low- and middle-income families of four $2,000 per year in tax savings thanks to the provisions in the law.

As Representative Smith reported:

> In fact, it is the working class who have made the biggest gains under the Tax Cuts and Jobs Act. Not only did working families get to keep more of their paycheck, but their paychecks grew the fastest compared to every other income group. America saw the lowest unemployment rate in 50 years because businesses had incentives to expand and bring production back to the United States. A year after passage of this historic tax relief, our economy grew at a full percentage point higher than the Congressional Budget Office had projected it would for that year. It is clear that the Tax Cuts and Jobs Act has made a real difference in the lives of hardworking Americans.

TCJA reduced the tax burden on families and businesses, while managing to bring in historic revenues to federal coffers. Tax revenues reached an all-time high of $4.9 trillion for fiscal year 2022, $900 billion higher than the Congressional Budget Office projected for 2022 when TCJA was signed into law and $1.6 trillion higher than before TCJA passed.[13]

One group that would be especially hit by rolling back Trump's tax cuts will be small business owners. A 20 percent deduction for small businesses, including limited liability corporations, partnerships, sole proprietorships, and S-corporations, is also set to expire by the end of 2025.

Most small business owners add their businesses' profit to their own personal income taxes. This is known as pass-through business income. According to the Tax Foundation, pass-through businesses make up more than 90 percent of all businesses in America and employ more than 50 percent of all private employees.[14] Because these business owners pay taxes based on individual income rates, they can face tax rates ranging from 10 percent to 39.6 percent at the federal level (if the TCJA's marginal rates expire). Additionally, many pass-through business owners must also pay self-employment and payroll taxes, which fund Social Security and Medicare. Then, they must pay state level taxes as well. As a result, the Tax Foundation reported these pass-through business owners pay 47 percent in taxes on average—and many exceed 50 percent.

If all the temporary provisions of the TCJA expire, small business owners—and all their employees—will be devastated. This will almost certainly mean they will be forced to raise their prices, lay off employees, go out of business, or all of the above. If half of the American workforce is suddenly put in jeopardy by tax hikes, our economy will at best grind to a halt—and at worst collapse. Our national debt will skyrocket because we'll have much less revenue due to the lack of economic activity. Even assuming small businesses can weather a tax hike on individual income, the TCJA permanently lowered the tax rate for big corporations to 21 percent. Should the pass-through income deduction go away, small businesses will be at a hugely unfair disadvantage, and American communities everywhere will suffer for it.

PRESIDENT TRUMP'S PLAN

President Trump is calling to make all individual income tax provisions in the TCJA permanent and provide further tax relief to Americans. He wants Congress to eliminate all taxes on tips that wage workers make, overtime pay, and Social Security payments. Also, Vice President Vance has called for raising the child tax credit to $5,000.

The tax-free tip proposal will be complicated to track, but I'm confident President Trump and his team can get it done. Eliminating income taxes on overtime pay for hourly workers and Social Security payments for seniors is a no-brainer. These proposals will immediately give significant relief to people in these tax brackets. For those who are still in the workforce, it will provide real incentive to work and succeed.

The COVID-19 pandemic crippled more than the general economy. In some ways, it collapsed the value of work—especially for young people who are new in or starting their careers. Across the country, many business owners still have job openings but no workforce willing to fill them. Many of these businesses have had to rely on the employees they do have to pick up extra shifts and work overtime to keep things moving. At a minimum, the people who are committed to work should not pay income tax on money earned after 40 hours a week. Congress should also explore what relief can be given to the employers who pay payroll taxes on overtime pay. This may require revising the rules proscribed in the Fair Labor Standards Act.

Critics of President Trump's proposal have claimed eliminating income tax on overtime pay could cost the federal government $680.4 billion over 10 years. The estimates are tremendously higher if you include all income and payroll taxes for employees and employers. However, an overtime tax cut could encourage workers to get back into the labor market and ease staffing issues across the nation. This means more workers would be paying taxes on their regular wages. It could also put more money in workers' pockets, who could then invest that money in their futures or their families. In addition to spurring economic activity, this could be a great way to create a path for many wage workers to get into the middle class. Those already in the middle class could grow their savings, pay down debt, live more comfortably, and add more growth to the economy.

Similarly, seniors who have worked their entire lives—paying into Social Security—should not be taxed when they receive the benefits they are owed. Period. Currently, seniors who make more than $25,000 a year (including half of their Social Security benefits) have half of their benefits taxed. Those who make $34,000 or more see an additional 35 percent of their benefits taxed. It is government robbery. Plain and simple.

The Committee for a Responsible Federal Budget estimates cutting these taxes would create a $1.8 trillion shortfall over 10 years.[15] Currently these tax revenues are marked for funding the

Social Security and Medicare Hospital Insurance trust fund. Many critics point to this estimate and others as a justification for continuing to take already-taxed money from American seniors. They say eliminating the taxes would make Social Security less solvent and endanger the future of the program. However, as I wrote earlier, the shortfall could likely be remedied by simply cleaning up Social Security and Medicare, eliminating waste, fraud, and abuse, and working to make our entire health care system more affordable.

Vice President Vance's proposal to increase the child tax credit by 150 percent to $5,000 also deserves consideration. This issue is dear to me. As I mentioned earlier, the Republican House invented the child tax credit as part of our 1997 tax cut legislation. At that time, it was a $500-per-child credit (roughly $975 in today's currency). When we first passed it, our goal was to help families who were struggling to be able to provide for their children. I don't think any of us knew the impact it would have. As a result of our 1997 legislation, more American children were lifted out of poverty than at any time in history up to that point. Over the decades I have personally met people for whom the child tax credit allowed them to provide for their kids and focus on creating a better future for their families. Even Biden's White House acknowledges the child tax credit "is one of the nation's strongest tools to provide tens of millions of families with some support and breathing room while raising children. It has also been shown to be one of the most effective tools ever for lowering child poverty."[16]

I hope Congress will consider Vice President Vance's proposal. It could improve—and even save—the lives of millions of Americans.

SIX

Americans and Immigration

A mericans have a long history of struggling with the issue of immigration.

Even before our nation's founding, when America was made up of British colonies, Benjamin Franklin worried that the number of Germans coming to Pennsylvania with their own newspapers, schools, and churches would drown out the English-speaking colonists. In the end, the Germans were assimilated into American society.

At the beginning of the American experiment, during the first Congress in 1790, the Naturalization Act defined the process of becoming an American citizen. Its terms reflected the times:

> ...any Alien being a free white person, who shall have resided within the limits and under the jurisdiction of the United States for the term of two years, may be admitted to become a citizen thereof on application to any common law Court of record in any one of the States wherein he shall have resided for the term of one year at least, and

making proof to the satisfaction of such Court that he is a person of good character, and taking the oath or affirmation prescribed by law to support the Constitution of the United States…shall be considered as a Citizen of the United States.

In a forerunner to the challenge we face in trying to distinguish between the Dreamers (immigrants who came to the United States as young children and grew up as Americans), the law went on to say of the new Americans, "the children of such person so naturalized, dwelling within the United States, being under the age of twenty one years at the time of such naturalization, shall also be considered as citizens of the United States."

There was no provision in this early period for how people could come to America. Immigration was open to those capable of undertaking it. As transportation capabilities advanced in the first half of the 19th century, immigration exploded. By the 1850s, hostility to newcomers increased so much that the Know Nothing Party was explicitly and aggressively anti-immigrant. It was founded during the chaos caused by the collapse of the Whig Party.

Abraham Lincoln, a former Whig politician turned Republican, disavowed the Know Nothings and courted immigrant newspapers and groups. This strategy paid off in votes for the presidential election and during the Civil War. German and Irish immigrants volunteered for the Union Army in huge numbers.

The first reference to citizens of the United States is in the 14th Amendment to the Constitution, which was ratified on July 9, 1868. It established the framework for modern citizenship within the law and the Constitution. The 14th Amendment states:

All persons born or naturalized in the United States, and subject to the jurisdiction thereof, are citizens of the United States and of the State wherein they reside. No State shall make or enforce any law which shall abridge the privileges or immunities of citizens of the United States; nor shall any State deprive any person of life, liberty, or property, without due process of law; nor deny to any person within its jurisdiction the equal protection of the laws.

After the Civil War, the American economy and population grew dramatically. As the number of immigrants from non-English-speaking countries increased, the desire to restrict immigration grew. By 1882, the resistance to open-ended immigration led to the passage of two restrictive bills. The Immigration Act of 1882 was the first time the United States tried to restrict immigration. It created a 50-cent fee for non-Americans landing at any port. The implementation of this law was contracted to the states. This landmark bill established a procedure for screening immigrants and prohibiting some of them from entering the country.

The 1882 Immigration Act also provided that convicts should be sent back to their countries of origin and established that every immigrant should be examined.

"If on such examination," the law stated, "there shall be found among such passengers any convict, lunatic, idiot, or any person unable to take care of himself or herself without becoming a public charge, they shall report the same in writing to the collector of such port, and such persons shall not be permitted to land."

Unlike the current chaos at the Mexican border, almost a century and a half ago, the United States implemented careful examinations of immigrants entering our country.

The second immigration act of 1882 was even more restrictive and targeted only Chinese immigrants. It was entitled the Chinese Exclusion Act. The law lived up to its name by instituting an absolute ban on Chinese workers coming to the United States. A decade later, Congress passed the Geary Act in 1892, which extended the ban for another decade. This law went a step further than excluding new Chinese immigrants. It required that Chinese immigrants already in the United States register and acquire a certificate of residence or face deportation. It was a big year for organizing an orderly immigration system. On January 1, 1892, the first immigrant was processed through Ellis Island. From then until 1954, more than 12 million immigrants would come through Ellis Island. Callista's grandmother came from Poland in 2007. When we went to Ellis Island, we looked up her paperwork. The contrast between the disciplined, orderly, professional approach of Ellis Island, and the disjointed, unruly, brazen chaos of our southern border could not be greater.

The one key group that was not affected by the Exclusion Act was the Japanese. President Theodore Roosevelt grew close to the Japanese when he helped negotiate the end of the Russo-Japanese War in Portsmouth, New Hampshire. (Roosevelt got the Nobel Peace Prize for his efforts.) He did not want to humiliate the Japanese, so he worked out an agreement that discrimination against Japanese in America (specifically the segregation of Japanese children in schools in San Francisco) would stop. In return, Japan would limit its issuance of passports to Japanese citizens to come to the United States. There was an exception for family members of people who were already in the United States, which led to many Japanese women suddenly marrying someone who was already in Hawaii.

Despite the professionalism of Ellis Island, the sentiment against immigration continued to grow. The Immigration Act of 1917, called the Asiatic Barred Zone Act, required a literary test for all immigrants over 16 years old for the first time. It prohibited immigration from the "Asiatic Barred Zone," including parts of Asia, the Middle East, and Russia.

Then, after World War I, a mood of American nationalism led to the strongest anti-immigration law ever passed. The Immigration Act of 1924 (the National Origins Act) used the 1890 census to determine how many people could come to America from each foreign country. The law put a 2 percent quota on each nationality (based on the number of immigrants by country of origin, counted in the 1890 census). It created a huge bias in favor of Northern Europe (whose immigrants had a larger presence in America) and against the rest of the world. For the first time, you had to have a visa to enter the United States.

The next great event in America's relationship with people of non-American origins was the internment of Japanese and Japanese Americans after the surprise attack on Pearl Harbor on December 7, 1941. This policy went into force on February 19, 1942, when President Roosevelt signed Executive Order 9066. It was a frightened overreaction to the attack. Ironically, it was not applied to the 160,000 Japanese who lived in Hawaii because the military said it was impractical. This was due to the key role the Japanese played in the Hawaiian economy and the amount of shipping it would have taken to move them to the mainland for internment. However, on the mainland, an estimated 120,000 Japanese were forced into internment camps, including 70,000 American citizens. It was a clear, shameful violation of their rights and liberties.

The Japanese internment was wrong, as indicated by Congress and President Ronald Reagan with the passage of the Civil Liberties Act of 1988. President Reagan apologized for the U.S. government's illegal acts, and the government paid compensation to the survivors. It should be noted that patriotic Japanese joined the American military during World War II despite the internment of their family members.

More than 33,000 Japanese Americans volunteered for the military. The Japanese American 442nd Regimental Combat Team was one of the most decorated units in the war. One of its members, Daniel Inouye, lost an arm to a grenade, won the Congressional Medal of Honor, and went on to become an influential and powerful senator.

As late as the 1950s, there was a consensus about controlling the border that insisted on securing legal immigration and deporting illegal immigrants. President Dwight Eisenhower presided over a mass deportation program (unfortunately called Operation Wetback), which deported over 1.5 million noncitizens who came to America without the proper legal documentation.

THE BREAKDOWN OF IMMIGRATION AND ASSIMILATION

The rise of the anti-American left in the 1960s began to break down the consensus on how to control the borders—and whether immigrants should learn to be American at all. Because the left had grown to despise American history and values, its members were opposed to acculturating immigrants into becoming American. This hostility also extended to programs designed to help Native Americans leave reservations and assimilate into American society.

The emergence of a militant civil rights movement extended into the immigration field. The quota system established under the 1924 immigration laws inherently favored Europeans and placed restrictions on non-European immigration. This was increasingly condemned as racial bias. The result was the 1965 Immigration and Nationality Act. Signed into law by President Lyndon B. Johnson in October 1965, it dramatically expanded immigration from Asia and Africa.

There was a tragic irony in the act being part of Johnson's Great Society. As Marvin Olasky proved in his landmark study *The Tragedy of American Compassion*, the Great Society replaced the principles that had worked in America for more than 200 years with a set of left-wing principles for welfare and immigration that were bound to fail. The Great Society represented a fundamental break with traditional America. It was based on a belief that money rather than culture was the key to success in America. It favored a system of learned dependence in which poor individuals were taken care of by the government. People were reduced from being citizens to being clients of the bureaucracy.

Further, the culture of the Great Society was dominated by a repudiation of traditional America as a racist, unequal society manipulated by the monied class against everyone else. As a young Congressman in the early 1980s, I learned how destructive this approach was for new immigrants. I recall a time when a hard-working and increasingly successful young Vietnamese man came to my office. He complained that his brother arrived in America and was captured by the welfare state bureaucracy and mentality. While the first brother worked hard and was rising in affluence, the second brother learned to live passively in public housing with food stamps and government handouts.

It hit me that the left's contempt for hard work undermines the work ethic in America. The left has clear contempt for the 40 million Americans who have had jobs at McDonald's, including Jeff Bezos. From the left's perspective, these hard workers take hamburger flipping jobs that are beneath them. The combination of the left's contempt for patriotism and their contempt for the work ethic began to make assimilation dramatically more difficult. Historically, immigrants came to America expecting to work hard so they and their children could become Americans.

This refusal to strengthen traditional America was compounded by the decay of support for controlling the border. In the left's view, borders were inherently racist and imperialist. Why shouldn't everyone be able to come to America if they wanted?

The recent Gallup World Poll that reported that 165 million people would like to come to America did not faze the left. The fact that such a mass migration of people from different cultures with work ethics would crush American society and culture was fine with the left. After all, the left viewed America as a bad place that did not deserve to survive. This open-border attitude combined with the explosive changes in communications and transportation meant that millions began to come into America illegally.

By 1985, the illegal immigration crisis became bad enough that a bipartisan majority formed around the Simpson-Mazzoli Act (for which I voted in favor). In return for the amnesty of an estimated 300,000 people, Congress committed to stopping the flow of illegal immigrants by controlling the border and pledged to create an effective program to make sure workers were here legally.

President Reagan wrote in his diary: "I'll sign it. It's high time we regained control of our borders and this bill will do this." The Simpson-Mazzoli Act provided amnesty for an estimated 300,000 illegal immigrants, but ultimately it was 3 million—a ten-fold increase over what we were told. And, of course, Congress never provided the resources to control the border or establish an effective employment verification system (something that the Chamber of Commerce and many business organizations deeply opposed). Looking back, it is incredibly frustrating and disappointing that the bipartisan law was not as effectively implemented as it should have been.

THE BIDEN DELUGE

In recent years, the magnet of American life combined with the declining cost of transportation has encouraged more people to accept the danger of illegally crossing the border. Many people have decided the risk was worth taking if they could live in America—a nation with a structure of freedom under the rule of law and opportunity for economic advancement.

President Barack Obama took some steps to slow down this avalanche of illegal immigration. Later, President Trump took serious and effective steps. By the end of 2019, he came close to getting the border completely under control. Then came the Biden deluge. It is estimated that during the Biden presidency, more than 7.5 million illegal immigrants—including a substantial number of criminals—flooded into the United States.

The American people were so upset by the increasing number of criminal gangs and violent illegal immigrants that it became one of the two biggest issues in the 2024 presidential campaign. Americans clearly felt something was wrong, unfair, and dangerous. At America's New Majority Project, we asked a number of key questions about illegal immigration. The results were striking.

As it related to the 2024 elections, we discovered that 77 percent of Americans oppose allowing illegal immigrants to vote, with 56 percent of voters preferring a Republican candidate who opposes allowing illegal immigrant voting to a Democrat who favors letting illegal immigrants vote. Further, 50 percent of voters thought that President Biden and the Democrats deliberately allowed illegal immigrants into the United States so that they would (hopefully) vote for Democrats. By comparison, just 42 percent disagreed with this assessment.

Leading up to President Trump's resounding victory, our polling at America's New Majority Project revealed that Americans see border security as the necessary first step to fixing our illegal immigration crisis. We found that Americans overwhelmingly support stronger measures to increase border security. Consider that 77 percent of Americans support hiring additional border patrol agents and 70 percent support declaring the border crisis a state of emergency, allowing for FEMA personnel and National Guard troop deployment to border communities.

Recognizing how open border policies have allowed for dangerous criminals to wreak havoc on American cities, communities, and families, 68 percent of Americans support designating drug cartels as terrorist groups. Sixty-six percent support instituting laws that make it easier to deport illegal immigrants.

People are so concerned about illegal immigrant crime they want local law enforcement to work with the federal government in tracking down the criminals. Most Americans (83 percent) support mandating that local law enforcement check the immigration status of an arrested individual who is suspected of being in the United States illegally. Moreover, a 67 percent majority agrees that state and local police should be allowed to arrest individuals suspected of being in the United States without legal permission.

Further, most Americans believe strongly that we should stop providing economic incentives to come to America illegally and that we should reform the asylum system. Polling from America's New Majority Project found that 72 percent of voters support mandating that every employer use e-Verify to ensure their employees are in the United States legally. Additionally, Americans recognize that the asylum system has long been abused and is in desperate need of reform. Accordingly, 75 percent support requiring asylum seekers to legally enter the United States, and 56 percent support disqualifying those who could receive protections somewhere else. A majority (70 percent) also support making the requirements for asylum seekers more stringent.

In his first week, President Trump implemented many of these immigration measures with the support of the American people behind him. In a blitz of executive actions, President Trump:

- Terminated Biden-era immigration policies, reinstituted the Remain in Mexico policy, and signed an executive order to establish a physical border wall;[1]
- Declared a national emergency at the southern border;[2]
- Issued a proclamation determining that the crisis at the southern border is an invasion under Article IV, Section 4 of the U.S. Constitution;[3]
- Signed an executive order giving the U.S. military authorization to develop a plan to deploy troops to the border;[4]
- Enacted an executive order halting federal funding for sanctuary cities, allocating resources for establishing detention

centers, and setting up Homeland Security Task Forces in every state to "faithfully execute the immigration laws of the United States;"[5]

- Implemented an order to augment vetting and screening protocols for people seeking a visa;[6] and
- Designated gangs and drug cartels as terrorist organizations, including MS-13 and Tren de Aragua.[7]

LEGAL IMMIGRATION

Seventy percent of the American people think illegal immigration is bad for the United States. However, it is important to remember that Americans deeply favor legal immigration.

Most Americans know people who have come to America legally and become good citizens and productive members of the community. President Trump's mother came from Scotland. His wife Melania came from Slovenia. As I mentioned earlier, Callista's grandmother came from Poland (as did her grandfather). It's no surprise that at least 73 percent of Americans favor legal immigration.

Callista and I recently made a documentary called *Journey to America*, which premiered on PBS. It told the life stories of nine remarkable people who came to the United States and contributed to making this a better country.

We must be resolved in stopping illegal immigration, but we must be equally resolved in streamlining the ability for competent, hard-working people to come to America and become Americans. Legal immigrants are a powerful source of economic and technological growth. Elon Musk, for example, is only the latest in a long line of people who make America wealthier and more technologically advanced. The wide-ranging skills, talents, and attitudes of legal immigrants are a key part of what makes America exceptional.

Legal immigration has long been a part of America's history. Consider that our first secretary of the treasury, Alexander Hamilton, was born on the island of Nevis, and the fourth secretary of the treasury, Albert Gallatin, was born in Switzerland. (Gallatin was responsible for funding the Louisiana Purchase, which doubled the size of the United States. He was so important that his statue now stands just outside the Treasury Building in Washington.) For generations, immigrants have made America exceptional. Sustaining legal immigration is as important as stopping illegal immigration.

THE DREAMERS

Finally, there is the difficult question of what to do about young people who were brought to the United States at such early ages that they have no memory of their former country and often no language skills except English.

There is a consensus that something must be done to provide them with a path to citizenship. However, the challenges are significant.

First, how do we legally define "Dreamers"? The definition must be codified in such a way that it helps those who have genuinely fallen into that limbo category but is not so expansive that it undermines the effort to stop illegal immigration.

Second, what are the legitimate tests of honesty, work, achievement, and desire to be an American that must be administered to forge a path to citizenship?

The American people recognize and agree that the Dreamers face a set of difficult and legally complicated circumstances and must be treated accordingly. In fact, a FWD.us poll found 71 percent of Americans are in favor of legislation that pairs border security funding with an earned path to citizenship for Dreamers. This includes 82 percent of Democrats, 73 percent of Independents, and 58 percent of Republicans.[8]

Further, according to a 2024 poll by UMass-Amherst/WCVB, 68 percent of Americans favor giving Dreamers American citizenship.[9]

Many Dreamers have shown remarkable motivation, initiative, and hard work. TheDream.US is a scholarship program that provides college and career assistance to undocumented immigrant youth. The average age of the program's first 11,000 scholarship recipients when they came to the United States was four years old.

In the last decade, TheDream.US has provided thousands of college scholarships to students at nearly 80 partner universities. Students who are a part of this program have a 76 percent college graduation rate and are committed to their future personal and professional success.

Ninety-four percent of the program's graduates with work permits are employed after six months. Many study and get jobs in nursing and health care, education and teaching, or STEM-related fields. These are fields that need more ambitious and hard-working employees.

From day one of his second term in office, President Trump has delivered on his promises to secure the southern border and resolve our nation's abounding immigration crisis. The American people agree that the first step of immigration reform includes controlling the border and making it virtually impossible to enter the United States illegally. It also requires deporting criminals who are in America illegally and reforming our system to make it easier for legal immigrants to come to America and achieve their own American dreams.

But amidst these transformative immigration reforms, we must not lose sight of this one final part of the process: developing a path to citizenship for the hard-working, motivated, law-abiding Dreamers.

It can be done, and it must be done.

SEVEN

Entrepreneurial Government

President Trump's decision to bring a wave of successful entrepreneurs into government may prove to be one of his most powerful contributions to making America great again.

Over the last 93 years, since the election of President Franklin Delano Roosevelt, the American system has grown more bureaucratic and centralized—and less accountable and competent.

Bureaucracies have a long history of delivering predictable results through systems of rules and processes. They grow in power until they become almost uncontrollable and impossible to reform.

Antony Jay's brilliant TV series *Yes, Minister* and *Yes, Prime Minister* should be required viewing for everyone who wants to manage and change bureaucracies. Jay was a senior adviser to Prime Minister Margaret Thatcher, and he pulled from real incidents of the civil service undermining Thatcher's policies. He then turned them into humorous TV episodes. Thatcher said it was her favorite program because it was so real. Jay went on to write a small but insightful book, *Management and Machiavelli*, which is extraordinarily helpful in thinking through effective management beyond bureaucracy.

One of the greatest problems with bureaucracies is the needs of the internal system become more important than the needs of the people the system is supposed to serve. The day-to-day comfort and convenience of the bureaucrats outweigh the desires and expectations of the customers (or taxpayers).

Bureaucracies tend to be ossified, obsolete institutions. The historically established principles and precedents on which the various bureaus are founded are slavishly adhered to—even when they no longer make sense. Following process and sustaining habits and patterns become end goals of strong bureaucracies.

Former secretary of defense Robert McNamara once observed that it was easier to acquire new multi-billion-dollar weapons systems than it was to change the coffee break schedule at the Pentagon.

McNamara's observation is related to a simple fact: people who tend to flourish in bureaucracies are comfortable in highly predictable systems with limited change. Bureaucrats nourish and train the next generation of bureaucrats, who then nourish and train the next generation of bureaucrats. It's a cycle. Eventually, the process becomes the measure of success even if it does not achieve the bureaucracy's original goals. In the Pentagon, efforts to change the bureaucracy are usually shrugged off. The permanent bureaucracy refers to presidential appointees as "the summer help." Civil servants, including those in the military, assume they can outlast presidential personnel.

Bureaucracies are not restricted to government structures. The gradual spread of the system—and the increasingly fluid relationship between federal agencies and the companies with whom they contract—have led many corporations to become bureaucratic. Taking bureaucracy out of government will require taking bureaucracy out of these big, entrenched firms (which spend a significant amount of time, money, and effort lobbying the government).

When Elon Musk was revolutionizing reusable rockets with SpaceX, he had a small team. It was less than 10 percent of the people assigned to develop rockets at Boeing. Of course, the Musk system required flexible, dedicated people willing to work long hours. An entrepreneurial achievement-oriented person is remarkably different from a process-oriented bureaucrat who is wedded to working 9 a.m. to 5 p.m. with long weekends and limited effort. This is the personality nurtured by bureaucratic systems.

This extraordinary work and achievement gap between entrepreneurs and bureaucrats is being tested by President Trump. His personnel choices—and his willingness to back up his appointees when they get into fights with the bureaucracy—represent serious stress tests on the system.

Entrepreneurs operate from a profoundly different model than bureaucrats. Entrepreneurs end each day asking, "Did we achieve what we set out to get done?" Bureaucrats end each day asking, "Did we follow the process correctly?" Entrepreneurs set big goals and then adapt constantly until they reach their goals. Bureaucrats set schedules based on process and are happy to achieve whatever can be done within that framework.

The natural pattern of bureaucracies is compounded by Congress creating new rules and new laws every time there is a problem. The challenge of managing the Pentagon is compounded by every congressionally mandated behavior. Each mandate may

seem reasonable on its own, but it becomes a mess when combined with the litany of previous instructions. The system becomes
red tape bound and can't function effectively.

In the George W. Bush administration, I helped a brilliant,
entrepreneurial medical doctor develop a new office of technological innovation in health care, which was going to be placed in the
Department of Health and Human Services.

All the paperwork was done. President Bush supported creating this new office. To celebrate its launch, Secretary of Health
and Human Services Tommy Thompson hosted a gathering of
about 200 health leaders at the Willard Hotel.

Thompson had been a successful governor (the longest serving
in Wisconsin history and the only one elected four times). He was
in the habit of getting things done.

As the new office was discussed, people came up with innovative ideas. Thompson would say "we can do that" or "I will appoint
a committee to work on that," etc. The following day, he was told
by the HHS general counsel that he had violated a whole series of
laws by promising actions that could only be undertaken within
the structure of official systems mandated by Congress.

While Thompson was getting briefed about the laws he had
potentially broken, the new entrepreneurial doctor was in a step-
by-step briefing on all the laws and bureaucratic rules he would
have to follow before he could make any progress on innovation.

When his legal briefings ended, he called and asked to come
see me. When he arrived that afternoon, he said he didn't know if
serious innovation in health care was even possible given all the
rules and regulations about which he had learned. All of his experience in successful achievement was blocked by the bureaucratic
mountain under which he was trapped.

Bureaucracies exist to guarantee a predictable outcome through a predictable system of rules and laws. They are designed to take normal people and give them an extraordinary capacity to manage things by having them work within historically proven rules and procedures.

The problem comes when the world starts changing and the bureaucracy hides in its precedents and regulations to avoid change.

Edwards Deming's work is a good example of why it is so hard for a bureaucracy to operate effectively in the modern world.

I had the good fortune of taking a 90-hour tutorial with Deming late in his career. It was astonishing how basic and yet profound his proposals were. The heart of Deming's system is continuous improvement. This system involves everyone from the janitor to the president of a company to be involved in constant improvement.

Deming's system of continuously improving quality worked so well it became the standard for Japanese industry after World War II. The annual prize for the best run company in Japan is still the Deming Award in honor of his impact in modernizing Japan and helping it become a world class producer of manufactured goods.

The contrast between Deming's continuous improvement and the American bureaucratic system became clear when Toyota and General Motors agreed to a joint venture in Fremont, California, in 1984. GM wanted to learn Toyota's lean manufacturing and management systems, and Toyota wanted to avoid tariffs on cars imported to America. The venture was called New United Motor Manufacturing (NUMMI). Thirty of Toyota's managers, who had been immersed in the Deming model, came in to help run a GM plant.

No major changes were made to the facility or the workforce. But GM workers were flown to Toyota plants in Japan for training. Further, all workers could offer ideas for improvement. There were a lot of ways in which the GM system was well behind the Toyota system. Consequently, the first year produced more than 4,400 specific ideas for improvement. Some were big ideas, but most of them were small tweaks. Detroit's initial reaction was to end the partnership. Any plant that needed 4,400 improvements was apparently too screwed up for GM to claim. However, the partnership endured more than two decades. Toyota ended up expanding on its own into the U.S. market. GM's bureaucracy never learned the lean manufacturing style and clearly missed the essence of Deming's involvement. Consequently, the NUMMI plant is now the Tesla Fremont Factory, after being purchased by Musk's company in 2010.

Now imagine trying to apply continuous improvement to the red tape bound federal system or the teachers' union–controlled public school systems that are failing in so many big cities.

We will know the Trump entrepreneurial offensive is working when we see rules and regulations that block continuous improvement being cut away.

Peter Drucker, the most influential management writer of the last 150 years, illustrated the challenges of effectiveness in a small classic called *The Effective Executive*. Drucker believed that effectiveness was different from efficiency. Efficiency involves doing something right. Effectiveness involves doing the right thing.

Drucker argued that all impacts had to be measured from the outside. Your customers' experiences should define how you focus your employees. Defining the end state of each bureaucratic activity using Drucker's definition of effectiveness would be a major breakthrough. The bureaucracy could then be reshaped until it achieved the defined end state.

The naval shipbuilding program is a perfect example of the collapse between desired end state and practical reality. During World War II, our ability to build ships was second to none. But that ability has simply collapsed as the bureaucracy, red tape, and union contracts have made it virtually impossible to build a modern warship quickly and inexpensively. Modernizing the American fleet has become impossible thanks to our unmanageable system.

Similarly, there are no defined acceptable outcomes that could explain the state of education in Baltimore. In 2023, there were 13 out of 32 Baltimore high schools in which zero students tested proficient on Maryland's math exam.[1] According to Fox 5 News:

> In those 13 high schools, 1,736 students took the test, and 1,295 students, or 74.5 percent, scored a one out of four. One is the lowest level, meaning those students were not even close to proficient.
>
> Last school year, Baltimore City Schools received $1.6 billion from taxpayers, the most ever. The district also received $799 million in COVID relief funding from the federal government. And still, not a single student tested at 13 city high schools scored proficient on the state math test.

In an entrepreneurial system, the shipbuilding system and the Baltimore school system would be massively overhauled almost overnight.

This bold entrepreneurial strategy designed to profoundly modernize government and make it more effective and less expensive will face eight major challenges:

First, there is no theory of successful long-term entrepreneurial government. We have had specific cases in which strong personalities have changed things, but when the personality retires, the system gradually drifts back to bureaucratic patterns.

Second, there are few existing entrepreneurial spaces in government. To some extent, the Defense Advanced Research Projects Agency (DARPA) is a pretty good model of continuous change. However, even within change-oriented institutions, there is a profound slowing down as bureaucracy overwhelms the urge to break out and innovate. Changes become smaller, slower, and more risk averse.

Third, we have no model for retraining millions of people who will have to run the new entrepreneurial system. Remember, many of them personally sought a calm, routine job with limited stress and change. We are now proposing they invest their lives in a much higher tempo, change-oriented system. That transition will be among the greatest challenges to the entrepreneurial impulse.

Fourth, one strategy may be to have small bureaucracies that outsource to flexible, lean entrepreneurial firms that focus on achieving measurable goals. This would be different from the current codependent system in which a large, slow government bureaucracy contracts with a large, slow private bureaucracy in a cost-plus, no risk relationship. The development of the Lockheed

Martin F-35 Lightning II fighter jet (the most expensive Defense Department program in history) is a case study in cost overruns with performance failures leading to no consequence for the contractor. The absurdity of the Boeing-NASA Space Launch System (SLS), which is many years behind schedule and many billions over budget, is another. In the case of the SLS, the development of SpaceX's reusable Starship will almost guarantee its demise. Only politics and lobbying have sustained the Boeing contract despite its obvious failure in cost and performance.

Fifth, a bold break from regular bureaucracy was outlined by Gavin Newsom before he became California's governor in a small book called *Citizenville*. Newsom took the concept of a popular digital game called FarmVille and applied it to the challenges of problem solving for a municipality. As mayor of San Francisco, he had some good, practical ideas for citizen involvement. As governor, he did not follow up on this bold de-bureaucratization effort. I suspect this is because the government employee unions who control Sacramento did not want to start shedding jobs as citizens took over the challenges of civil society. There are hundreds of opportunities to use modern technology to empower citizen involvement in ways that would have been impossible a generation ago.

Sixth, as the concepts of entrepreneurial government become clearer, all the in-house educational and training systems should be shifted to that model and away from the bureaucratic precedents, processes, and systems.

Seventh, as the federal drive for a transition from bureaucratic to entrepreneurial models accelerates and intensifies, there should be a major effort to involve state and local leaders and governments. State and local leaders can identify zones of bureaucratic and regulatory interference from the federal government that can be eliminated or made entrepreneurial. State and local leaders can also be encouraged to develop their own models and undertake their own experiments in more dynamic, less expensive environments. Whenever possible, the various state and local government associations should be recruited to help educate their members and host training sessions on the new models. Their members should share successes and difficulties in making the transition. There are only 537 elected officials at the federal level. There are 519,145 additional elected officials in the United States. There could potentially be a lot more people working to develop entrepreneurial government.

Eighth, whenever new problems are analyzed and new opportunities are developed, there should be a bias toward the innovative, new, less expensive, more convenient citizen-centric approach instead of the usual bureaucratic response.

The shift to an entrepreneurial model—and the appointment of successful entrepreneurs to key positions—may be one of the biggest changes President Trump and the Make America Great Again movement make to the functioning of government in the United States. They will face ferocious and formidable opposition. They will also face the natural and inevitable failures of trying new things and approaching big new changes. If they persevere, they will change history for the better and create a dramatically more effective, stronger United States of America.

EIGHT

Education for Survival

The crisis in American education is deep. It affects every level from preschool through graduate school. Millions of adults have had such bad education that they find it hard to earn a decent living or be fully informed citizens.

I have a passionate commitment to learning (although not to traditional education). Having taught in high school and college early in my career, I have some sense of the challenges of the classroom. The real crisis in American education was driven home for me 42 years ago. In April 1983, I attended some of the kickoff press conferences and meetings that launched "A Nation at Risk: The Imperative for Educational Reform." This report was the result of a year and a half of effort by 18 leaders in education, government, and business. They served on the National Commission of Excellence in Education, which President Ronald Reagan created in 1981. The report was stark in its condemnation of the American educational bureaucracy. It asserted, "Our nation is at risk...the educational foundations of our society are presently being eroded by a rising tide of mediocrity that threatens our very future as a nation and a people."

The commission then put into perspective just how bad our educational system had become:

> If an unfriendly foreign power had attempted to impose on America the mediocre educational performance that exists today, we might well have viewed it as an act of war. As it stands, we have allowed this to happen to ourselves. We have even squandered the gains in student achievement made in the wake of the Sputnik challenge. Moreover, we have dismantled essential support systems which helped make those gains possible. We have, in effect, been committing an act of unthinking, unilateral educational disarmament.

The commission went on to report: "Our society and its educational institutions seem to have lost sight of the basic purpose of schooling, and of the high expectations and disciplined effort needed to attain them."

Keep in mind: this was more than 40 years ago. President Reagan insisted on the importance of the commission's work. He said, "There are few areas of American life as important to our society, to our people and to our families as our schools and colleges." A substantial effort to improve education grew out of "A Nation at Risk." As a junior member of Congress, I participated in a series of education reform public events around the country. Secretary of Education Ted Bell played a major role in bringing groups together and communicating how big a problem our education system faced. A decade later, his communications director, Tony Blankley, became my press secretary and did a great job while I was Speaker.

As part of this reform effort, I was involved in three different projects. While teaching at what was then West Georgia College (now the University of West Georgia), I got involved with the Rich Computer Center at Georgia Tech. I participated in an experiment involving the Autographic Learning Facility, or ALF. It was an effort to develop distance learning in the pre-internet age. The technology was too clumsy and difficult.

Then I took speech money I made as a congressman and invented a program called Earning by Learning. The concept was simple. I strongly believe in John Mauldin's assertion that "incentives work." I thought it was strange that we kept trying to get young people to learn by incentivizing everyone but them. With Earning by Learning, we went into public housing projects and paid elementary school students $2 a book for every book they read during the summer. These were simple books written for second- and third-graders, so it was easy for the adult volunteers to ask a few questions and get a sense of whether students had actually done the assignment.

I learned how deep the problem of educational failure was going to be in our first year. In Villa Rica, Georgia, we had a second-grader who read 83 books and earned $166. (In 1984, this was a lot of money, especially for a second-grader.) I thought this would launch her on a successful learning future, but it had the opposite impact. She went back to school that fall and was rapidly bored. The school curriculum allowed no opportunity for people who had already passed their grade in capability. As a result, she was considered a troublemaker.

Years later, I learned how pervasive this problem was when Callista and I met with U.S. Supreme Court Justice Clarence Thomas. He agreed to swear Callista in as ambassador to the Holy

See. (The presidential swearing in is ceremonial, but there is an earlier administrative swearing in that marks her official standing.) Justice Thomas told us about his childhood. As a young Black child in segregated Savannah, Georgia, he secretly went to the white library. He explained that if he had gone to the Black library, he feared his classmates would discover how much he was reading and pressure him to be what they considered normal. It simply didn't fit the cultural norms for young Black children at the time to care about learning, Justice Thomas told us. This challenge of cultural hostility to learning or achieving is a major problem in poor neighborhoods. It is a significant part of why it is so hard to get dramatically better educational results in communities that reject education.

So, we learned that incentives work. When we set up Earning by Learning in public housing in Douglas County, Georgia, the kids were skeptical—even hostile—to our proposal. They were so used to being cheated, they thought we were tricking them to read all summer with no intention of paying them. We modified the program so they could get paid every week.

The results were electrifying. From a small start (six or eight students), the program grew every week. The reason was simple. When the ice cream truck came to the neighborhood, the students who were in the program had money and could buy ice cream. Their friends were jealous and would ask where they got it. The answer would be "I read some books." Their friends promptly asked to be let into the program. By the end of the summer, we had dozens of students participating. It was a great success.

I talked about Earning by Learning on the House floor (where C-SPAN carried it to hundreds of thousands of viewers) and in speeches around the country. To my delight, other groups started to set up their own versions. In every case with which I was familiar, the program worked. Poor children read far more than they would have without an incentive plan that made sense—namely cash. Even $2 per book had a big impact.

The other great project in shaking up the failing education bureaucracy emerged in Milwaukee, Wisconsin. Polly Williams was the chairwoman for Jesse Jackson for President and a state legislator. She developed a school choice plan for poor students trapped in bad schools. She called it the Milwaukee Parental Choice Program and targeted poor families in rough neighborhoods. She collaborated with Republican Governor Tommy Thompson, and they passed a bold school choice reform in 1990. I worked with them in publicizing the concept around the country. Today it is a dominant concept in reforming and improving education.

Yet, after 42 years of handwringing and reforming, American education levels continue to be totally unacceptable. The clearest example of unacceptability is the Baltimore City Schools system. Chris Papst of Fox 45 Baltimore has been reporting on the extraordinary collapse of the system for years. He made an award-winning documentary called *Learned Helplessness* about the consequence of a failing school system.

According to Papst's reporting, there are about 75,000 students in 32 schools. Of those, 13 are high schools with more than 6,500 students total. In 2023, Fox 45 Baltimore discovered that in these 13 schools, zero high school students tested proficient on the state math exam. Across the whole system, only 10 percent of the 75,000 students tested proficient. At the same time, Baltimore City Schools had a $1.6 billion annual budget.

Fox News Baltimore reported:

"This is educational homicide," said Jason Rodriguez, deputy director of People Empowered by the Struggle, a Baltimore-based nonprofit…"There is no excuse," he said. "We have a system that's just running rogue, and it starts at the top…"

Of the 32 high schools…if 13 had zero students test proficient, that means 40 percent of Baltimore City high schools could not produce a single student doing math at grade level. The list of 13 schools includes some of Baltimore's most well-known high schools, including Patterson High School, Frederick Douglass, and Reginald F. Lewis.

But that's not the only alarming finding we made. In those 13 high schools, 1,736 students took the test, and 1,295 students, or 74.5 percent, scored a one out of four. One is the lowest level, meaning those students were not even close to proficient.

Last school year, Baltimore City Schools received $1.6 billion from taxpayers, the most ever. The district also received $799 million in Covid relief funding from the federal government. And still, not a single student tested at 13 City high schools scored proficient on the state math test.

"So, it's not a funding issue. We're getting plenty of funding," said Rodriguez. "I don't think money is the issue. I think accountability is the issue."

Six years ago, in 2017, Project Baltimore produced a similar report, where we analyzed state test scores and found 13 City schools had zero students proficient in math. Many of the schools from 2017 are also on the

2023 list, including Patterson High School, Frederick Douglass, the Reach! Partnership School, New Era Academy, Coppin Academy, and Achievement Academy.[1]

Think of the lives ruined by the expensive Baltimore City Schools bureaucracy, which apparently thinks everything is fine as long as the paychecks keep coming. There is no connection between performance and payment. There is no pressure to rethink or reform the system. From the viewpoint of the education and union bureaucrats, the system works—it's the parents and students who are failing. Trying to reform the system is almost impossible because it has nearly $2 billion to spend—and direct contact to the public. The reformers have tiny budgets and limited reach.

While Baltimore City is the most infamous and well-studied case of big city education failure, there are educational horror stories in too many other cities. There are stories of students graduating from high school unable to read their diplomas. In many of the big cities, up to one-third of students simply do not show up (even though they are on the rolls for the purposes of the schools getting paid by the state). In some systems, attendance is taken only two or three times a year. I have been told in some districts, those days are free pizza days designed to draw back the students who have, in effect, dropped out. It is fraud, but it is also business as usual in too many of the biggest, unionized, and corrupt systems.

While Baltimore City may be an extreme case, the overall record of American education indicates that "A Nation at Risk" unfortunately failed to turn around the decay and ineffectiveness on which it focused. Linda Gorman, writing in Econlib, tackled the question of when American education started to decline.

She reported that despite economic growth and high academic achievement through the first half of the 1900s, American students' test scores started dropping in 1967 and kept falling through the 1980s.

As Gorman reported:

The achievement decline cannot be blamed on inadequate spending. Between 1960 and 1995, annual per pupil spending in the United States rose from $2,122 to $6,434 in inflation-adjusted 1995 dollars. By 1999, the United States was spending an average of $7,397 per K–12 student. Spending in other industrialized countries averaged $4,850. Only Switzerland, at $8,194 per pupil, spent more than the United States. In industrialized countries, student scores on the Third International Mathematics and Science Studies tests are uncorrelated with spending. Though per capita U.S. spending is high and the academic achievement of its fourth-graders is above average, its eighth-graders score in the middle of the pack, and twelfth-grade achievement is consistently among the lowest of the countries studied.[2]

In other words, the longer you stay in the American school system the further behind advanced countries you become. Gorman also found per capita student spending had no correlation to achievement within the United States. From 2000 to 2001, per student spending in America's 100 largest public school districts ranged from $4,413 to $13,577 (an average of $8,859). Gorman reported achievement in those districts varied widely and had no connection to spending.

By comparison, private schools had lower per student spending and better academic achievement. As Gorman wrote:

> In 1990, a RAND Corporation study showed that Catholic high schools in New York City had higher graduation rates and better test scores than that city's public high schools despite similar student bodies drawn from rough neighborhoods. The Catholic schools excelled because they elicited dramatic performance improvements from marginal students, apparently by providing more orderly environments for learning. At $3,500 per student, the Catholic schools also spent almost 50 percent less than the public schools.

The problems of K–12 education involve simple competence in basic skills and basic knowledge. We now have millions of supposed graduates who can't read, write, or do basic math. How can they earn a living? How can they learn and reason enough to be good citizens? President Reagan warned of the danger of failing schools in 1981 when he said: "If we are to guard against ignorance and remain free, …it is the responsibility of every American to be informed."[3]

The crisis we face in education is ultimately a crisis of our survival—as an informed, self-governing country and as a workforce capable of being productive.

WHY EDUCATIONAL ATTAINMENT IS IN DECLINE

While we worked to develop effective 21st-century learning while I was in Congress, it became obvious we were trying to solve the wrong problems. Our reforms have overwhelmingly been focused on schools and classrooms. Yet, the key to a dramatically better informed and more capable citizenry may be outside the traditional educational bureaucracy. It may be virtually impossible to achieve our optimum level of learning by trying to improve the current education bureaucracy—and force the teachers' unions to accept change.

As I thought about the scale of learning we will need to be successful as citizens and competitors in a worldwide economic system, I was reminded of President Dwight Eisenhower's rule about problem solving. Eisenhower said: "Whenever I run into a problem I can't solve, I always make it bigger. I can never solve it by trying to make it smaller, but if I make it big enough, I can begin to see the outlines of a solution."[4]

We need to take the same approach to rethinking learning in America. Our goals should be approached within a hierarchy of learning, training, and educating.

First, we want to maximize the ability of every American to learn. This means ensuring they acquire the initial tools of learning—reading, writing, and basic math. In the age of Google, Wikipedia, YouTube, and ChatGPT, if you have the basic skills and are patient and focused, you can learn just about anything. The teacher-dominated classroom, with set hours and long periods of sitting, is increasingly an obsolete model.

In the age of industrialization, when we were acculturating people to work in factories by arriving on time, meeting production goals, and following a foreman's orders, the current classroom-teacher model made sense. The more we bureaucratized teaching, the less effective it became. The more we focused on unionized work rules, the more we drove passionate learning-oriented teachers from the system. Many good teachers take pay cuts to leave public bureaucracies and go to schools where the focus is on students and learning rather than on work rules and union requirements. Furthermore, there are clear problems with the group model of lumping students together. Some students need more activity and exercise time. Forcing them to sit for long stretches is painful. Some students learn quickly. Other students learn slowly. Both can learn, but forcing them into a one-way curriculum and schedule model maximizes stress and minimizes achievement.

In a similar vein, learning by doing often works dramatically better for many students than learning by memorizing. I am astounded at the number of friends and colleagues who routinely Google or YouTube how to fix their cars, paint a room, or cook a gourmet meal and learn enough to complete their projects.

Roger Schank was a remarkable education reformer. He believed most of our current academic requirements came from academics deciding what they enjoyed and wanting to replicate themselves. He argued people learn rapidly and completely when they have a need to learn something, and they learn slowly and ineffectively when they are learning something they are forced to study. Schank built training programs for businesses so their employees could learn new skills and knowledge quickly when they needed it. He specifically did not try to get employees to memorize general information that they could not immediately apply.

With online learning, games, videos, phone apps, and other technology, it is possible to revolutionize the speed, depth, and convenience of learning. When my wife, Callista, was the U.S. ambassador to the Holy See in Rome, Italy, we took daily language lessons by computer. There were daily immersion challenges you had to complete to progress. As a result, we picked up day-to-day conversational Italian surprisingly quickly. Imagine a series of focused literacy programs online that would enable Americans of any age and culture to learn conveniently 24 hours a day.

With a little creativity we could eliminate illiteracy in America—and it's a real problem. According to the National Literacy Institute, roughly 40 percent of students nationwide cannot read at grade level. This includes 70 percent of fourth-graders from low-income households. Further, 21 percent of American adults were illiterate in 2022.[5] And this is not a function of immigration or students with second languages. The institute reports that two-thirds of the adults who are illiterate are native born. Only one-third are born outside the United States. For far too long, far too many of our schools have failed to teach the basics. We now have a huge number of illiterate Americans who can hardly be fully informed citizens, competitive workers, or active participants in society. The National Literacy Institute estimates that illiteracy costs the United States about $2 trillion a year.

I suspect that many of those with literacy challenges have smartphones. In fact, the smartphone should be seen as the school of the future. It is available 24/7. It is almost always with you and can be used intermittently at your convenience. Both our health and learning systems should be rethought with smartphones—or other personal technology—at the center. Far from keeping phones out of schools, we should be figuring out how to put schools in the phones.

Training is a different challenge than generalized learning. Training imparts a particular set of skills and knowledge that enable you to be productive in a particular field. As Mike Rowe has emphasized for years, we have a cultural values mismatch. We push far too many people into getting degrees that lead them into low-paying jobs. Meanwhile, many scorn the kind of training that could lead people into high-paying jobs.

As John Gardner warned a generation ago, "The society which scorns excellence in plumbing as a humble activity and tolerates shoddiness in philosophy because it is an exalted activity will have neither good plumbing nor good philosophy: neither its pipes nor its theories will hold water."[6]

We must rebuild the sense that all work has dignity—and working with manual or trained skills does not stop someone from learning in their spare time. Being interested and informed about the larger world, and the government we elect, is an imperative part of free citizenship. I have a friend who records history lessons for retired or semi-retired people who now have time and opportunity to learn because they are curious. As he puts it, his primary market is a retired dentist who finally has the time to focus on learning about interesting things.

This eclectic approach to learning and training would lead to profound new ways of measuring achievement. Too much of today's extraordinarily expensive education system focuses on activity rather than achievement, process rather than progress, and teaching curricula rather than helping students learn what they need to succeed in life.

The scale of change we need in K–12 education is staggering. But it is nothing compared to what's needed in the higher education bureaucracy.

Support staff at major universities almost always outnumber the faculty—and sometimes the students. This is a big clue that it is going to be difficult to create change in our public colleges and universities. Higher education reached its peak effectiveness a generation ago. Originally, higher education was devoted to preparing people with useful, specialized knowledge that would enable them to succeed in the world. In 1908, almost a third of all students in public universities were in engineering. Today it is about 5 percent.

Now, the higher education establishment focuses on getting students to learn to belong to higher education institutions. The narcissism and self-love of the faculty and staff lead them to want to recreate themselves in the next generation. So, they encourage students to follow in their footsteps, even if it is economically irrational. Universities suffer from an enormous amount of make-work, paperwork, and a self-indulgent faculty that leans ever more to the left.

There has always been a degree of contempt and snobbery among academics. In effect, if you go out in the world and make enough money to contribute extensively, your money is admired but you are not. That is why so many conservatives are shocked when their generosity toward their alma maters lead to more endowed chairs for people who despise them. The arrogance of the academics is strengthened by the sheer amount of money their institutions now have. It makes no sense for Harvard to be tax-free when it has a $53.2 billion endowment—and is an ideologically driven politically biased bastion focusing on producing the next generation of left-wing heroes. We should rethink higher education funding, accreditation, and influence.

The higher education industrial complex will fight with all its resources, including networks of influential people, to protect itself from reform. Yet, reform is essential if we are to get back to true institutions of higher learning. Education is the Achilles heel of American survival. If we can't produce citizens capable of learning and thinking for themselves, the process of self-government will die. If we can't produce people capable of doing the complex work of the modern age, the American economy will die.

Any serious national security strategy for America must include a dramatic rethinking of education at every level.

NINE

The Enormous Challenge of Health and Health Care in America

H ealth and health care may be the largest, most complex challenges in America. We currently spend about 17 percent or more of our economy on health care. This compares with about 3 percent spent on national defense. So health care is almost six times the cost of national defense.

But this comparison is not enough to capture the difference in complexity. The 3 percent of our defense spending goes through one single, albeit inefficient, institution—the Department of Defense. Our dramatically bigger health care expenditure includes decisions by individuals and families; businesses providing health insurance benefits; insurance companies; local, state, and federal governments; and national programs. These include Medicaid (administered by the states with federal supervision), Medicare, Tricare (for the Defense Department), the U.S. Department of Veterans Affairs, the Federal Employee Health Insurance System (administered through private insurance companies), and the Indian Health Service.

Because health care is a matter of life and death, it is of great importance to every American.

I encountered the politics of health care when I first ran for Congress in 1974. Listening to people on the campaign taught me about the concerns of patients, doctors, hospitals, pharmaceutical companies, and governments. It opened my eyes to insurance and government cost structures and a host of legal issues. I have been involved with the issues of health and health care for the last 51 years.

After I left Congress, I helped found the Center for Health Transformation. It sought to bring together all the stakeholders in health to discuss positive solutions that would improve our lives while lowering costs. Then, in 2003, Anne Woodbury and I published *Saving Lives and Saving Money*. This book had been previewed and approved by Senator Bill Frist, a world-class heart and lung transplant surgeon who became Republican leader in the Senate and whose family had founded a successful hospital chain (HCA).

In *Saving Lives and Saving Money*, we made two arguments designed to shift the focus of the Bush administration. The first was about the rhetoric surrounding health care reform in Washington. It was captured in the title of the book. Health is a moral rather than an economic issue. You must save lives, and then you can focus on saving money. The sense that money has become more important than health alienates people from the health system. Health care can be the difference between life and death, pain-free and painful living, and a full life and an increasingly limited one. People are sensitive to anything that implies money is more important than human beings. Because of this intense concern that health should come first, people react strongly when decisions are explained in financial terms.

The second argument was about the root causes of the dysfunction of the current health care system: the poor health of the American people and a broken marketplace. To be successful in lowering costs and increasing access, we must focus just as much on health as we do on health care. This is because one of the root causes of our unaffordable system is high demand. Approximately 86 percent of all health care spending goes toward treating chronic diseases. Many are largely preventable. But for the most part, they cannot be cured—only managed once they develop.

This is why President Trump's campaign promise to "make America healthy again," in partnership with Robert F. Kennedy Jr., is so important. Outside of specific issues such as COVID-19 and opioids, it is the first time the overall health of the American people has broken through as a serious campaign issue. President Trump and RFK, Jr. are reminding us that many health decisions about nutrition, exercise, and other activities occur before one encounters the health care system. These decisions can improve the health and lengthen the lives of Americans while dramatically lowering costs.

We also need to create a much more open, transparent, and patient-empowering health care system. It should trust Americans to make informed decisions about their own health and how their health care dollars are spent. Health care will never fully be a typical consumer marketplace. Being treated for a disease or injury is not like buying a car or a television. However, there are basic market fundamentals that can be brought to bear to improve the patient experience in the American health care system.

In the 22 years since writing *Saving Lives, Saving Money*, I have written dozens of other books that explore the challenge of reforming our health system. In *Trump and the American Future*, for instance, I wrote four chapters—more than 20,000 words—detailing principles and policies essential to fixing the health system. I provided examples of places where they are being successfully applied to deliver high-quality and low-cost care. I will try not to repeat this material (however, sadly, much of it is still relevant). Instead, I intend to offer a high-level overview of key concepts to understand recent developments in health care that help explain the failure of Washington's attempts to reform the health system. I'll also include principles for achieving real, effective change.

PRISON GUARDS OF THE PAST

It is a sad comment on how difficult it is to reform the health system that the book *Saving Lives and Saving Money* is as relevant today as it was 22 years ago. The health system has proven to be dramatically more difficult to reform than I would have thought possible when I left the Speakership.

In fact, the more politicians have attempted to reform the health care system, the more expensive it has become—and the less Americans like it. A recent poll by Scott Rasmussen shows a 20-point drop in the number of Americans happy with their health insurance since the passage of the Affordable Care Act (Obamacare) in 2010. The simple fact that it took me years to learn (and much of Washington still does not understand) is that there is no "health system" as such. You can't design a sweeping reform for the entire health system, because there is no way to implement it.

The health economy is made up of hundreds of different subsystems, each seeking to protect its own interest and position of authority. The concept of general reforms gets shrugged off. The different power and spending centers pursue their own interests rather than the larger general reforms theory suggest should work.

In fact, many of the elements of the health system systematically work to stop progress in health or health care if it would cost them money or prestige. Their interests transcend any national interest as far as they are concerned. In fact, you can think of the health care system as a totally irrational system filled with people behaving in a completely rational way within the context of that system. Of course, they all convince themselves they are acting out of virtuous concern for the patient rather than self-interest. This is mostly baloney.

I encountered a clear example of this pattern in 2016, when I was introduced to Visibly (then known as Opternative). Visibly offers online eye acuity exams for glasses and contact prescriptions that can be conducted using your smartphone. The results are sent to an optometrist who verifies the results and writes a prescription.

In response to this innovation, the lobbying group that represents optometrists went to war against the company. They argued that Visibly's online vision exams were a threat to public health because they did not include an eye health exam. This is typically done at the same time patients go to the optometrist to get their prescriptions renewed. This is despite the American Optometry Association's own guidelines that recommend an eye health exam every two years for adults below 60, compared to every one year for eye acuity exams.

The result of their efforts was a series of lawsuits that delayed rollout of Visibly's service. There are bans in several states that still exist today. As I wrote in a *USA Today* op-ed in 2016, "The next time you worry about the high cost of health care, consider how many different groups and organizations have lobbyists working to kill competition and stop the technological progress that could help bring costs down."[1]

This vivid example is typical of new technologies in health care—and any innovation or reform that threatens established revenue models. For instance, price transparency in health care is supported by more than 90 percent of Americans. Price transparency is good for saving money on non-emergency medical procedures. It creates competition to lower costs for everyone. It is also an issue of fairness. Patients should understand their options before consenting to treatments.

One of the biggest accomplishments of the first Trump administration was an executive order that required price transparency from hospitals and insurance companies for all medical procedures. However, even after the rules were finalized, it was remarkable to watch hospitals drag their feet in complying with the rules. When President Biden took office, the health care industry found a more sympathetic ear. President Biden walked back some of the transparency requirements and was lax on enforcement. According to an analysis by Patient Rights Advocate, hospital compliance in posting all prices fell in 2024.

With examples of anti-progress and self-interested maneuvering like this, I came up with the concept that the past has prison guards protecting it while the future only has publicists. The imbalance between the two is enormous. It slows down progress in solving our health challenges.

"DO NO HARM" CAN LEAD TO "MAKE NO PROGRESS"
Another significant obstacle to change is the culture within medicine that understandably discourages risk-taking.

The Hippocratic Oath emerged about 2,500 years ago and is still the most influential set of moral instructions for physicians. It insists, "I will do no harm or injustice to [patients]." One of the great problems with bold change in the health system is the danger of doing harm. If something works imperfectly—or more expensively but it does work—there is an enormous weight against trying something new and untested.

This deep and legitimate bias against harming people makes change in the health system inevitably slower and more cautious. It also leads to a real bias toward doing what you learned in medical school when you were young rather than rushing to the newest fad 30 years later—even if the fad offers the promise of better outcomes at lower costs. The power and aggressiveness of the American trial lawyer system, and the deep American predilection for suing people, makes risk-taking in medicine even more dangerous. For a doctor or hospital to have a bad outcome is to invite an expensive and time-consuming lawsuit. It is one further inhibitor to adopting new and better treatments. The new techniques may have flaws that bankrupt the adopting institutions.

HEALTH INSURANCE IS NOT HEALTH CARE. HEALTH CARE IS NOT HEALTH.

Another reason why past attempts from Washington to reform health care have failed is that they are focused on the wrong thing. Washington fails to understand that health insurance is not health care, and health care is not health. Health insurance (be it through private or government coverage) is how most health care is purchased. Health care is the treatment that Americans receive from doctors and other providers. Health is the degree to which Americans are free of illness or injury.

Here in lies the challenge to making America healthy again and fundamentally fixing our broken health care system. There have been many serious examinations of what leads to good health. Most of these come to the same conclusion—the health care we receive plays only a small role (about 20 percent) in determining health outcomes. Most of the rest comes from the lifestyles we lead and the environments in which we live. A surprisingly small amount is determined by our genetics.

This means trying to improve the health of the American people by trying to improve the health care they receive in a medical setting is already difficult. What Washington usually does is even more hopeless if our goal is to improve health. When politicians talk about "health care reform," they are usually focused on the first item—health insurance. The reforms are usually changes in the way health insurance operates (such as requiring it to cover more procedures or patients) or changes to the way Medicare and Medicaid pay doctors.

Some of these reforms have merit simply as a matter of being good stewards of taxpayer money or to financially protect patients. But they will have limited impact on the real health of most Americans. Thus, they will not be enough to meet the goal of "saving lives and saving money" or President Trump's goal to "make America healthy again."

WHY "MAKE AMERICA HEALTHY AGAIN" IS ESSENTIAL TO FIXING OUR HEALTH CARE SYSTEM

When thinking about the health of the American people as it relates to how to fix the American health care system, we can think of two broad groups of Americans. The first group is those without chronic health conditions. These Americans have routine, inexpensive health expenditures, as well as random health expenditures from short-term illness or injury. These random expenditures can be quite expensive, but they are small enough in number that their costs can be affordably spread out across a coverage pool.

The second group is made up of those who have chronic illnesses. These Americans have routine and expensive health expenditures to treat their conditions, as well as a much higher likelihood of random health expenditures due to their underlying illness. Eighty-six percent of all U.S. health care spending goes toward providing treatment for these Americans suffering from chronic disease. In fact, 50 percent of all U.S. health spending goes toward the treatment of 5 percent of Americans.

Any real strategy to tackle the cost crisis in health care must include a system for moving people from group two into group one and preventing people from group one from joining group two. Unfortunately, our health care system is not designed to do this. In fact, perhaps the best way to understand what is broken about the American health care system is to think of it as a "sick care" system rather than a health care system. This helps to understand certain contradictions inherent in American health care. It explains how life expectancy is now stagnant or even dropping while medical technology and treatments keep improving. It explains why we are better than ever at treating diseases while Americans have more diseases than ever before. It explains why health care spending is consistently increasing faster than inflation, gobbling up more of the economy. Yet profit margins at hospitals (the single largest cost center in health care) are relatively modest.

Eighty-six percent of our American health care spending goes toward the treatment of chronic diseases, a large percentage of which are preventable. Despite this, most of what we refer to as prevention in medicine is actually early detection. For an example of this, look at the list of preventative services for adults that health insurance companies are required to cover with no co-pay.[2] It is mostly screenings, not prevention.

This is because almost all of the incentives in the system—from our medical training to the financial pressures to the general cultural patterns of the American lifestyle—lead to an extreme bias toward dealing with the chronic disease epidemic with highly specialized, disease-specific doctors. Doctors prescribe pharmaceuticals and costly medical procedures to manage the diseases after they appear, instead of helping patients prevent and reverse them with lifestyle modifications.

Of course, pharmaceuticals and medical procedures have their place and are needed. But we should be thinking about healthy food and exercise as medicine, too. Other interventions take place outside a medical setting but are proven to improve health and health outcomes. For instance, the number of close friends and family you have has been shown to have a direct impact on your health.

HEALTHSPAN VS. LIFESPAN—CONFRONTING THE LIMITS OF OUR SICK CARE SYSTEM

For more than a century, improvements in medicine (and overall living conditions) led to a dramatic increase in the average lifespan of the American people. In 1900, the average age of death in America was 47 years. By 2015, it had nearly doubled to its peak of 79.4 years. However, progress since then has stalled, and even been reversed. The reason is that we have reached the limits of our sick care system to continue these improvements. Even as lifespan increased over the decades, the average age of developing a chronic illness remained steady. In fact, recent years have seen Americans developing these diseases earlier than ever before. As the average age of Americans increased, that meant a growing proportion of our population was living with at least one chronic illness. Today, according to the National Health Council, 60 percent of American adults have at least one chronic illness, and 40 percent have two or more.

This is why we need to start treating "healthspan"—the average age before Americans develop a chronic disease—as important a public health metric as "lifespan." Simply put, we can no longer improve the latter without improving the former. Chronic illness tends to compound. Once we develop one, we are more likely to develop another. Furthermore, the likelihood of developing a chronic illness increases as we age, and Americans are, on average, getting older.

These two accelerants turn treating chronic disease into a game of "whack-a-mole." Our highly specialized, single-disease-focused medical system that values treatment over prevention simply gets overwhelmed as multiple conditions emerge.

As President Trump and his health care team develop their agenda to make America healthy again, healthspan should be adopted as the key metric to measure success.

Deeply engrained cultural patterns in medicine and America, however, will take a while to reverse. Making America healthy again should be considered a multi-decade project that will take place over multiple administrations. Establishing healthspan as a key public health metric and developing strategies to increase it would be a significant accomplishment for President Trump over his term. It can create the foundation for future success.

THE ENORMOUS POTENTIAL OF LIFESTYLE MEDICINE

Lifestyle changes can prevent, treat, and often reverse the progression of a vast majority of the most common and costly chronic diseases in America. This would improve the lives of the American people, increase our productivity as a nation, and drive down health care premiums and the burden on taxpayers. If you doubt the potential impact of lifestyle modification, consider the work of Dr. Dean Ornish, founder of the nonprofit Preventive Medicine Research Institute and pioneer of what he calls "lifestyle medicine."

In 2010, I worked with Dr. Ornish to get Medicare to cover his lifestyle medicine program for the reversal of heart disease. This was the first time Medicare covered a program of lifestyle modification for treating and reversing heart disease. Getting coverage is important to make it financially accessible to patients and to spread awareness and interest among doctors. The program consists of:

- A whole-foods, minimally processed, plant-based diet;
- 30 minutes per day of moderate aerobic exercise and strength training;
- An hour per day of stress management, such as meditation (which may include prayer), stretching, and breathwork; and

- Two hours per week of support groups for patients and their partners.[3]

Coverage includes a nine-week, 72-hour course featuring instruction and practice in each of the four areas of the program. Furthermore, Dr. Ornish's company sends patients their first two weeks of meals in the mail at no cost to them while they are learning to cook healthy foods, shop, and eat out. This is an intense program, but it has a shockingly high compliance rate of around 80 percent after one year.[4] For comparison, typical medication adherence rates for chronic disease medication are only 50 percent.

Dr. Ornish attributes this high compliance rate to its effectiveness in improving symptoms and key biomarkers—and in genuinely enhancing the quality of patients' lives. Participants report having more energy and less pain, and being happier. The program provides patients with a sense of empowerment, community, and meaning. As Dr. Ornish says, "Joy of living is a much better motivator than fear of dying."

Last year, Dr. Ornish and his research partners announced results of a groundbreaking randomized clinical trial (the gold standard when it comes to proving effectiveness of medical interventions) showing that the same lifestyle medicine program used to reverse heart disease can also be used to often halt and reverse early-stage Alzheimer's disease.[5]

Results after 20 weeks showed overall statistically significant differences between the intervention group and the randomized control group in cognition and function...

There was a statistically significant dose-response correlation between the degree of lifestyle changes in groups and the degree of change in most measures of cognition and function testing. In short, the more these patients changed their lifestyle in the prescribed ways, the greater was the beneficial impact on their cognition and function...

The announcement goes on to note that these same lifestyle modifications adopted earlier in life could likely prevent Alzheimer's disease as well. This is particularly important given new technologies able to predict people's likelihood of developing the disease. Previously, there was little someone could do with that knowledge other than worry. Now, they potentially have a plan of action. By contrast, only three Alzheimer's drugs have been approved by the Food and Drug Administration (FDA) in 20 years. All three only slow down the rate at which the disease worsens, have significant side effects, and are expensive.

THE HEALING POWER OF COMMUNITY

In America, we spend a lot of time arguing about various diets. Advocates for vegetarian, ketogenic, Mediterranean, paleo, and other diet programs vie for supremacy (and market share). To be clear, I am not advocating for one program over another. (It is worth noting, however, that they all seem to emphasize eating whole, minimally processed foods.)

Dr. Ornish's diet is vegetarian, but when you talk to him, he is most passionate about the power of the fourth part of his program: the support groups. Humans are intensely social creatures, but new technologies such as home entertainment systems and smartphones have led to increased isolation. The rise of secular ideology and the accompanying decline of church attendance is another major factor that has led to a loss of community and meaning in people's lives. Numerous studies show that people who regularly attend religious services have better health outcomes than those who do not.[6]

This has profound implications on the mental and physical health of the nation. In fact, there is growing evidence that thinking of mental and physical health separately is a false dichotomy. A 2023 report from the U.S. surgeon general raised the alarm on America's epidemic of loneliness. The report said that "the mortality impact of being socially disconnected is similar to that caused by smoking up to 15 cigarettes a day."

A key challenge for President Trump and his health team will be finding appropriate ways to increase genuine socialization and community engagement in America. The 250th anniversary of America in 2026 provides one potential opportunity to renew civic pride and engagement. The United States should also study the impact of recent laws passed in countries such as Australia that prevent minors from using social media apps that often increase social isolation. If the health benefits are positive, we should consider adopting something similar in the United States.

A CONFLICT OF VALUES

We need to take seriously the implications of the potential impact of lifestyle medicine to radically shift the trajectory of America's health and, therefore, health spending. I am hopeful President Trump, RFK, Jr., and the entire health team of this new administration will embrace creative and aggressive ways to create incentives to patients and doctors to embrace it.

Let's face it: Americans generally understand that eating more vegetables and exercising is healthy. They know eating high fat and sugary foods and being sedentary is not. Yet, for most of us, the threat of health problems down the road is not enough motivation to make changes today.

This is why in addition to covering lifestyle medicine programs for those already sick, we should seriously consider financially motivating Americans to follow versions of them to prevent sickness. It makes no sense that in the U.S. we will pay almost nothing to keep our citizens well but enormous amounts once we get sick. Sixty percent of all health care spending is funded by the government. Even private health care spending can be thought of in collective terms because so much of it is run through health insurance companies funded by premiums, which most of us pay directly or indirectly as health benefits.

Once someone develops a chronic disease, lifestyle medicine can have a dramatic short-term impact on patient well-being and overall health spending. That's less true for those who have not yet developed a chronic illness but may be on the path to developing one. For those patients, well-being would improve, but not as dramatically. For the insurance companies, cost savings would be further down the road. Given insurance turnover rates of around 30 percent, the savings on those patients don't necessarily materialize for the payer.

I understand the idea of financially rewarding people to be healthy offends certain sensibilities. For one, there is a deep strain of self-reliance that has been a key part of the American tradition.

Financially motivating people to take proper care of themselves seems at odds with this. Furthermore, if you are the type of person who is naturally attracted to wellness, you may not understand how and why others are averse to it.

But there is proof of the success of these sort of programs. The Cleveland Clinic recently enacted a program in which they gave employees $2,000 off their insurance premiums if they engaged in healthy lifestyle and improved key health indicators. The program is an unqualified success—it has, over time, saved the employees and the Cleveland Clinic hundreds of millions of dollars.

Consider: if it takes a $2,000 financial benefit to motivate employees of one of the most recognized hospitals in the world to be healthier, don't you think most Americans not already surrounded by health and health care would need something similar as well?

HARNESSING THE SCIENCE OF AGING BIOLOGY

Even as we embrace the power of lifestyle medicine to address the chronic disease epidemic and increase our healthy longevity, we should be investing in biopharmaceutical treatments that do the same. One of the most promising fields of research for developing these preventative therapies addresses the other root cause of chronic disease: aging.

There is a difference between your chronological age (the number of years you have been alive) and your biological age. Biological age is a measurement of how well your cells perform certain functions essential to good health. Chronological age, of course, has an impact on your biological age, but they are not the same thing. Aging biology science (or geroscience) is the study of the relationship between these cellular mechanisms behind aging and our body's deterioration as we age, particularly as it relates to our susceptibility to age-related chronic diseases.

The field of aging biology has made some remarkable advancements over the past few decades.

After gaining an understanding of the biological mechanisms behind aging, the field's scientists have produced research showing there are interventions that can have a direct impact on these cellular functions, slowing down—and in some cases reversing—the advancement of your biological age.

One intervention has been covered already—healthy living. It turns out a big reason why healthy living works well is because it has a direct impact on these biological hallmarks of aging in your cells. Better cell function leads to better overall health. For instance, Dr. Ornish's lifestyle medicine regimen has been shown to increase telomere length. The shortening of telomeres in our cells is considered a major driver of aging.

We should also be looking to biopharmaceutical options to prevent disease. America is the world leader in biopharmaceutical research and development. This is an enormous advantage for our country. A big part of transforming our sick care system into a health care system will be channeling this scientific and economic power into the advancement of health—in addition to the treatment of disease.

There are two broad strategies for accomplishing this. The first is to increase funding for aging biology research at the National Institutes of Health (NIH). Increasing basic science funding creates more material that biopharmaceutical companies can use to develop therapies. Currently, aging biology research is housed within the National Institute on Aging (NIA). This would seem to make sense, but most of the budget of the NIA goes toward studying age-related diseases—particularly dementia—rather than the root causes of the disease: aging. This is typical of our disease-centric, specialized health care system. We study disease, not health. We need a robustly funded, separate institute dedicated to studying healthy longevity and aging biology at the NIH, one that could coordinate and cross pollinate with the other institutes focused on specific diseases.

Second, we need to develop new pathways for preventative therapies at the Food and Drug Administration. Currently, to get a drug approved, you must show that it has a beneficial impact on the progression of a disease or its symptoms. This can range anywhere from an outright cure for the condition to simply slowing its progression. This makes sense if your goal is to treat disease after it has been diagnosed, but what if your goal is to prevent the disease from occurring in the first place, which is the promise of treatments that target the biological process of aging? There is currently no clear path for these sorts of therapies. As a result, most biopharmaceutical companies using aging biology research as the foundation for their therapies are conducting clinical trials trying to show they can treat disease rather than prevent it. Treating age-related chronic disease by targeting the underlying biology of aging that causes it is certainly promising, but preventing it is far more exciting and potentially impactful.

At Gingrich 360, we work with the Alliance for Longevity Initiatives to advocate for policies that will promote healthy longevity in America, with a particular focus on harnessing our biopharmaceutical industrial base to develop treatments aimed at improving health by targeting biological aging. I encourage you to visit its website and learn more about our efforts.

THE OZEMPIC DILEMMA

For some, there is a tension between encouraging healthier living to prevent and treat chronic disease and investing in biopharmaceutical treatments to do the same. Many of the people who are the biggest advocates for the former criticize our health system's overreliance on drugs, so they are hostile to the latter. They argue that drugs have side effects and are often expensive, while lifestyle changes are more affordable and only have positive side effects, so they should be prioritized.

We are seeing this tension play out in real time with the debate over the new GLP-1 receptor agonist weight loss drugs like Ozempic and Wegovy. When the drugs first came on the market, they were approved as a treatment for type 2 diabetes. This made them significantly different from other diabetes medications, and indeed most medications to treat chronic diseases. Rather than target the disease or the symptoms directly, the weight loss drugs target the underlying condition (obesity) that leads to the insulin resistance and other dysfunction characteristics of diabetes. Recently, brands of these types of drugs were approved as a treatment for obesity itself.

In many ways, this is a breakthrough, but there is a dilemma: There are 115 million Americans who qualify as obese. Should we really be willing to spend hundreds of billions of dollars a year on these drugs when eating healthier, exercising, increasing social engagement, and other lifestyle interventions could potentially have the same impact, with fewer side effects and much less cost?

There is a lot to consider here.

First, increased uptake will lead to competition between brands, which will lower the prices of obesity medications.

Second, when determining if the costs are worth it, you must consider the downstream health and financial impacts of coverage. A less obese population would be happier and more economically productive. We would also spend less on diabetes, heart disease, and other chronic diseases. It could be that aggressively treating obesity, even at great expense, is worth the long-term investment.

Third, these medicines are relatively new. We need to carefully monitor their long-term impact on patients and their evolution as new versions are released. We are already learning that a high percentage of people who go off these weight loss medications once they reach their goal weights report gaining it back again. It may be that coverage needs to be contingent upon the patient successfully modifying their lifestyle to incorporate more healthy foods and exercise. The choice may not be between medication or lifestyle changes, but instead the optimum use of both.

We need robust studies with long-term tracking of patient outcomes that examine all these factors. My recommendation for the Trump administration is to set the shibboleths aside and let the data speak for itself—remembering that we must put patient health first. Our mantra must continue to be first save lives, then save money.

TECHNOLOGY EMPOWERING PARTICIPATORY HEALTH

A key component of embracing lifestyle medicine will be empowering patients with the information they need about their health to make informed decisions and take care of themselves. Many health care organizations focused on transforming our health care system to one that emphasizes prevention follow the P4 theory: health care should be predictive, preventative, personalized, and participatory.

In many ways, our health system is the opposite of those four Ps, particularly the last one—participatory. There is an old expression that "nobody washes a rental car." This is because we have no sense of ownership of a rental car and see no reason to take care of it. Unfortunately, America's health care system encourages patients to treat their health as if it is a rental car. Medical knowledge is treated as sacred text only to be deciphered by the priestly class—doctors and scientists. Too many doctors get frustrated by patients who do their own research and want to play a role in designing their own treatments.

To be fair to doctors, this attitude is partly a consequence of the demands to see a high volume of patients every day while having to deal with an extraordinary amount of paperwork from the insurance industry. Most doctors just don't have enough time to spend with patients to be truly collaborative. This same attitude applies to patient data. Medical systems are highly possessive of patient data and resist making it available to patients in a way that allows them to easily move between providers. Indeed, medical systems and insurance companies see patient data as their property, rather than the patients' property. This means they are averse to any development that creates patient data outside their control.

This aversion is running headlong into conflict with the rise of personal health monitoring technologies such as Apple Watches or FitBits. In recent years, there has been significant progress getting many of the health monitoring features of these devices approved by the FDA as safe and effective. There is a tremendous psychological difference between getting real-time feedback about your health and lifestyle decisions and getting the results of your blood tests once or twice a year at medical checkups. Advances in robotics and distance monitoring technologies should also enable the dramatic expansion of self-care, at home care, and the ability of family and neighbors to care for their loved ones with less stress.

This rise in real-time data should empower doctors to work with patients in using the data from this continuous monitoring to actively manage their health. Doing so, however, will require a culture shift in medicine.

HOW MEDICARE CAN BE PART OF MAKING AMERICA HEALTHY AGAIN

Earlier, I made the case that trying to improve health through health care payment reform is difficult. However, there is one area where it makes sense to try and improve health through payment reform—and that is among the sickest Americans. Since chronic illness increases with age, Medicare is a prime space to use payment reforms to improve the health of patients and in the process save money.

The reason it makes sense is that people with multiple chronic illnesses utilize health care far more than others. In the typical fee-for-service way of paying for health care, providers are paid per episode of care. This means that doctors and hospitals have no direct financial incentive to help their patients better manage their diseases. In fact, you could argue they are negatively incentivized because doing so would result in lower utilization of health care services and less revenue.

The alternative to fee for service is value-based care. This encompasses a wide range of payment models. But the basic idea is to structure payments to doctors in a way to incentivize better health outcomes in patients. Medicare Advantage is uniquely designed to take advantage of value-based care arrangements to achieve better health and lower costs. Since the program was created in 1997, enrollment has steadily grown. Last year, more than half of all Medicare enrollees chose a private Advantage plan over traditional Medicare (Part A).

In traditional Medicare, the government pays providers directly. In Medicare Advantage, however, the government pays insurance companies a set amount per senior they enroll in their plans, and it is up to the company to manage costs for all their members within that global budget.

This sounds like typical commercial insurance (with the bulk of the premium being paid by the government, instead of an employer or individual) but has one critical difference. In Medicare Advantage, the government pays the insurance companies more to enroll sicker patients. These additional payments make it extremely valuable for insurance companies to work with the doctors in their networks to help these patients manage and mitigate their chronic illnesses. They do this by striking value-based care arrangements with doctors and doctor groups, where they are paid more if the patients they manage consume fewer expensive health care services—particularly preventable hospitalizations.

In traditional Medicare, there are similar value-based care arrangements that the government will strike directly with providers. These are called Accountable Care Organizations (ACOs). Properly structured, these arrangements keep patients healthier and happier. This keeps them out of the hospital and costs less money. For example, estimates are that poor medication adherence leads to 125,000 deaths and an additional $300 billion per year in hospitalizations, additional medical appointments, and other complications. In a typical fee-for-service model, doctors would get paid for diagnosing a patient and writing a prescription. However, they have no direct financial incentive to see if the patient was taking his or her medication or taking it correctly. If doctors and doctor groups are paid more if patients stay out of the hospital, they are directly incentivized to make sure their patients are correctly taking their medicines.

This is a great model that has produced significantly improved health outcomes and lower costs where it is done correctly. We work with several health care provider companies that specialize in taking care of the sickest seniors. Their patients are happier and healthier, and the companies are profitable. It is a win-win-win for patients, doctors, and taxpayers.

THE CHALLENGE—COMPLEXITY BREEDS COST AND CORRUPTION

However, there are real challenges and downsides to value-based payment systems that need to be confronted. The first challenge is they are enormously complicated. Typical fee-for-service payments, in traditional Medicare or commercial insurance, produce a large volume of transactions. However, they are relatively straightforward. A doctor provides a service, and the payer pays for it.

Value-based payment arrangements require an enormous amount of bureaucracy, patient data collection, rules, and regulations. All this complexity adds costs and can make doctors feel micromanaged by the payer, rather than serving the needs of the patient. This is particularly true of doctors who see a blend of

Advantage, Part A, Medicaid, and commercial insurance patients. All the different rules and payment structures can be overwhelming.

Value-based payment arrangements, particularly in ACOs, can also drive consolidation in health care. Consolidation is a natural response by the provider to these arrangements. If they are going to be judged based on patient outcomes, they want to make sure they are in control of as many points at which the patient touches the health care system as possible. Consolidation in health care markets gives providers more market power, enabling them to negotiate higher payment from commercial insurance. A 2022 RAND Corporation study showed that hospital mergers can raise prices by up to 65 percent. The Federal Trade Commission estimates mergers can lead to price increases of 40 to 50 percent.[7]

However, just as the pressure on Advantage insurers to reduce health care utilization can lead them to focus on prevention and wellness among their enrollees, it can also lead them to simply make it harder for patients to receive care. A senior hospital expert said to me recently that the fight over money has "become a real war." Doctors and hospitals feel they are engaged in a constant fight with private and government insurance agencies to get paid. The cost in time and worry has begun to undermine the entire system.

Even before United Healthcare CEO Brian Thompson was murdered in December 2024, there was growing attention to the amount of prior authorization requirements in Medicare Advantage, whereby doctors must first receive approval from the insurance companies before they can administer care.[8] This has led to growing doctor and patient outrage because it looks as if the insurance companies are violating the moral compass by which Americans believe health care should be guided—patients before profits.

It is also leading to a crisis of physician shortages. Many got into medicine to help people, but they are finding it impossible to do so within the demands of our bureaucratic health system. This has led to what doctors describe as a professional crisis of "moral injury." Physicians have a suicide rate double that of the total population. The problem is particularly pronounced among women. The suicide rate for female physicians is 250 percent to 400 percent higher than the total female population (the male physician suicide rate is 70 percent higher than the total male population). A July 2024 poll showed that nearly two-thirds of doctors don't want their children to work in medicine.[9] (While I don't have hard data to support this, anecdotally I will tell you that the happiest and most satisfied doctors we have met during our work on health care at Gingrich 360 are those who do not accept health insurance. This allows them to focus completely on patients.)

In a real sense, the system has evolved to be the opposite of my 2003 book's title. Instead of "saving lives and saving money," the current system focuses on "saving money and then saving lives." The entire pre-approval process that gives power to a doctor, nurse, or bureaucrat who has never seen you over the doctor who is directly treating you is a symptom of the sickness of the system. It should be possible with modern analytical systems to return power to the doctor and then monitor their aggregate behavior over time without putting patients at risk. We can also avoid having doctors feel micromanaged by an anonymous person in whom they have no trust.

The massive complexity that Medicare Advantage inspires also creates loopholes that allow insurers to make money while doing little to nothing to improve patient health. For instance, the feature in Medicare Advantage whereby insurers are paid more to cover sicker patients is essential to avoiding what happens in the under-65 individual market—where insurers go out of their way to discourage sick people from enrolling. (The Affordable Care Act required insurance companies to cover people with pre-existing conditions. But there are other ways of discouraging enrollment by sick patients—such as by not including the best specialists in their provider networks.)

However, this feature also has a bug—it incentivizes insurance companies to make their enrollees look as sick as possible. A yearlong investigation by the *Wall Street Journal* showed that doctors who work directly for Medicare Advantage insurance companies—particularly UnitedHealth Group—diagnose their patients with far more diseases than independent ones who contract with them. Even these independent doctors diagnose at a higher rate for their Medicare Advantage patients than their traditional Medicare patients.[10]

The Advantage companies argue that this is evidence of the system working as intended—the sickest patients are attracted to the higher quality care that Medicare Advantage plans incentivize from health care providers. There is likely some truth to this. However, the same investigation also exposed that Medicare Advantage insurers received $50 billion in extra payments over three years for diagnoses that were never treated.[11] So, either these patients were not actually sick, or they were not getting the treatment they need. Either way, the system is not fully working as intended.

This loophole in the structure of these extra payments undoubtedly needs to be addressed. But attempts to audit to ensure diagnoses actually lead to treatment will create more overhead, paperwork, bureaucracy, and compliance costs. This is typical of attempts to fix our enormously complicated system—every reform seems to create a new set of problems. Getting the fix right will be a significant challenge for President Trump and his health team.

FIXING THE BROKEN MARKETPLACE

The fact that we have a sick care system instead of a health care system is one of the two major reasons why our system is so broken. Addressing this requires reorienting the system around the prevention of disease, rather than just treatment. Embracing lifestyle medicine, incentivizing therapies that have the potential to prevent disease, and new technologies allowing patients to monitor and manage their health are key strategies in achieving this transformation.

The other major reason why our health system is so broken is that the market for health care goods and services is dysfunctional. There are dozens of ways that it is broken, but let's focus on five.

1. Lower Supply, Higher Demand

As the American population gets older and sicker, demand for health care is rising. A functioning market would respond to rising demand with rising supply to meet the need. However, the supply of doctors relative to that growing demand is falling. In fact, the United States has fewer doctors per capita than almost every other developed country.

We already discussed the morale problem among doctors due to the profit-maximizing, micromanaging, overly bureaucratic health care system. This is part of the problem. But we can't overlook the impact of naked self-interest leading to the shortage.

Physician groups, particularly the American Medical Association (AMA), are a significant reason why we have a shortage of doctors in America. These groups control accreditation of doctors. They consistently create more spots for specialists, who are paid more than general practitioners. This is despite an ongoing and severe shortage of primary care doctors in America. The AMA has also successfully lobbied against efforts to allow nurses to deliver health care and to bring foreign trained doctors to the United States.

The AMA couches all its objections in the language of patient safety. However, it is easy to see how limiting the supply of health care benefits its members. It's basic economics—rising demand with falling supply leads to higher prices. It is worth noting that the self-interest of the physician groups raises prices and creates health care deserts—particularly in poor rural areas. These are areas where access to basic health care services is limited or non-existent. Estimates are that 30 million Americans live in health care deserts. This is a direct result of the supply shortage. Higher demand for health care and falling supply of doctors means physicians can be choosy about where they practice—and most are going to choose wealthier urban or suburban areas.

Hospital trade groups have also conspired to limit patients' options for care. For instance, during the drafting of Obamacare, the American Hospital Association successfully lobbied Congress to include a restriction on physician-owned hospitals from being included in Medicare. State-based Certificate of Need (CON) laws are also manipulated by providers to reduce choice. These certifications are needed to open medical facilities in most states. Remarkably, the boards that decide whether to award the certificates are stacked with representatives from providers in the area. Of course, they're going to do everything they can to limit competition.

Overcoming the lobbying of the interest groups will be a major battle for President Trump. But it is vital to increasing access to care, lowering prices, and making America healthy again.

2. The Problem with Health Insurance

Second, the use of third-party payers (such as health insurance companies or public health coverage) to pay for most health care services in America has created a self-perpetuating cycle of increasing costs. In a normal market, the purchaser is the one who receives the good or service from the provider. In health care, however, the purchaser is a third party—such as an insurance company—while the patient receives care from the provider. (Of course, ultimately, it is the patient who pays, either in higher premiums, higher taxes, or lost wages.)

This creates an adversarial relationship between the three parties, in which the payer fights the provider to save money, the provider fights the payer to get paid, and the patient fights to understand just what the heck is happening.

The purpose of insurance is to turn large, unpredictable expenses into small, predictable ones. But as we've reviewed, most health care spending is not unpredictable—it is spent on chronic disease. Once someone is diagnosed with a chronic disease in our current sick care system, their health expenses associated with that condition become predictable and often last the rest of their lives. Even for routine care, such as checkups and visits for minor medical issues, insurance is not an efficient vehicle for paying for health care. Car insurance, for example, doesn't pay for routine maintenance such as oil changes. Even minor scrapes and fender benders are paid out of pocket. It's only the unexpected, large expenses that are handled by car insurance.

If you've ever been in a car accident or suffered property damage, you've experienced the frustration of filing a claim and going through the approval and reimbursement process. Now imagine how much more expensive car insurance and car maintenance would be if that process had to be repeated for every oil change, tire rotation, air filter replacement, scratch, and dent. That's the reality of health care in America. It's no surprise then that from 1975 to 2019, the number of health care administrators in the United States grew by 831 percent while the supply of doctors grew by just 200 percent.[12]

One possible solution to the problem is to remove the third-party payer from as much of health care as possible (such as all non-emergency care), putting patients in direct control of most of the health care spending in America today. You could do this while still providing Americans with financial protection through money deposited by employers or the government into health savings accounts to use for most routine care, and then by providing catastrophic insurance on the back end to take care of emergencies. This would create real competition for most health care services, making the system more efficient, patient-friendly, and affordable.

The challenge is that costs are so high now, and the system is so complicated, that most Americans understandably get spooked by the idea of having to pay directly for most of their care, even if the money they spend is provided by the government.

So, Washington tends to focus on finding ways to hide costs from patients, such as requiring insurance to cover more services. This insulates more of health care from market forces, which leads to more bureaucracy and middlemen and higher prices and premiums. Washington then responds by creating subsidies to make higher premiums more affordable. This continues the vicious cycle. Breaking that cycle to empower patients and introduce true competition in health care will be one of the biggest challenges for President Trump.

3. Pricing Chaos

There is another way health insurance and other health coverage programs add complexity to the health care system—they make it virtually impossible to determine how much health care services cost. Contracts between health insurance companies and providers include negotiated reimbursement rates for every possible billable medical procedure. Each procedure is represented by a five-digit number called a Current Procedural Terminology (CPT) code. In 2024, there were 11,163 CPT codes.

Health insurance providers are often part of dozens of different health insurance networks, plus Medicare and Medicaid. They also have a price for those without insurance and often a separate, discounted price for patients willing to pay cash up front. The result is each medical procedure can have dozens of potential prices depending on the patient's coverage provider. All this complexity leads to enormous price variation for the same procedures between providers—and even within the same provider.

This is beginning to change. President Trump's 2020 price transparency executive order for hospitals and insurance companies required disclosure of all negotiated prices in machine-readable files that can be accessed by patients and aggregators.

Turquoise Health is one of those aggregators. In 2024, it released an analysis showing that since transparency requirements were imposed, price variation in health care has shrunk. The highest 25 percent of prices dropped by 6.3 percent. The lowest 25 percent of prices increased by 3.4 percent, and the middle 50 percent dropped by 1.1 percent.[13]

This is modest progress, but in a truly functioning market, we would see a steeper drop toward the lowest prices. Instead, we see more of a convergence toward the middle. One barrier toward true competition is that the pricing information is still too difficult to access for many patients due to a lack of enforcement and weakening of the rules by the Biden administration. More fundamentally, however, many patients don't have an incentive to take advantage of price transparency because of the structure of their health coverage.

For instance, a patient may have the same co-pay no matter what provider they see. Or, say a patient has a $2,000 deductible, and they require knee surgery. Whether they choose to have it at the less expensive outpatient surgery center or in a more expensive hospital, they're going to pay $2,000. And, of course, if the patient has already met their deductible, they pay almost nothing out of pocket.

President Trump can act at the executive level and work with Congress to reinvigorate and strengthen his price transparency rules throughout the health care industry. But to see the true impact, they also must take the next step and find ways to truly incentivize American patients to seek out better value providers.

4. The Middlemen Problem

The inefficiencies of the third-party payer system have created a labyrinth of bureaucracy in the health care system. Every part of the system is grabbing for power and dollars at the expense of the patient. Government mandates and rules designed to protect patients in this system create additional complexities that add cost to the system. This gives rise to the fourth big problem with the health care marketplace: middlemen. Health care is awash in middlemen, each taking advantage of inefficiencies, bureaucratic requirements, or complexity within the system.

These middlemen tend to line up on either side of the divide between the payer and provider in the payment system. They all provide services to help either side handle all the bureaucracy and complexity. Of course, all these intermediary organizations just add to the complexity and costs. It is a self-perpetuating cycle. More bureaucracy leads to more middlemen, which creates more bureaucracy.

One of the most problematic middlemen in health care are pharmacy benefit managers (PBMs). PBMs are massive companies that negotiate discounts on drugs on behalf of insurance companies. There is nothing wrong with bulk pricing discounts. That's common in most industries. But PBMs go beyond this.

First, they create formularies that dictate what medicines patients can access. This is essentially putting their own judgment over that of doctors, pharmacists, and patients. Second, they have complicated payment mechanisms that create opportunities for mischief. One of those payment models is spread pricing, in which they reimburse pharmacies at a lower price than they charge insurance companies. They pocket the difference as profit. PBMs will also claw back payments from pharmacies and push patients toward pharmacies they own through a parent company.

Manufacturer rebates are another PBM payment mechanism that has played a major role in the escalation of drug prices in America. These are payments made from the manufacturer to the PBM in exchange for higher formulary placement. The problem is the savings don't flow to patients at the pharmacy counter. They are kept by the PBMs and insurance providers. Furthermore, rebates incentivize manufacturers to raise their list prices for medicines, enabling them to offer larger rebates to PBMs while still making a comfortable profit. These higher prices make their way down to patients who often pay the list price for the medicines before they reach their deductibles. We see similar patterns in other group purchasing organizations in health care, such as for medical devices and durable medical goods. These organizations are adding minimal value while extracting a lot of wealth from patients and taxpayers.

Republican and Democratic members of Congress have introduced many bills designed to reform PBMs, but most are killed by intense lobbying pressure. President Trump and Congress could pass real legislation to curb the worst of these industry practices. This could be a real area of bipartisan cooperation.

5. The Innovation Challenge in Biopharmaceuticals

As much as we want to embrace the potential of lifestyle medicine to treat and prevent chronic disease, we also want a robust engine of biopharmaceutical innovation to produce treatments and cures for conditions that emerge despite it.

Estimates are that it takes roughly $2.4 billion to get a treatment to market. That's a lot of sunk cost for the biopharma companies, manufacturers, and their investors to make up to make their investment worthwhile. Furthermore, they need to make enough money to make up for all the drugs they invested in that did not make it to market.

In short, we need to strike a balance between affordability for patients and taxpayers and maintaining the incentives for continued innovation and drug development. The government, as the largest payer of health care in America, is ill-suited to be the one to set appropriate prices. Its bias will always be in favor of paying less, even if that leads to less innovation. Its short-term budget concerns will always trump the long-term goal of more effective treatments.

We saw this after President Biden signed the Inflation Reduction Act, which included new powers for the government to determine how much certain drugs should cost. Pharmaceutical companies immediately announced they were discontinuing research and development on certain potential therapies because the risk and reward calculation had changed.[14] Similar programs that dictate the prices of drugs by government fiat will have the same problem. Instead, we should focus on solutions that eliminate the ability of PBMs and other middlemen to drive up costs for patients, accelerate approval of lower cost generic drugs, and plug coverage holes in Medicare.

The nature of advancements in biopharmaceutical science poses another challenge. Medicine is becoming increasingly personalized to individual patients. This is producing remarkable improvements in effectiveness—particularly in cancer—but it makes the treatments much less scalable compared to ones that are identical for every patient. These treatments are naturally going to cost much more.

We are also beginning to see approval of more disease cures, as opposed to treatments. This is a dramatic step forward for patients, but it comes with challenges around pricing and affordability.

A vivid example of this challenge can be seen with the breakthrough cure for hepatitis C that was introduced in 2014 by Gilead. Previous treatments required a lifetime of continued treatment, but this cured hep C with a three-month regimen of one pill per day. The treatment was expensive—around $80,000—but this is far less than the approximately $1 million that a hep C patient accrues over his or her lifetime.

In the first year after the treatment's release, Gilead made around $10 billion off the treatment, but each subsequent year it declined. By the end of year three, the company's stock had dropped significantly because by curing the disease, Gilead literally eliminated its customers. I don't want to overstate the problem—the company made significant profits, but the most profitable drugs tend to be the ones that require patients to take them over a lifetime.

President Trump and his leaders at the FDA, as well as Congress, should develop ways to ensure pharmaceutical companies are maximally incentivized to produce cures. This could involve creating bonds that fund the purchase of cures by the government and other payers when they are released, to allow maximum availability to patients, and that are paid back to bond purchasers using the savings accrued from avoiding decades of treatment.

WHY I AM STILL OPTIMISTIC ABOUT SAVING LIVES AND SAVING MONEY

Despite all the difficulties outlined in this chapter, I am convinced we are on the verge of a dramatic revolution in our ability to keep people healthy and to have them live much longer.

The work being done on longevity by doctors, researchers, and entrepreneurs is going to lead within a generation to the average person being able to live to 115 or more and have the energy and health of a 60-year-old where they are over 100. The focus on better nutrition and better preventive public health strategies will begin to bring down the cost of health care and increase the relative health of all Americans. The development of artificial intelligence, real-time online communications, and robotics will lead to independence for millions who today would end up in institutional settings under other people's control.

America has always broken through the prison guards of the past. The Pony Express could not survive the spread of the telegraph. The stagecoach and wagon train could not compete with the railroad. Passenger trains were dominant in the 1930s and 1940s, but the airplane rapidly replaced them for most long-distance travel. Vaudeville could not compete with movies. Movies had to change dramatically to compete with radio and television.

The rotary phone and the tens of thousands of operators placing calls have been replaced by dramatically different self-serving systems that have grown into handheld computers of enormous power (an iPhone has far more computational power than the Saturn 5 rocket, which took Americans to the moon).

We are living in an age of enormous breakthroughs in science, technology, and engineering. Every year we have new tools, new insights, and new capabilities. The sheer advantage of intelligent systems, personal knowledge and power, and constant innovation will presently break the health system loose in ways we can barely imagine.

Each single step may seem relatively small, but the cumulative innovation, adaptation, and adoption will be amazing. We are on our way to a health system that truly saves lives and saves money.

TEN

Security to Survival

The decline of the American system relative to the range of opponents and competitors we have is creating a threat to our survival. I have studied national security for 67 years. I started in August 1958, when my dad was stationed at Seventh Army headquarters in Stuttgart, Germany. As a young student, I wrote a paper on the balance of world power with the help of the Seventh Army librarian. Today, I believe we are in enormous danger.

In fact, I think we are in the greatest danger of losing America to foreign adversaries since General George Washington crossed the Delaware River on Christmas Day, 1776. The threats to our survival come from a wide range of growing failures in the American system. Our news media has decayed into focusing on sensational trivia and extreme partisanship. This makes it extraordinarily difficult to develop a serious national conversation. Politics is dominated by short ads on social media and television. There is little space for communicating complex issues. Further, communication happens so fast, it is hard to consider long-range, important challenges. Short-range noise obfuscates everything.

It is hard for candidates to develop powerful but complicated messages about the real threats to America. Their time is absorbed by constituent demands, fundraising, and today's hot-but-irrelevant drama. The challenge is compounded for candidates by having to deal with reporters who know little, study less, and rely on 30-second sound bites.

We are also weakened by memories of past greatness. France could not believe an emerging German Empire could beat it three times in a 50-year period. The British military planners couldn't imagine the Japanese would occupy the great fortress at Singapore from the land. They planned all their defenses against a seaborne threat. Similarly, America came out of World War II as the greatest military power on the planet. The U.S. accounted for about half of the world's economic activities. Virtually all our commercial competitors had been bombed and were in ruins. Faced with what was perceived as a Soviet effort to take over the world (as described by George Kennan in "The Sources of Soviet Conduct"[1]), we developed a grand strategy of knitting together the free nations in a coalition large and powerful enough to contain the Soviet Union. We determined it would eventually fall behind technologically and economically and crumble.

National Security Council Paper 68, issued in April 1950, outlined the strategic situation and defined the containment strategy. It would lead to the Soviet Union disappearing 41 years later. NSC-68 may have been the most insightful and effective strategic document in American history. It is worth reading today as a model for the strategic plans we should have but do not.

With the collapse of our only global rival, Americans fell into a combination of hubris and amnesia. We decided we had won a final victory over tyranny. Francis Fukuyama wrote *The End of*

History and the Last Man in 1992 arguing that the future would belong to the democracies. Most Americans were happy to believe their elites when they said the world was now safe. President George H. W. Bush went to Congress on January 29, 1991, and proclaimed a new world order of states working together to stop violence between nations. Americans felt they had been given permission not to worry.

For a decade, Americans developed amnesia and took a recess from thinking and preparing for a dangerous world. This explains the enthusiasm for President Clinton's focus on progress at home. It also explains why President George W. Bush thought his experience as governor of Texas had prepared him to be a domestically focused president of the United States. On September 11, 2001, the fantasy ended. Americans were tragically forced to remember the world is always dangerous—and we must be prepared for it.

Journalist Robert Kaplan warned that the elder Bush's new world order was a delusion in a 1994 *Atlantic Monthly* article titled "The Coming Anarchy."[2] Kaplan asserted that the new world order was dreamed up in nice, air-conditioned, four-star hotels and restaurants. The world he had been covering as a journalist was moving in the opposite direction. Violence was spreading, not shrinking. Primitive forces were pushing modern Western civilization back. The conflicts and hostilities that had been suppressed by the two great alliances during the Cold War were now rebounding. Military forces of the civilized countries shrank during "the peace dividend" under the pressure of paying for endlessly expanding welfare states.

Six years after his article, in January 2000, Kaplan turned the essay into a remarkable book, *The Coming Anarchy: Shattering the Dreams of the Post Cold War*. Nearly twenty months after that tragically prescient book was published, the American dream of invincibility and safety was shattered by 19 terrorists and three hijacked commercial jets. By the end of that day, 2,996 people were killed. The younger Bush administration's reaction to the terrorist attacks was in many ways the end of the period of American dominance that had begun in World War II.

First, the investigation into the terrorist attacks was rigged. Establishment leaders ensured that key people were placed on the commissions to protect the Clinton and Bush administrations from accountability. The Democrat and Republican administrations had made serious mistakes in failing to go after Osama bin Laden. The Clinton team was deeply frightened by the disaster in Somalia (captured in the movie *Blackhawk Down*). They were extraordinarily risk averse to getting involved in third-world fights. Furthermore, Clinton's team had no interest in Afghanistan. They thought it was a remnant of the Cold War. Clinton administration national security adviser Sandy Berger once boasted to me that they had finally gotten the CIA to withdraw assets from Afghanistan because it no longer mattered.

The Clinton White House lawyers repeatedly blocked opportunities to kill bin Laden. The CIA analyst who had been assigned to getting rid of him got so angry about their obstruction he was demoted. He was reassigned to less important matters and allowed to stay until he could draw his pension. Ironically, then–secretary of defense Bill Cohen told us in a meeting with the Hart-Rudman Commission members that we were going to eventually get hit by an attack. He said there were simply too many threat indicators being detected to think we could stop everything. The Clinton opposition to an effective intelligence service was such that I personally forced a $1 billion increase in the 1999 budget. After the

9/11 attacks, CIA director George Tenet told me this addition was critical to the system being able to operate (which led to my having remarkable access to the intelligence community going forward).

The Bush team was Russian- and European-centric. It failed to pay attention to the warnings about terrorist threats to the United States. So, the immediate tragedy for America after the disastrous loss of life was the willful avoidance of confronting the truth. For those in power, it wasn't worth it if it meant the Democrat or Republican administrations would suffer political costs. The second, much worse tragedy was the inability of the American national security system to recognize we were in a new world. The systems, doctrines, and structures necessary to defeat the Soviet Union were wrong for the new, totally different series of conflicts in which we were about to engage.

It must be understood that the 23-year, failed involvement in Afghanistan—and the continuing involvement in Iraq, Syria, Jordan, and the rest of the Middle East—have been debilitating. They have weakened the will of the American people, drained a huge amount of resources (an estimated $8 trillion), cost thousands of lives, led to declining morale in the military, and led American political and military leaders to mislead themselves and the American people.

Even relatively small wars can force leaders to focus on issues and problems that are much smaller than the real threats to the nation. Iraq and Afghanistan took up an enormous amount of mental energy available to American leaders from 2001 to now. Large bureaucratic structures such as the defense and state departments build momentums of activity that sustain themselves. Furthermore, their information silos restrict how they think—and what they are allowed to think. I learned this lesson when we created the Rumsfeld Commission on the ballistic missile threat to the United States in 1998. The commission found that intelligence analysts were bound by what they were allowed to see. They were not allowed to share compartmentalized information with other analysts. When Secretary of Defense Donald Rumsfeld and his team would move from silo to silo and ask, "What if you knew this," suddenly the analysts described much different outlooks on the ballistic missile threat.

President Clinton and I created the Hart-Rudman Commission in 1998 to review American national security requirements. It was the most comprehensive report since the 1947 National Security Act created the modern Defense Department. It was led brilliantly by retired air force general Chuck Boyd (the only Vietnam prisoner of war to achieve four stars). The commission looked at total national security and not just at the Defense Department. The Hart-Rudman Report concluded that the greatest threat to the United States was a weapon of mass destruction in an American city. We asserted it would probably come from a terrorist group.

This was 1998. It was totally outside the framework of traditional military capabilities. We proposed that we needed a Department of Homeland Security structured to be capable of dealing with three simultaneous nuclear events in three different cities. In fact, Senator Warren Rudman called me the father of homeland security in a Senate hearing. Unfortunately, the system for heavy civil reconstruction, mobile health care, and strong law enforcement and disaster response was never developed. Instead, Congress pushed together a whole series of agencies that proved virtually impossible to manage into a Department of Homeland Security.

As recently as the 2024 hurricane disaster in North Carolina, the department proved it would be hopeless in trying to cope with a major, national calamity such as a nuclear attack on a city.

A second major danger is the electromagnetic pulse (EMP) attack, which could eliminate all electricity capability. An EMP attack could render useless cars, refrigerators, televisions, communication devices, and a host of other important everyday electronics. My good friend Bill Forstchen, who has been my coauthor for several books, lives in Black Mountain, North Carolina. He wrote *One Second After*, a novel that describes the devastating and immediate impact of an EMP attack. One EMP weapon detonated at 100,000 feet over Omaha, Nebraska, could take out electricity in about one-half of the country. It is probably the greatest danger. Nuclear war would hurt both sides so badly that it is hard to imagine a rational state starting one. An EMP attack is initially bloodless. Its impact is in destroying the infrastructure that we rely on for modern life. And it can be done with one bomb. Every time North Korea launches a satellite, I worry about its potential to be carrying an EMP device.

This is a perfect example of the gap between national security and national defense. Remember, the fortresses of the French Maginot Line sat impotently while German tanks went around the northern flank. The great sea-facing cannons of Singapore were useless as Japanese troops bicycled down the Malay Peninsula to capture the fortification. Similarly, if we don't develop the defenses against an EMP attack we could lose a war in ten minutes, despite having the most powerful military on the planet.

There are several big national security threats that would not show up in a national defense analysis. This siloing of thought and analysis was driven home to me in December 2005. Rumsfeld asked me to review the overall situation in Iraq. It was clear we were mired down in a mess and did not have a firm strategy to win the war. As importantly, we had no plan to establish conditions for us to leave. I investigated the various reports on Iraq (a country I had first reviewed in depth 15 years earlier with support from then–secretary of defense Dick Cheney). Rumsfeld sent a team to Iraq to thoroughly evaluate what needed to be done. He asked them to brief me before they briefed him.

When the team finished walking through what they had learned, and I finished reading their report, I made an obvious comment. The report said the key to Iraq was jobs, electricity, and the economy. However, the report began with a discussion of the security situation and ended with a set of recommendations focusing on the security situation. When I pointed out the contradiction between the analysis and the prescription, their response was that security was the DoD's job. Electricity and jobs were handled by the State Department. So, the keys to victory were outside the Defense Department's area of responsibility. It was clear the State Department lacked the organizational structure and resources to solve the most important requirements of a stable pro-American Iraq.

Our system is simply not designed or trained to develop holistic views of challenges. It cannot create a vision of what America needs and then design strategies for success. Nor can it effectively delegate implementation of the strategies to systems that are designed and trained to win. Virtually no aspect of the system is held accountable for achieving the goals defined by the political system elected by the American people. Instead, strategies are constantly redesigned to fit within the comfort zones of the bureaucracies responsible for them. The classic example is the Joint Army and Navy Board for coordinating the navy and war departments after the Spanish-American War. Created in 1903, it was supposed to ensure that the two services had compatible strategies.

When Pearl Harbor was attacked on December 7, 1941, and the Philippines were hit the same day, there was a clear requirement for a joint army-navy strategy to save the American forces in the Philippines. It turned out that 38 years after the Joint Board was created, the two services had developed radically different strategies for the Philippines in case of war with Japan. The army felt its forces could hold out for three months until the relief force was brought by the navy. The navy had planned for a three-year campaign to defeat the Japanese navy and then get to the Philippines.

General George Marshall directed General Dwight Eisenhower—who had served in the Philippines and knew the people they were trying to rescue—to see if there was a way to get forces to the islands. Eisenhower was forced to report that it was hopeless. The forces in the Philippines had to be sacrificed while America rebuilt its capabilities and focused on winning the larger world war with the Axis powers. Failing to plan—or lying to yourself while planning—can have devastating results in lost lives and catastrophic defeats.

Despite these historic examples, the American system has been unable to develop an effective approach to our strategic survival. In fact, we fail to recognize how many challenges are vital to our survival—and how desperately we need a focus on achievement rather than efforts. In all too many of our systems, activity is confused with achievement. People respond to failure by promising more sincere effort. They don't think through why they failed and what has to change to succeed.

Albert Einstein is apocryphally quoted as saying, "Insanity is doing the same thing over and over again and expecting different results." Whether he said it or not, this kind of insanity infects virtually all our large public and private bureaucracies. When confronted with clear failures, they simply ignore reality and insist on doing more of what is already failing.

THE ORPHANS OF AMERICAN SURVIVAL

If America is to survive in an increasingly dangerous, complex, and fast-moving world, we must deal with the key elements of national power that have been orphaned.

America currently has 12 strategic orphans that need nurturing. Each of these orphans is essential to American survival in a dangerous world. Each is a key component of national security even though they may only be partially or not at all a function of national defense. The Pentagon must be aware of them, but it can solve only a few of them by itself. For most strategies, other agencies and leaderships must be engaged.

CREATING A GRAND NATIONAL STRATEGY

America historically had a grand national strategy. We would create the largest economy in the world and attract immigrants willing and eager to work. We would educate our citizens to a higher level than other countries and rapidly innovate. We would make heroes of successful inventors and entrepreneurs to encourage others to follow in their footsteps. We would build a navy capable of protecting our borders and send Americans forth as traders and missionaries across the world. That strategy worked brilliantly through World War II. Despite its decay afterward, it retained enough momentum to win the Cold War with the Soviet Union.

Today, there is no American grand strategy. President Trump's sense to Make America Great Again comes the closest to a grand strategy, and it has the support of slightly more than half the American people. The Make America Great Again movement must become more detailed and attract a broader coalition to become a stable, implementable grand strategy. It is historic that President Trump developed and articulated a grand strategy—and then won the argument with the left about which direction was better for America. Now, this vision must be expanded into a series of areas that have no clear driving strategy.

EDUCATION CAPABLE OF MEETING OUR CHALLENGES

If we can't produce scientists and engineers capable of inventing the future more rapidly than our competitors—and workers capable of implementing that future—we will inevitably be overwhelmed. We will simply become an uncompetitive nation in a world that will deal brutally with the weak. We need a deep overhaul of learning for K–12 with an emphasis on achievement, not activity. We need to focus on results, not effort. We need a strong system of apprenticeships and vocational learning to ensure a workforce capable of maximum productivity.

Our higher education system was once the best in the world. Now it is dominated by woke culture that teaches falsehoods, imposes phony ideological principles, and has abandoned academic rigor. It also received far too much funding from unaccountable foreign governments and other distorting sources.

Too many Americans have been (and continue to be) cheated by the collapsing K–12 system. We need an effective, time-limited, convenient system of adult education to help those who the educational system has failed over the past half century.

There is no replacement for fixing our education system. If we continue to produce people who have not learned—or who have learned things that are not true—we will not survive as a country.

AN EMP DEFENSE THAT WORKS

We need an immediate crash program to protect ourselves against an EMP attack. The entire electric grid must be hardened against EMP. Future production of electric products, including cars (electric and traditional), must have EMP protection. We need a serious and thorough evaluation of all our EMP vulnerabilities and a plan to fix them within three to five years.

SURVIVING LIMITED NUCLEAR EVENTS

In a world of rapid proliferation of nuclear weapons, we must assume nuclear attacks are possible. Terrorist groups could acquire them through theft, blackmail, or deliberate provision by an enemy that wants to hurt America.

As we have seen with various natural disasters, our emergency response capabilities are sadly limited. Every study of the effect of a nuclear weapon on a major city is horrifying. We have been sleepwalking and hoping nuclear attacks could not happen. Alternatively, we have convinced ourselves that in an all-out nuclear war, nothing would be left. Both views have allowed us to avoid serious, methodical, professional development of a nuclear attack minimization program dedicated to rapid response, recovery, and rehabilitation.

We called for precisely such a capability in the Hart-Rudman Commission Report, and we still need it. It could save hundreds of thousands of lives, and it would dramatically strengthen our disaster recovery capabilities.

AN INDUSTRIAL BASE FOR THE AI AGE

President Trump has correctly focused on rebuilding the American industrial base. We need to once again become the arsenal of democracy we were in World War II. However, we must reshape tax, regulatory, subsidy, and procurement policies to maximize the growth of a new late 21st-century AI-empowered economy. It will be far more effective than rebuilding the industrial base of the past.

BECOMING A SPACEFARING NATION

President Trump outlined the American destiny in space on June 18, 2018:

> We don't want China and Russia and other countries leading us. We've always led—we've gone way far afield for decades now, having to do with our subject today. We're going to be the leader by far. We're behind you a thousand percent.
>
> America's vital interest in space lost out to special interests in Washington, except, of course, for the senators

and congressmen here...But all of that is changing...My administration is reclaiming America's heritage as the world's greatest spacefaring nation. The essence of the American character is to explore new horizons and to tame new frontiers. But our destiny, beyond the Earth, is not only a matter of national identity, but a matter of national security. So it is important for our military. So important.

When it comes to defending America, it is not enough to merely have an American presence in space. We must have American dominance in space. So important.

Elon Musk has expanded this vision to include colonization of Mars so humans will become multi-planetary and capable of surviving a disaster on Earth. The development of the Starship with its ability to lift 100 people or 150 tons of material into orbit—and do so 10 times per rocket—is the beginning of a revolution.

Every aspect of space, from aviation regulations and environmental requirements to NASA's own overly bureaucratic proliferation of rules and regulations, must be reviewed. Space is to the 21st century what air power was to the 20th century. We must become spacefaring people. We must have the ability to protect our assets and people in space.

REDEFINING NATIONAL DEFENSE STRATEGY AND PROCUREMENT

Captain Alfred Thayer Mahan, the great historian of naval dominance, remarked that "no bureaucracy can be expected to reform itself." This is why developing a national defense strategy and inventing a procurement system to replace, not reform, the current procurement system must be imposed from beyond the Defense Department.

If North Korea fired one missile at the United States, the odds are high that it would get through. If China or Russia fired several missiles simultaneously, the odds are high that they would get through. We have watched in the last few years as the Israelis, with American help, have defeated most of the missiles fired at them (literally thousands as of this writing). We know it is possible.

The problem of ICBMs is harder than the systems the Israelis have defeated. Even traditional ICBMs come in much faster. Hypersonic weapons that are maneuverable will be even harder to defeat. The combination of the two arriving at the same time is a hard problem. President Reagan's vision of a space-based missile defense system is still the right vision. We did not have the technology 40 years ago. We could have it now. We should develop a space-based system that works against all avenues of attack. We are vastly bigger than Israel, and we must defend a dramatically bigger area—against opponents who can come from any direction.

Investing in technology and testing and then fielding a 99 percent effective missile defense system should be a high priority. It should be protected from other organizations seeking to use its money.

A STRATEGY FOR IRAN

The Iranian theocratic dictatorship has hated America since its founding. For more than 40 years, Iranian leaders have chanted "death to America." Ayatollah Ali Khamenei even went on

Iranian national television to reassure the country that "death to America" and "death to Israel" were statements of policy, not political slogans.

For its entire history, the Iranian dictatorship has been the principal state funder of terrorism (something our State Department has routinely reported every year). There have been several diplomatic initiatives trying to reason with and guide the Iranian dictatorship. In a Defense Policy Board meeting in 2008, then–secretary of defense Robert Gates reminisced about his experience with Iranian diplomacy. He was deputy to President Jimmy Carter's national security adviser Zbigniew Brzezinski in a meeting with the Iranians in 1979. Carter wanted to find some way to accommodate the new revolutionary regime. The Americans offered a series of concessions. After each one, the Iranian revolutionaries said, "We don't care about that. We want you to turn over the shah so we can publicly execute him." The Americans repeatedly offered positive steps and the Iranian zealots repeatedly gave the same answer. When it finally became clear the Americans would not deliver the shah, the Iranians left the meeting. A few weeks later, the American Embassy was seized in violation of international law, and the American diplomats became hostages for the next 444 days.

Gates concluded his story by saying that anyone who thought there were moderates in the dictatorship were delusional.

Despite the reality of hatred and support of terror by the mullahs—and their steady efforts to get nuclear weapons—there is no strategy for regime replacement. We have consistently assumed the mullahs were inevitable and irreplaceable. The result is continued war against Israel by Hezbollah and Hamas, continuous attacks on Western shipping by the Houthis, and steady Iranian support for terrorism around the world.

We need a strategy that helps the Iranian people take their own country back from a dictatorship that has trapped, imprisoned, and impoverished them. It says a lot about the American establishment that despite more than 40 years of open hostility, we still have no strategy except accommodation and diplomacy with a regime we assume is unchangeable. This must change.

DEFEATING RADICAL ISLAM

One of the tragedies of the George W. Bush administration was the speed with which it abandoned thinking seriously about radical Islam. Bush's staff was afraid that even the use of the term "radical Islam" would alienate all of Islam. They were reinforced in this belief by Islamists themselves.

One of the earliest and most consistent analysts of the rise of militant Islam was Mark Steyn. He warned more than 20 years ago that the rapid migration of unassimilated Muslims into Western countries would inevitably change the countries' character and ultimately undermine Western civilization. The massive anti-Semitic, pro-genocide, and pro-Hamas demonstrations on our college campuses is a good example. The arrest warrants issued for Israeli prime minister Benjamin Netanyahu and former defense minister Yoav Gallant for war crimes and crimes against humanity in Gaza by the International Criminal Court is a similar natural outcome of the collapse of Western values. The number of supposedly decent democratic countries that have said they would honor the International Criminal Court's arrest warrant for a popularly elected leader in a free society while he is fighting for his country's survival is another example of the collapse of Western moral courage. We have no strategy for overcoming radical Islamists. With each passing year, they gain strength.

WINNING UNCONVENTIONAL WARS

Vietnam, Afghanistan, post-Hussein Iraq, Syria, Hamas, Hezbollah, Boko Haram, the Houthis, etc. The list seems almost endless. As Kaplan warned in *The Coming Anarchy*, the challenge of violence to the organized civilized world is going to grow greater.

It is a stunning commentary on the culture and structure of the American military that it could wage war for 23 years in Afghanistan and lose to a supposedly inferior force. The fact is the Taliban had the commitment, staying power, and willingness to endure casualties that enabled it to outlast the Americans. Our problem was, we had no theory or strategy for decisive victory. We tried to wear them down, and they wouldn't quit.

The inability to learn from defeat began in Vietnam. We started training programs for South Vietnam in 1961. We left in 1973, and our South Vietnamese allies were defeated in 1975. As Lieutenant Colonel John Nagl makes clear in his remarkable book *Counterinsurgency Lessons from Malaya and Vietnam: Learning to Eat Soup with a Knife*, the army simply would not learn from the British in Malaya or from their own mistakes. In an equally remarkable book, Colonel Harry Summers Jr. took to heart a conversation he had at the end of the Vietnam War. He told a North Vietnamese colonel that the Viet Cong never beat Americans on the battlefield. The colonel replied that was beside the point, the

Viet Cong won the war. Summers wrote *On Strategy: A Critical Analysis of the Vietnam War* to explore what Prussian general Carl von Clausewitz and other past military minds could teach us in rethinking our strategies for limited wars. The fact is: We have learned no key lessons for our military or political leadership. We have brought together no key lessons for the other government aspects of national power. We are unprepared today to do any better in the next unconventional campaign.

It is a strategy and doctrine gap that has disturbing implications in a world in which we are almost certainly going to face unconventional opponents in unavoidable fights.

CONVINCING THE AMERICAN PEOPLE

None of these strategies will work unless the American people understand them at a general principles level, support them as necessary, and remain committed to them through disappointments and difficulties.

President Abraham Lincoln said, "In this age, in this country, public sentiment is everything. With it, nothing can fail; against it, nothing can succeed." And it is still true. When we have developed a grand national strategy, the American people must understand and support it. When we have developed the orphan strategies, the American people must come to understand and support them.

General Washington used Thomas Paine's two great pamphlets, *Common Sense* and *The Crisis*, to sustain popular support throughout the eight years of the war for independence. He had *The Crisis* read to his soldiers as they boarded boats to cross the Delaware River on Christmas Night, 1776.

President Lincoln knew he had to maintain popular support throughout the four long years of the Civil War. He used emissaries to go around the country. He regularly held what he called public opinion baths of open receptions at the White House. Lincoln spent a great deal of time on some of the finest political writing in American history. The Gettysburg Address was a clear moral appeal that said if you abandon the war, you abandon those who gave their lives for the cause of the Union and freedom. Read it as a political pamphlet, and you will understand how extraordinary Lincoln's mastery of public leadership was.

We may not be able to match Washington or Lincoln, but each of us who believes in the importance of American survival—and freedom as a way of life—must understand our first job is to understand what must be done. Our second job is to help our fellow Americans understand why it must be done. Only then, when the American people are with us, can we truly focus on implementing the necessary strategies.

ELEVEN

A Defense System
That Works

Within the larger framework of a national strategy, there is a practical reality. If a nation can't defend itself against military attack, subsequent strategies won't matter.

Creating a national defense system that works is a serious feat. The system must keep up with technological change. It must keep focus on war winning rather than war fighting. It must provide opportunities exciting enough to recruit and retain the best people. And it must be efficient and cost-effective. Eliminating waste in a militarily useful way will be critical. All these challenges must be met and overcome if America is to remain free and safe.

We must confront the massive, bureaucratic, and complex defense system that we built over the last nine decades. The great bureaucracies we developed to win World War II and the Cold War have gradually built a momentum of their own. In his January 17, 1961, Farewell Address, President Dwight D. Eisenhower warned about the gradual alliance of the Pentagon and giant corporations. He said they could merge into an unaccountable and uncontrollable force aimed primarily at defending their own self-interests. As a five-star general whose entire career had been in the army until he became president, it is worth considering Eisenhower's warning in detail:

> A vital element in keeping the peace is our military establishment. Our arms must be mighty, ready for instant action, so that no potential aggressor may be tempted to risk his own destruction.
>
> Our military organization today bears little relation to that known by any of my predecessors in peace time, or indeed by the fighting men of World War II or Korea.
>
> Until the latest of our world conflicts, the United States had no armaments industry. American makers of plowshares could, with time and as required, make swords as well. But now we can no longer risk emergency improvisation of national defense; we have been compelled to create a permanent armaments industry of vast proportions. Added to this, three and a half million men and women are directly engaged in the defense establishment. We annually spend on military security more than the net income of all United States corporations.
>
> This conjunction of an immense military establishment and a large arms industry is new in the American experience. The total influence—economic, political, even spiritual—is felt in every city, every state house, every office of the Federal government. We recognize the imperative need for this development. Yet, we must not fail to comprehend its grave implications. Our toil, resources and livelihood are all involved; so is the very structure of our society.

In the councils of government, we must guard against the acquisition of unwarranted influence, whether sought or unsought, by the military-industrial complex. The potential for the disastrous rise of misplaced power exists and will persist.

We must never let the weight of this combination endanger our liberties or democratic processes. We should take nothing for granted. Only an alert and knowledgeable citizenry can compel the proper meshing of the huge industrial and military machinery of defense with our peaceful methods and goals, so that security and liberty may prosper together.[1]

President Eisenhower understood how large systems operate. He helped create the modern American military. In the early 1930s, Eisenhower was assigned to study the industrial mobilization base that would be needed in a major war. He understood exactly the system he was warning against.

All bureaucracies become self-defending and self-serving. It is an iron law of bureaucracies. In the case of the Department of Defense, you have to include the enormous corporations that are intertwined and codependent with the Pentagon. They form what Eisenhower dubbed "the military-industrial complex" 64 years ago. With six decades of evolution, the public and private bureaucracies developed an incestuous relationship to protect and enrich each other. This relationship has become a major hindrance to developing an affordable, modern, and technologically evolving system of military power.

The challenge of leading giant bureaucracies is compounded by the culture of self-preservation. None of this is new or peculiarly American. Consider that the French had more tanks than the Germans in 1940. But their culture forced them to break up the tanks to help the infantry, which dominated their military. Another classic example of culture defeating reality is the French series of defeats at Crecy (1346), Poitiers (1356), and Agincourt (1415). In three catastrophic defeats over a 69-year period, the culture of the French aristocracy forced it to rely on heavy cavalry. In each case, the English use of the long bow and their willingness to fight on foot led to disastrous casualties. These catastrophic losses almost destroyed the French's ability to remain a nation.

In the American system, Colonel David Johnson's brilliant book *Fast Tanks and Heavy Bombers: Innovation in the U.S. Army, 1917–1945* outlined the capacity of culture and bureaucracy to reject reality. He described how Army Chief of Staff George Marshall asked the chief of cavalry to brief him on what they had learned from the German use of tanks in Poland and France during the Blitzkrieg (lightning war). He was astounded at the answer. The cavalry had carefully analyzed the German system of armored warfare. The chief of cavalry concluded that they needed trucks pulling horse trailers to bring the horses close to the forward edge of battle so that they would be fresh when the cavalry needed them to fight tanks.

Marshall listened in amazement and thanked the chief for an enlightening briefing. When the chief left, Marshall told Beetle Smith, his assistant, to retire the man by the end of the day and close the office of the chief of cavalry. It took a leader of Marshall's courage and toughness to change obsolete and deeply resistant systems in the U.S. Army and modernize our forces to win the war.

Later, during the Cold War, there was pressure for continuous modernization. The Soviet Union was a big opponent. It was modernizing at a sufficient pace that the American military was pressured to evolve and use technology. However, even during the Cold War, the impact of corporate and government bureaucracy was beginning to take hold. Once the Soviet Union disappeared, the defense contractors worried about their bottom lines. Meanwhile, the military senior leadership became increasingly politicized and unwilling to make waves by forcing innovation against internal and corporate resistance. Congress compounded the problem of inertia and change resistance by adopting more regulations. This led to shallow thinking, limited planning and less testing and doing.

Elon Musk has proven that cutting-edge breakthroughs occur only in organizations with cultures that accept failure as part of the process. He had several rockets blow up as he developed the ability to build a reusable rocket that could land and be reused. At the time, he would cheerfully tell the press that SpaceX learned a lot from the failure, and it will help solve problems and get to a successful rocket. SpaceX was a private company with a failure-acceptance mindset that tolerated successful failures—as long as Musk thought it was getting them closer to their goal. Government bureaucracies have a much more risk-averse attitude. They know that careers can be ruined if tainted with failure. They also know that enough failure guarantees congressional hearings in which someone must be a scapegoat.

Bureaucracies naturally build more regulations and implement more procedures to minimize risk. But these mazes of red tape minimize progress or make it so expensive that advancements can't be developed.

General Bernie Schriever was the legendary, forceful, and charismatic developer of the American intercontinental ballistic missile system. He once called a successor and commented on his successor's 17 successful flights with no failures. His successor beamed with pride until Schriever said the man and his team weren't trying hard enough. Schriever understood that real progress requires real risks. Safe, mistake avoidance systems minimize the chance for new developments. Similarly, as the bureaucratic incest between the military and the giant corporations has grown stronger, it has become harder for new ideas to break through. People become satisfied with existing contracts and relationships. Actual competition breaks up the game and causes powerful institutions (military, bureaucratic, and corporate) to lose power and money.

Adam Smith, in *The Wealth of Nations*, warned, "People of the same trade seldom meet together, even for merriment and diversion, but the conversation ends in a conspiracy against the public, or in some contrivance to raise prices."[2] Consider the network of lobbyists, consultants, and self-protective activities between the various elements of the military and the companies with which it works. It is clear our defense system gets what it is comfortable with rather than what it needs to keep America safe and free. This is dangerous.

Congress has tried to control the acquisition process by piling up regulations, which has led to more paperwork. This crowds out small companies that can't afford the time to fill out the paperwork. As a result, large corporations that have entire departments dedicated to doing Pentagon paperwork become stronger. In Congress, I represented the company that made virtually all the airport baggage handling carts. The company's product was good, and its cost was competitive. They provided baggage carts to a wide range of domestic and foreign airlines, including Aeroflot. Despite their ability to produce exceptional baggage carts at competitive prices, they refused to bid on the military requirement for baggage carts. They felt strongly that they did not want their lean, aggressive, hard-charging workforce to get sucked into a slow, paperwork-ridden bureaucracy.

When I arrived in Congress in 1979, I was deeply pro-defense. The collapse of support for the military was a result of the anti–Vietnam War movement and President Jimmy Carter's anti-military attitude (even though he was an Annapolis graduate who had worked for Admiral Rickover in the nuclear navy). Together, they had lowered morale, weakening our ability to be effective militarily. As long as Carter was president, I was deeply committed to expanding federal defense spending.

The senior military was so desperate for pro-defense elected officials in the post–Vietnam War era that I got to work with a wide range of people. In early 1981, I began working with Bill Whitehurst (second-ranking Republican on the House Armed Services Committee), Dick Cheney, Gary Hart, Sam Nunn, and about a dozen other members to develop the Military Reform Caucus. With funding secured, we wanted to study how to develop a more effective and less expensive defense system. The Military Reform Caucus routinely met with a wide variety of defense intellectuals, who gave the caucus a pretty good introduction to the basics of military power and the things that could be dramatically improved.

The biggest result of the caucus was the drafting and passage of the Goldwater-Nichols Department of Defense Reorganization Act of 1986. It moved the system from a siloed service focus to a joint commitment. This forced all of the services to learn to work with each other. It was clearly the boldest and most decisive reorganization of the Pentagon's operations since the National Security Act of 1947. Five years of work had gone into thinking through and then passing the Goldwater-Nichols Act. On the House side, I had the opportunity to be the third witness in favor of the bill, after retired chairman of the joint chiefs General David Jones and retired chief of staff of the army Shy Meyer. (It was telling that the two military supporters had both retired.)

Despite a year-long study by the Center for Strategic and International Studies—and a great deal of work by the House and Senate Armed Services Committees as well as individual members—there was still deep and virtually unanimous senior military hostility to the idea of jointness. This included resentment that Congress would impose it. In fact, every one of the senior generals and admirals opposed Goldwater-Nichols. They felt it diminished the power of their positions and blurred or undermined the authority of the services.

We were able to overcome all this opposition because of a single historic event. When the United States liberated Grenada in October 1983, it turned out that the army and navy radios could not connect with each other. An army captain was forced to go to a pay phone, call a friend in the Pentagon using his personal credit card, and ask his friend to tell the navy that the radios were not communicating. When this story came to light, it raised a question of simple systems incompetence that no four-star could defend or answer. This abhorrent failure made it easy to definitively explain to members of Congress how badly the system needed an overhaul. In a meeting I attended aimed at recruiting a key Republican to support the bill, Senator Barry Goldwater said, "The f—ing system just doesn't work."

Today, virtually everyone agrees that jointness has been a great success and a return to the siloed services of pre-Goldwater-Nichols would be a huge mistake. There are earlier examples of presidential and congressional imposition of change on defense systems resistant to change.

After the disastrous inability to mobilize for the Spanish-American War, Secretary of War Elihu Root imposed reforms on the dysfunctional army command structure. Drawing in part on the German General Staff model, he created a professional system with a general staff. He modernized the National Guard. He founded the Army War College to continue the evolution of thought in the military. In 1925, after the emergence of air power in World War I, President Calvin Coolidge created the Morrow Board (named after its chair, Dwight Morrow) "to study the best means of developing and applying aircraft in national defense." The board recommended several changes. These included adding an assistant secretary of war and an assistant secretary of the navy. Also, the board recommended adding a seat on the general staff for an individual from the Army Air Corps (renamed by the board to emphasize more independence from the regular army than its earlier title of Army Air Service).

The most important impact of the Morrow Board may have been the fact that its only Democratic member of Congress was Carl Vinson of Georgia. Vinson went on to chair the Naval Committee and later the Armed Services Committee. He authored the 1934 Vinson-Trammel Act, which called for the building of 92 major warships. Before World War II, he authored three additional naval construction bills, including the Two Ocean Navy Act. The navy—which defeated Japan and the German submarine, and landed Americans all around the world—was the product of Vinson's leadership and foresight. Virtually all the ships used to defeat Japan were authorized before Pearl Harbor.

The greatest civilian leadership intervention in the modern military may have been President Franklin Delano Roosevelt's commitment to building 50,000 aircraft per year. In 1938, the United States had produced 1,800 military aircraft. As the Germans conquered Europe, Roosevelt wanted to emphasize air power. So, in May 1940, he called for 50,000 aircraft to be made per year. This posed an important problem for General Marshall, who was the army chief of staff. Marshall wanted to build a 200-division army. He explained to President Roosevelt that with the manpower needed to construct (and then man) 50,000 aircraft per year, he could never build an army the size he had planned. Roosevelt firmly responded, "We are building 50,000 aircraft a year, so figure out how many divisions that permits." Marshall had to drop his plan from 200 divisions to 89.

In retrospect, FDR's commitment to airpower was the correct response to technological change; a change that was impossible for the bureaucracy to adopt on its own.

TRANSFORMING—NOT REFORMING

The scale of change we need in the Department of Defense is not a mere reform of the current system—it is transformational. Any effort to reform the current system will fail. First, it will be targeted at improving the present, when preparing for the future is needed. Second, the enormous layers of bureaucracy and culture will absorb the reforms and twist them until they have become part of the current mess.

A simple example of the scale of change we need can be found in the Pentagon itself. The Pentagon opened in 1943 so 26,000 people could use carbon paper, manual typewriters, and filing cabinets to manage a worldwide war. Today, we have computers, laptops, iPads, and smartphones. I have never been able to get a serious estimate of how the speed and volume of information flow in the Pentagon has increased since the 1940s. But it has to be on the order of one million times more efficient than the time of manual typewriters with carbon paper. Yet, we still have 26,000 people in this gigantic building.

I often tell people we would get a better defense system if we reduced the Pentagon to a triangle and turned the other two-thirds of the building into a museum of national defense. The underused people with modern technology spend all day creating work for each other to seem busy. They just aren't very productive or effective.

So how could we proceed with a transformational change of national defense?

President Trump must continue to insist on transformational change for the entire government. He must take the lead ensuring that people understand that transformational change includes the Department of Defense. Only President Trump's personal leadership can arouse the American people to demand transformation, insist that all the elements of the federal government help (beginning with the Office of Management and Budget), and convince Congress that transformation is not a partisan position, but a matter of national survival.

Congress must undertake a profound transformation of its own. The current narrowly regulatory, pork-for-back-home-oriented, lobbyist influence system permeating Congress is one of the greatest threats to transforming national security. The scale and density of regulations cripple any effort to transform the Defense Department. The muscle of giant corporations and their lobbyists inhibits any effort to move toward an agile rapidly evolving system. The pork barrel approach to protecting unnecessary jobs and favoring obsolete facilities inhibits needed changes and encourages a psychology of defeatism in the defense system. It lets people hide behind congressional interference as an excuse for not doing anything. Then-congressman Dick Armey's brilliant invention of the base closing system has saved more than $20 billion. By some estimates, it has reduced costs by about $5 billion a year. Congress needs to develop a whole series of regulation-ending approaches. It should replace failing systems rather than reform them. A large part of transforming the American national defense system lies in Congress, not the Pentagon. We desperately need a generation of congressmen and senators willing to transfer authority and power back to the Defense Department, so it can modernize and transform as the times require.

Our discussion of national defense and development of the needed components must start in the future and work back to the present. We are guaranteed to fail if we start with the current system and try to modernize and reform it. This process of imagining the future and then working to create it (while weaning away and leaving behind the parts that are unnecessary) has a long history in successful defense planning and implementation. Alfred Thayer Mahan's vision of the dominance of navies provided the intellectual ammunition for Theodore Roosevelt, Henry Cabot Lodge, and others to insist on building a modern navy in the 1890s.

The war games played at the Naval War College in the 1930s led Admiral Chester Nimitz to say, "The war with Japan had been re-enacted in the game rooms here...in so many different ways that nothing that happened during the war was a surprise—absolutely nothing except the kamikaze tactics toward the end of the war."[3]

It is likely that the war in the Pacific was several years shorter and much less costly in American lives because of the power of the naval war games. They shaped the culture, professional military education of the officers, and the planning in the theater. General Billy Mitchell's pioneering work developing the 1919 air campaign plan—and the books he wrote after World War I—laid the basis for virtually everything the modern air force has done. Alvin and Heidi Toffler's vision in their groundbreaking book *The Third Wave* convinced the army to develop AirLand Battle. In a dramatic break from the past, this forced a cooperative process with the air force.

General Bill Hartzog told me while in charge of planning for the future of the army that you must go out on a hill 20 or 30 years from now and look around. Then, when you understand what you will need in that world, you come back to the present and begin to think through the bridges to achieving that future. If you start planning in the present, you will never be bold enough. You will simply be extending what you are already doing. Marginally improving the world of the present is not the same as preparing for the future.

We must imagine the probable technology of 2050 or 2060, then think through the doctrines that would use that technology. Then we must think through the structures that would be needed to implement the doctrine and use the technology. Finally, we must approach Congress to support the changes this thought exercise will reveal. That is a transformational rather than reform approach to rethinking where we are and where we must go. It will also tell you how to prioritize which changes you need immediately, which you must work toward, and which can be out-year projects (you can't do everything at once in a system of this size and complexity).

In addition to the culture of defense, the executive and legislative branch components involved with defense are at the heart of the transformation. It is impossible to transform any system unless the people are willing to adjust to the change. If enough people adjust to the change, you will, by definition, have changed the culture. Unless the culture is changed, the system will inevitably fail. No matter how many structures and systems you change, if the people implementing them don't adapt to them, they will undermine them and return to the previous system.

This cultural change inside the Department of Defense must be reinforced and strongly supported by the White House and Congress. If these powerful institutions try to sustain the past or block and undermine the future, it will be dramatically harder to transform our national defense and meet the challenge of emerging technology and competitors. A significant part of the cultural change must come with members and, equally or more importantly, with their staffs. This means that the new defense leadership must focus on educating their executive and legislative branch colleagues rather than merely lobbying them. Getting people well enough educated in the requirements of national survival will lead them to ask the right questions and support the right budgets.

In an ideal world, the members of Congress and their staffs, the key executive branch members (especially those in the White House, OMB, the Department of State, and intelligence agencies), and the entire Department of Defense (uniform and civilian), would work to develop a doctrine of transformation. The doctrine of transformation would blend Musk's lessons from Tesla and SpaceX, Peter Drucker's sense of effectiveness and customer orientation, Edwards Deming's focus on continuous improvement and dramatic increases in efficiency, and Antony Jay's model for replacing bureaucratic rules and regulations with human leadership and human cooperation.

There is an entire body of literature on delegating decisions and authority to the people doing the work rather than trying to control them through detailed regulations and red tape. The concept of transformation inevitably requires accepting failures and the need to continue innovating and thinking until things start working. That requires decentralization and delegation, rather than top-down efforts to control by detailed processes.

If transformation sounds dramatically different from what we are currently doing, that is because it is. It is more powerful but much more complicated psychologically, especially in fostering trust and localized leadership. The current acquisition system must be replaced rather than reformed. The current system has accumulated hundreds of thousands of pages to guarantee fairness, detailed oversight, mistake minimization, and avoidance. It is a blueprint for behavior so detailed that even an untrained person won't make a major mistake if they follow the detailed rules and regulations from the last 80 years. (Some regulations are so old that they've been around since the creation of the Department of Defense, and in other cases, since the time when the U.S. had a War Department and a Navy Department.)

Congress will never successfully reform the current process because it is too complicated. It is filled with too many arcane details, most of which were adopted for perfectly good reasons but together have made everything more and more complicated. Congress should start with a blank slate and look at the acquisition process and controls of the most dynamic and rapidly evolving companies. At a time when Apple produces a new cell phone every year, procurement must evolve to meet the pace of changing technology.

The greatest breakthroughs are occurring in small startups, many of which are purchased within a year or two by bigger corporations that find acquisition more reliable and less expensive than trying to develop everything internally. The defense acquisition system must have similar agility.

There are two considerable complexities in the defense acquisition of bold, new, and sometimes radically different, but more powerful, capabilities. First question: Is there a doctrine for the new technology's application to winning that makes it profitable to acquire it? The purpose of the Defense Department is to win wars and, ideally, to be so strong that no war occurs. Winning wars is inherently different from just meeting customer demand in a marketplace. The new technologies must be useful and applicable in a war-winning system. Second, the military at any given moment is fielding a complex set of capabilities and activities. How does the fascinating new development fit into the existing infrastructure of war-winning?

These two requirements inherently make even rapid defense acquisition somewhat more complicated than purely civilian, customer-oriented technology. Their closest analog may be new health system innovations that must fit into large hospitals' culture and operating systems. Since health care at its most intense is a life and death event, it may be a useful analog to study in developing a new defense acquisition system.

Just as Goldwater-Nichols was a profound break in the single-service model of organization, the new 21st-century rapid, affordable acquisition system must be a profound break with the paper ridden, detailed process, cumbersome system we have today. Congress must combine transformational-oriented military leaders and the best acquisition practitioners in the private sector to develop the new model of 21st-century rapid, lean acquisition. When the model is clear, before allowing a theoretical model to upend the largest acquisition system in the world, it ought to be tested in a series of acquisition war games to see how it would work in practice.

This transformational approach to national defense will require a thorough rethinking of professional military education. From basic training to the command and staff colleges, and from the war colleges to the specialized general officer courses, the challenge will be to develop learning to fit a transformational design of defense. If we really want a cultural change in the Department of Defense (and for that matter, in the foreign service and the intelligence community), then the courses professionals are required to take must be transformational. This is clearly not the case today.

This need for a transformational professional education system will lead to a profound rethinking of what people need to learn, how to update it as we learn more, and how to keep everyone at every level aware of the latest knowledge requirements as the world keeps evolving and transformation continues. One of the greatest requirements for America in developing a much more effective system of national security is developing the courage to invest time, energy, and leadership to rethink our failures. This is true across the entire national security system.

Historians will marvel that the United States lost in Vietnam, failed in Iraq, clearly lost in Afghanistan—and did not develop a thorough rethinking of what worked and what failed. As a first principle, we must be in the business of winning wars, not just fighting them. We should look back at each case and determine under what circumstance, if any, the war could have been won. We must look soberly at the gaps in our thinking, doctrine, training, organization, and equipment. In every case, we should also look at the role of the White House and Congress and the degree to which they helped or hurt in the cause of winning the wars. We should apply all these lessons to thinking about the various competitors we face today—or those we will face in the future. Here's the central question: Given what we have learned from this profound rethinking of our past, how should we behave in preparing for a war-winning future?

Finally, a significant amount of effort must go into rebuilding morale, pride, and commitment in the military. We have more than 337 million Americans. We need about 1 percent committed to the survival of our country. We need a style, a sense of purpose, a call to service and duty, and an intensity of team building that will enable us to attract and keep the best and the brightest.

On February 24, 1981, President Reagan went to the Pentagon to present the Congressional Medal of Honor to Sergeant Roy Benavidez. That simple gesture of honoring a brave person in the Pentagon sent a signal that the Vietnam War's anti-military attitude and President Carter's contempt for the military were in the past. With Reagan, a new era of taking our defense seriously arrived. With morale and commitment, there is often a psychological component of recognizing the dedication of our men and women in uniform, how dangerous their work is, and how much all of us owe them for protecting America.

The pathetic efforts at diversity, equity, and inclusion in the Biden-Harris administration are rapidly being replaced by the proud patriotism of the Trump-Vance administration. Enlistments will rise, re-enlistments will increase, and the morale and effectiveness of those who risk their lives to defend us will skyrocket. These are the reforms we need to make America safe in an increasingly dangerous world.

TWELVE

Artificial Intelligence and the Endless Frontier

The ongoing explosion in artificial intelligence (AI) capabilities will be one of the major characteristics of the next 50 years. The emergence of electricity generation, internal combustion engines, and modern chemistry changed life dramatically between 1870 and 1920. Now, the various capabilities of AI will be felt throughout virtually every aspect of life.

We have achieved massive computational power, which enables us to undertake a remarkable range of tasks with speed and accuracy. But this is not AI in itself. There is a steady movement toward computers that are capable of learning, evaluating, and growing in capability on their own. Think of it as the difference between directed capability and self-guiding capability. Both are powerful. Directed capability is the dominant form today, but genuine artificial intelligence is becoming more possible.

We are already seeing AI in a wide range of applications. Every year, Apple introduces a new and improved cell phone. Tesla is pioneering information gathering and real-time autonomous vehicles, including a robot taxi that has no steering wheel or pedals for braking or accelerating. In fact, Tesla has a database of everyone who has ever driven a Tesla. It may be the largest AI training database in the world. It is an example of how Elon Musk develops many areas with a long view toward their ability to improve the world.

The extraordinary increase in computing power and the steady drive toward miniaturization has enabled us to put more capabilities into smaller spaces. As an example, drones can be built with extraordinary information processing capabilities. We see these new military capabilities being used in practical ways in Ukraine and in the Israeli conflict with Iran and its allies. The shift in combat power was first shockingly displayed when the Russians initially attacked Ukraine on February 24, 2022. The Ukrainian use of modern weapons was an enormous shock. Three weeks earlier, Chairman of the Joint Chiefs of Staff General Mark Milley had said he thought the Russians would be in Kiev in three days if they invaded Ukraine. The difference between the conventional defeatist view and the reality of what happened was the Ukrainian use of autonomous vehicles.

In particular, they had drones and missiles that flew over tanks, identified them autonomously, and then hit them from above where their armor was weakest. Disastrous vehicle losses (including the trucks that carried ammunition, food, and gasoline) meant the Russians were stopped, devastated, and finally forced to retreat. Ukraine used even more elegant and advanced autonomous capabilities to drive the Russian Black Sea Fleet back into Russian ports—while destroying several Russian warships. This was a mismatch of multi-million-dollar ships being destroyed by vehicles costing tens of thousands of dollars. The Russians also developed a wide range of drones and other autonomous weapons.

When America sent 31 of its best main battle tanks to Ukraine, Russian drones took out one-third of them. New technologies of defense against drones will be necessary for tanks to be successful again on the emerging battlefield.

While there are clear military uses for advanced computing and artificial intelligence, it is only a tiny part of the wave of revolutionary change. This technological change will shape the lives of everyone for the next two or three generations. In that time, we will develop a clearer understanding of the new capabilities and their limitations, dangers, and uses.

The scale of change bearing down upon us is a vindication of one of the most prescient books written about science and creating a better future. Vannevar Bush was the most important American scientist in the first half of the 20th century. As a professor at the Massachusetts Institute of Technology, he did much of the early work on computing. He later became president of MIT. As World War II approached, Bush was recruited for a series of jobs that ultimately gave him a leadership role with some 6,000 American scientists. In 1945, he wrote an essay, "As We May Think," that stimulated a great deal of thought about computers and computing over the next several decades.

President Franklin Delano Roosevelt wrote Bush in November 1944 and asked him to do a report on the future of scientific research. When President Harry Truman replaced Roosevelt on the latter's death in April 1945, Bush presented him with what became the decisive 241-page paper on government and science entitled "Science: The Endless Frontier." Bush believed that the future was virtually limitless. He argued that government funding of scientific research would accelerate the development of a wide range of capabilities to help people. Science played a steadily expanding role during World War II, with the Manhattan Project to develop the atomic bomb. There was a growing belief that scientific research could lead to a better future with greater options, more prosperity, and better lives.

Belief in the power of systematic knowledge to create more powerful solutions led to a wide range of institutions with substantial budgets. The National Science Foundation (NSF), the Defense Advanced Research Projects Agency (DARPA), the National Aeronautics and Space Administration (NASA), the National Institutes of Health (NIH), and a host of other agencies all grew out of this notion. Resources were allocated. Smart people were attracted, and knowledge was expanded. The computer you use was largely invented in its basic functioning through a series of government-funded research projects. The jet airplane was largely funded by the development of military aircraft. The great breakthroughs in modern medicine grew out of enormous amounts of research done at the NIH and elsewhere. (The human genome project actually started in the Department of Energy.) The internet was originally developed by the government to have a decentralized system of communication that could survive a nuclear war.

When I was Speaker, we balanced the federal budget for four straight years. We did so by cutting spending in many federal agencies. However, we doubled the budget for the NIH. We were convinced by private sector pharmaceutical company executives that the steady flow of new knowledge from government-funded research was the engine driving improvements in health and in defeating disease.

Since President Richard Nixon declared war on cancer in 1971, a lot of money has been invested into understanding and treating cancer. Survival rates have steadily improved. Many cancers that would have been death sentences a generation ago are now curable or manageable. The momentum toward early detection and cures for virtually all cancers is enormous. The breakthroughs have extended far beyond cancer. I have a brother and sister who have each had a lung transplant. Both are leading completely active lives. They would likely have not survived a generation ago. My sister-in-law had a liver transplant. She also would have died a generation ago. She is leading a full life enjoying her family and traveling as though she had never had a problem. A good friend's son needed three delicate heart operations by the time he was three years old. Today, he is in college playing soccer. He has every expectation of leading a full life.

The next phase of these scientific advances will include treating and curing Alzheimer's, Parkinson's, and other complex and currently incurable diseases and conditions.

The endless frontier of science has created opportunities far beyond our health. On February 20, 1962, John Glenn became the first American to orbit the earth. With the technology of that era, it was a daring and dangerous undertaking. There was a reason a marine test pilot was in the capsule. Sixty-three years later, more people are going into space, including civilians. Musk's Starship will be able to carry 100 passengers at a time. Space tourism is now a game only for the wealthy, but within a generation it could become the equivalent of a high-end cruise ship.

I cite these historic examples to make a specific case. What we are about to experience is an extension and a deepening of a process of systematic learning and development that started in 1945. Large computational systems, mass data collection, artificial intelligence, and artificial general intelligence (further down the road and sobering in its potential threat to humans) will all lead to enormous changes in what we know and can do. In short, our lives are on the edge of a series of more powerful revolutions than we can imagine. There are factors that really make this dramatic acceleration different and more powerful than any past period of dramatic new knowledge.

First, there are simply a lot more scientists, engineers, and entrepreneurs investing their money and lives in understanding new knowledge and applying it profitably. The result is a flow of capital on a scale that no one could have imagined in 1945 when Bush was writing. The capital available to Google, Microsoft, Meta, Apple, Amazon, Tesla, and SpaceX dwarfs government programs (although they are also heavily involved in government contracting, and federal funds are a significant part of their ability to do research and development). The model of venture capital starting with small enterprises is widely understood. Tens of thousands of ambitious entrepreneurs are in the marketplace seeking new ideas, developments, and opportunities to create the next big breakthrough. There are an amazing number of would-be Steve Jobses, Elon Musks, Bill Gateses, etc., working seven days a week on shoestring budgets to see if they can develop the future. The sheer scale of today's inventing, developing, and marketing systems dwarf anything Thomas Edison or Henry Ford could have imagined.

Second, the speed of information flow enables new discoveries and knowledge to reach would-be entrepreneurs with a speed that did not exist even 20 years ago. There is an emerging ecosystem of scouts looking for breakthroughs and then connecting them to capital. This will accelerate turning knowledge into products and services. In fact, this system of using new knowledge to transform existing systems is so pervasive it has led to the old order using law and culture to inhibit the changes.

The classic example of protecting the past against the future is the European decision to pursue regulation rather than innovation. If you look at the most dynamic, technologically advanced companies, they are overwhelmingly American, Chinese, and Japanese. India, Israel, and Taiwan are also making significant contributions. (Taiwan dominates the world in making computer chips. It accounts for 68 percent of the regular chip production and an estimated 90 percent of the most advanced chips necessary for artificial intelligence.) At some point in the last 30 years, European elites concluded they simply could not innovate fast enough without breaking up their cultural and political networks. They had grown up around the dominant industries of the 1960s and 1970s. The European Union decided it could use regulation to limit innovation. The result is the steady decline of Europe as a competitor. It cannot attract the capital and talent necessary to compete with the emerging knowledge-based companies. The speed of acquiring and disseminating new knowledge is going to continue to accelerate. The countries that encourage are going to become wealthier and militarily stronger. The countries that hide from the future behind legal structures that protect the past will grow relatively poorer and weaker.

Third, the big breakthroughs led to an amazing number of spin-offs and smaller breakthroughs. Ford developed the assembly line, uniformity of parts, and low-cost mass production of cars. This set the stage for gas stations, motels, highway maps, local car dealers, car washes, pizza deliveries, and an amazing array of jobs and entrepreneurial opportunities. All the current developments in science and technology are going to lead to a huge number of new opportunities. Energetic, ambitious people will try to imagine market opportunities. For example, a decade ago, who would have believed that Instagram could build such a huge market that Portuguese soccer player Cristiano Ronaldo could have 632 million followers and earn $3.23 million per post on the platform. Who would have believed that he would be starting for Al Nassr in the Saudi League and the Portuguese National team.

The Trump campaign was the first American political campaign to recognize that new media was competing with and in some cases displacing old media. The number of podcasts President Trump did—and the reach into different audiences it gave him—was an example of being aware of how technological change was being reflected in societal behavior. This is an example of the new knowledge being used to displace the old, dominant systems.

Who knows how many new companies and professions will grow out of the current scientific and technological revolution? What we do know is countries that encourage this kind of entrepreneurship will be wealthier, have far more opportunities, and be stronger militarily. They will also develop far more prestige than countries that hide from the future and prop up the past.

Fourth, systems of gigantic scale will generate knowledge in quantities and forms we have never known. We experience new technology writ small. It is our cellphone, Apple Watch, and the way we make airline and hotel reservations. Yet, behind all this is an emerging worldwide series of huge systems. The giant systems empower the individual capabilities.

When I was young, we lived in France while my dad was serving there in the army. Making a call back to the States to talk to our relatives was an all-day project. We had to go to the Orleans

Post Office to ask for access to the Atlantic trunk line. They would call Paris and be told what time of the day the line would be available. Then, we would go back to the post office at the designated time and place an expensive, usually brief, call back home. The first time my daughter Kathy called me on her cell phone from France, while I was in a car driving in Georgia, I realized I was living in revolutionary times. Speed, access, and cost of technology was falling rapidly. This process of speed, convenience, and lowered cost has accelerated and spread to many kinds of information gathering and analysis. Tesla is a good example of the coming scale of information—and how it will be translated into our lives. Every Tesla is an information machine. It gathers up huge volumes of data about traffic conditions, driver patterns, mechanical behavior of the car, and other information. All of it is being stored at Tesla's gigantic information center. It is now probably one of the largest centers of data in the world. After all, every drive generates huge volumes of data. Part of Musk's passion about massive computing and artificial intelligence is the degree to which this will monetize Tesla beyond any plausible auto company value. Tesla is best understood as an information company with cars rather than a car company with information. This also explains its market capitalization.

The same kind of information gathering, analysis, and dissemination is occurring in health and health care. With every passing year, we know more about the human body. Doctors once relied on the lessons they had learned in their lifetimes and their intuition about what those lessons meant for you. Now, it is becoming possible for doctors to tap into gigantic databases that include thousands (and in some cases millions) of cases that resemble yours. We will presently have quantifiable best practices and outcomes on a scale that will radically transform the practice of medicine and open up a system of real-time, self-managed health.

Finally, we are living in a revolution of general knowledge and personally applied knowledge. You get an example of personally applied knowledge every time your computer brings you information you did not request. Recently, a friend of mine got an email from Open Table saying that he apparently liked Italian food and there were 10 good Italian restaurants near him. It is helpful and a little frightening to know how much the larger system knows about you. Callista loves the way her pictures get organized and displayed by her cell phone, which will take a year, a place, or a face, and build a presentation with music around it. It is intrusive and amusing, but it is clearly beyond her control unless she wants to kill that app.

We will learn more about the human genome and then we will apply that to learn more about your personal genetic makeup. We will learn much more about how people learn. This will transform education. The mid-19th century industrial model of standardization is currently boring students and frustrating teachers, and is totally out of synch with how the rest of our lives are lived. The age of artificial intelligence will be as big a change as the shift from agriculture to industry was in the 19th century. We have barely begun the journey, and it is going to accelerate and proliferate.

A final word of caution: people as brilliant as Musk and Henry Kissinger are worried that artificial general intelligence will eventually dominate—and even eliminate—the human race. Kissinger was so concerned that he coauthored *The Age of AI: And Our Human Future* with Eric Schmidt and Daniel Huttenlocher. I think we are a long way from that danger, but it is something that deserves a lot more long-term thinking.

In his remarkable work *I Robot*, Isaac Asimov in 1950 was writing about a robot detective in 2035 Chicago (it seemed a long way away back then). Asimov built into his story the laws of robotics that were designed to prevent any robot from hurting humans. It might be worth revisiting that concept and wondering how it would apply to artificial general intelligence and even if it could be. But for now, and for the foreseeable future, the revolution in computing and artificial intelligence is going to lead to dramatic economic growth, much better health care, a revolution in education, and dramatically greater military capabilities. It must be a major asset in thinking about how we solve America's problems.

THIRTEEN

Americans in Space

The second Trump administration has a magnificent opportunity to achieve decisive American leadership in space. President Trump outlined and began implementing this vision in his first term.

The dual emergence of Elon Musk as a close adviser and Jared Isaacman leading NASA gives the American space development capability an enormous boost. The less publicized—but no less impressive—work by Jeff Bezos at Blue Origins, Eren and Fatih Ozmen at Sierra Nevada Corporation, Kam Ghaffarian at Axiom Space, and the dozens of emerging entrepreneurial startups represents a revolution in our space capability.

There are three vital areas of space activity that will shape the future of humanity.

First, there is a military component. President Trump recognized this when he convinced Congress to create the Space Force in December 2019. It is vital that the United States dominate military capabilities in and from space. We must drop the concept of pinning China's capability as our benchmark and instead go all-out to develop science, technology, and bold new doctrines and organizations. We must pull so far out front that China and others trail us for decades. This will require a dramatic overhaul of our slow, cumbersome, timid bureaucracies. It will also mean devoting the resources necessary to be the dominant force in space.

Second, NASA has led the world in classic science missions and broadened our understanding of the solar system and beyond. However, NASA's decades-long effort to protect the disastrously expensive Space Launch System, Orion manned spacecraft, and the Gateway space station to orbit the moon have killed important scientific projects that could provide invaluable new knowledge. This means radically shrinking NASA's 18,000-person bureaucratic system and using the dramatic collapse in modern launch costs to develop a more robust and daring scientific program in space.

Third, the emerging commercial use of space is already a $570 billion industry. It is projected to rise to $1 trillion a year by 2040. With the steady decline in launch costs, every effort should be made to grow commercial space activities. This can become the underlying resource and test bed from which the military can learn in peacetime and mobilize in war time.

Musk's passion for colonizing Mars to become an interplanetary species and avoid extinction from a single catastrophic event led him to develop reusable rockets. He reasoned that you could never get enough launches to colonize Mars if you had to build each rocket. His success creating reusable rockets lowered launch costs enough to enable him to create Starlink—thousands of satellites sustaining worldwide communications. Profit from Starlink is funding the development of the reusable Starship, which will presently start colonizing Mars. This is the kind of vision turned into practical achievement that will proliferate as we get greater experience in space.

These developments in military, scientific, and commercial space are a significant part of President Trump's vision to Make America Great Again. President Trump's commitment to space led him to create the Space Force. It also led him to resurrect the National Space Council. The council was established in 1989 by President George H. W. Bush but was disbanded in 1993 by President Bill Clinton. The Clinton-Gore team had a limited, Earth-focused vision of space. The administration was eager to submerge American space activities into international projects with Russia and other countries.

In June 2017, President Trump resurrected the National Space Council and gave it a mandate to dream big and plan for the moon, Mars, and beyond. As he said:

> With the actions we are launching today, America will think big once again. Important words: think big. We haven't been thinking so big for a long time, but we're thinking big again as a country. We will inspire millions of children to carry on this proud tradition of American space leadership—and they're excited—and to never stop wondering, hoping, and dreaming about what lies beyond the stars.

At the first meeting of the National Space Council, Vice President Mike Pence outlined the following clear goals:

1. Refocus America's space program toward human exploration and discovery—launching American

astronauts beyond low-earth orbit for the first time since 1972.

2. Establishing a renewed American presence on the moon to build a foundational system for space activities beyond Earth's reach. The moon will be a stepping-stone, a training ground, a venue to strengthen our commercial and international partnerships as we refocus America's space program toward human space exploration.

3. From the moon as a foundation, America will be the first to bring mankind to Mars.

4. Renew America's commitment to creating the space technology to protect national security. America must be as dominant in space as it is on Earth.

5. Promote regulatory, technological, and educational reforms to expand opportunities for American citizens and ensure that the U.S. is at the forefront of economic development in outer space.

6. American industry must be the first to maintain a constant commercial human presence in low-earth orbit expanding the economy beyond the planet. We'll strengthen our economy, as we unlock new opportunities, new technologies, and new sources of prosperity.

7. We'll inspire our children to seek education in science, technology, engineering, and math.

8. Our nation will bring American values to this infinite frontier. We will renew the American spirit itself and rekindle our belief that America can accomplish anything.

President Trump outlined the key strategic objective for America in space on June 18, 2018.

We don't want China and Russia and other countries leading us. We've always led—we've gone way far afield for decades now, having to do with our subject today. We're going to be the leader by far. We're behind you a thousand percent.

America's vital interest in space lost out to special interests in Washington, except, of course, for the senators and congressmen here...

But all of that is changing. We know that. My administration is reclaiming America's heritage as the world's greatest spacefaring nation. The essence of the American character is to explore new horizons and to tame new frontiers. But our destiny, beyond the Earth, is not only a matter of national identity, but a matter of national security. So important for our military. So important. And people don't talk about it.

When it comes to defending America, it is not enough to merely have an American presence in space. We must have American dominance in space. So important.

The key challenge for the American space program is the president's 2018 commitment to "American dominance in space."

I worked closely with the first Trump administration to develop an aggressive, comprehensive change from the limited programs of the Barack Obama years. This was a great breakthrough in vision, scale, and intensity.

My commitment to space goes back to the eighth grade when I began reading *Missiles and Rockets* magazine. It covered the Russian pioneering effort with Sputnik and then President John F. Kennedy's challenge to go to the moon. I grew up reading Isaac Asimov, Robert Heinlein, and other science fiction writers. So, I really believed in space as a realistic and essential part of our future. Psychologically, I watched *Star Trek* as a documentary. It made sense to me that we would go where no one had gone before. It also made sense that the ship would be American (the USS *Enterprise*). I felt that my mission was to help us get a few steps closer to that vision.

Unfortunately, after we reached the moon, momentum declined. The fateful decision was made to build a shuttle that could be reused. But it was fragile and costly. It represented a shift back toward an Earth-focused rather than solar system–oriented NASA.

When I got to Congress, I introduced HR 4286 "to establish a national space and aeronautics policy." The 15-page bill outlined a bold, aggressive policy to permanently establish Americans in space. It included a call for reusable rockets to reduce the cost of getting into space. As a sign of how strongly I believed we had to move large numbers of Americans into space, the last page of the bill drew on the Northwest Ordnance of 1787. It outlined how a colony could self-organize under the Constitution and then apply for statehood. When I hear Musk talk about the importance of colonizing Mars, I feel vindicated in pointing the way 44 years ago.

President Reagan supported our desire to develop a more powerful and exciting future. NASA allowed a lot of its younger (under 35) scientists and engineers to come to long dinners with Congressman Bob Walker and me. (Walker later became chairman of the House Committee on Science, Space, and Technology.) We challenged these younger space enthusiasts to brainstorm what could be done if they had no budgetary constraints. The result became two chapters in a book I wrote called *Window of Opportunity*. My intention was to encourage the Reagan administration to be pro-science and technology. Those two chapters still stand up well as guideposts for a bold American space policy.

Inspired by the younger NASA scientists and engineers, Walker and I introduced and passed an amendment to allow NASA to spend $400 million developing a reusable rocket that could land and then be launched again. NASA hired Lockheed Martin, but they could not get it done. The space program was limping along with the same single-launch system Wernher von Braun developed for the V-2 rocket in World War II. Rockets were bigger and more powerful, but they remained expensive single-use systems. The ultimate dinosaur in this development was the Space Launch System under NASA's Artemis program. As Michael Bloomberg described it:

> There are government boondoggles, and then there's NASA's Artemis program. More than a half century after Neil Armstrong's giant leap for mankind, Artemis was intended to land astronauts back on the moon. It has so far spent nearly $100 billion without anyone getting off the ground, yet its complexity and outrageous waste are still spiraling upward. The next U.S. president should rethink the program in its entirety.

The SLS program was a reminder that NASA followed the normal bureaucratic pattern. It was remarkable, agile, and entrepreneurial at its founding. Then, it gradually grew mistake-averse, rules-dominated, and timid. It created a self-protecting alliance with Boeing to build a giant old-fashioned rocket. The NASA and Boeing bureaucracies undertook a symbiotic commitment to hide from facts and seek more money. Results didn't matter. The NASA-Boeing alliance was protected by Alabama senator Richard Shelby, who was chairman of the Senate Appropriations Committee and ferociously protective of the NASA presence in Huntsville, Alabama—even if it was the wrong thing for America and the space program. The Boeing bureaucracy produced overruns and failures, and repeatedly missed delivery dates.

Unfortunately, for Boeing and NASA—and fortunately for America—a dramatic breakthrough came that made the Space Launch System definitively and irrefutably obsolete. Musk was driven by a passion with which I could identify. He wanted to colonize Mars to make humanity a multi-planetary species. Unlike most visionaries, Musk was also a brilliant engineer and an extraordinary entrepreneur. At a young age, he made a lot of money in internet startups. He was confident he could launch companies and had the money to do so.

When Musk founded SpaceX in March 2002, it was for the purpose of developing rockets that would make it possible to colonize Mars. Note, he didn't aim to visit or explore Mars. He meant to colonize Mars. Musk concluded that the expensive transportation system was the key obstacle to his goal. So, he learned how to build reusable rockets, which would lower costs. As a result, SpaceX lowered the cost of getting a satellite into orbit by 90 percent. This was maybe the most deflationary event of the last 20 years.

Musk has an amazing willingness to fail quickly and learn rather than hesitate and have long planning sessions. This is a key to SpaceX's success. When rockets blow up, Musk doesn't fret. He immediately analyzes what was learned from the failure. The current workhorse for SpaceX is the Falcon 9 rocket. It has nine engines and launches most of the cargoes delivered by SpaceX. However, the future workhorse will be the Starship, which will have enormous capacity. The third version of the rocket will have 39 raptor engines. It is an amazing engineering achievement and is made more astonishing by the fact that the Starship can come back, land, and be reused.

The reusable version of the Starship will carry 150 tons or 100 passengers. Musk's goal is to build enough Starships—and be able to turn them around quickly enough—to have at least one launch every day. This will be a revolution in cost and frequency of launches. It should change all current planning for humans in space. The combination of reusability and the first mass production line for rockets will give SpaceX the potential to revolutionize all our planning. The bureaucracies remain far too cautious and timid. Starship is not an improvement over the traditional rocket. The Starship is a revolution in capabilities comparable to the railroad replacing the stagecoach.

The difference in cost and capabilities became vividly clear when Boeing proposed to launch a scientific package to Europa (a moon of Jupiter's) for $2.5 billion. SpaceX replaced Boeing for $178 million. So, the new reusable system saved the taxpayer more than $2.3 billion. This combination of radical cost declines and radical capability increases is exactly what an entrepreneurial approach to science, technology, and engineering create. It is the opposite of the large entrenched bureaucratic systems.

As brilliant and daring as Musk is, he is not alone in pioneering huge entrepreneurial space capabilities. Jeff Bezos founded Amazon and is nearly as wealthy as Musk. He has created Blue Origins, which is focused on developing sustainable space-based activities near Earth. Bezos is following a slow, methodical approach to developing high-quality engines and reusable rockets.

Aside from Bezos, there are many other new startups trying to develop new and less expensive approaches to getting into space.

One imperative of this emerging entrepreneurial space industry will be an aggressive overhaul of space-focused regulations that make it more expensive, more time consuming, and harder to launch rockets. Highly regulatory and detailed systems used by the military, NASA, the Federal Aviation Administration, and others must be thoroughly reviewed. Their rules should be reevaluated and modernized to minimize lost time and money for emerging new technologies.

Many difficult decisions must be made to accelerate the American adventure into the solar system.

The current NASA bureaucracy is wedded to a combination of the Space Launch System and the lunar Gateway space station. The system would orbit the moon and be a way station for astronauts going down to the surface of the moon. Both projects are expensive. The Space Launch System is estimated to cost $4 billion for each time it launches. The Gateway is projected to cost more than $5 billion to build and possibly $1 billion a year to maintain.

As Mike Bloomberg observed in the *Economic Times*:

Unfortunately, that's not all. To build Gateway, NASA is adding a second stage to the Space Launch System, called

Block 1B, that is six years behind schedule, expected to cost $5.7 billion and will add about $1 billion to every launch. To accommodate Block 1B, the agency is erecting a new launch tower called ML-2, which is expected to cost $2.7 billion, more than seven times initial estimates, and doesn't have a plausible completion date. (The company building ML-2 has billed the government for 850,000 overtime hours in the past two years.)

These two exorbitant bureaucratically defended obsolete systems have crowded out other projects. Meanwhile, NASA is canceling or postponing promising scientific programs—including the Veritas mission to Venus; the Viper lunar rover; and the NEO Surveyor telescope, intended to scan the solar system for hazardous asteroids—as Artemis consumes ever more of its budget.[1]

Clearly, a great deal of change is needed if America is to accelerate its role in space. Before President Trump announced a person to lead NASA, one well-informed analyst told me a new NASA administrator should have six key change-oriented capabilities.

1. A commitment to large-scale space settlement and ultra-low-cost access to space.
2. Proven ability to influence national space policy.
3. Deep knowledge of (and commitment to) commercial space development and commercial space partnerships from the government and private sector sides.
4. A willingness and commitment to decisively transform NASA, including major program cancellations, RIFs,

center closings, etc. The administrator can't be friends and neighbors with traditional NASA personnel and cannot care what the NASA/contractor community thinks of him or her.

5. Significant knowledge or experience of how NASA works, including the embedded players who will resist change and try to undermine the White House.

6. An ability to build bipartisan coalitions to reinforce and sustain major changes in the long term.

Jared Isaacman is a remarkable choice to lead NASA. He fits perfectly with President Trump's recruitment of successful entrepreneurs who can provide the energy and drive it will take to move the gigantic federal bureaucratic system.

In Walter Isaacson's amazing biography of Musk, he described Isaacman's credentials as a successful entrepreneur and a deeply committed space enthusiast:

Instead, for SpaceX's first civilian flight, he chose a low-key tech entrepreneur and jet pilot named Jared Isaacman, who displayed the quiet humility of a square-jawed adventurer who had proven himself in so many fields that he didn't need to be brash. Isaacman dropped out of high school at sixteen to work for a payment-processing company, then started his own company, Shift4, that handled more than $200 billion in payments each year for restaurants and hotel chains. He became an accomplished pilot, performing in air shows and setting a world record by flying around the world in a light jet in sixty-two hours. He then cofounded a company that owned 150 jets and provided training for the military and defense contractors. Isaacman bought from SpaceX the right to command a three-day flight—named Inspiration4—that would become history's first private orbital mission. His purpose was to raise money for St. Jude Children's Research Hospital in Memphis, and he invited a twenty-nine-year-old bone-cancer survivor, Hayley Arceneaux, to join the crew, along with two other civilians.

"The customer wanted to go higher than the International Space Station," [William] Gerstenmaier explained, referring to Isaacman. "He really wanted to go for the highest he could. We briefed him on all this orbital debris stuff. He and his crew understand the risk and accept it." "Okay, great," replied Musk, who respected people willing to take risks. "I think that's fair, as long as he's fully informed." Later, when I asked why he had not opted for the lower altitude, Isaacman said, "If we're going to go to the moon again, and we're going to go to Mars, we've got to get a little outside our comfort zone."

Isaacman was so thrilled that he offered $500 million for three future flights, which would aim at going to an even higher orbit and doing a spacewalk in a new suit designed by SpaceX. He also asked for the right to be the first private customer when it was ready.

With Musk and others continuing to drive better, faster, and less costly rocket launch capabilities—and Isaacman forcing dramatic deep change on NASA—the stage is set for an extraordinary American era in becoming a spacefaring nation. There are several areas that must be developed to achieve this goal.

OPPORTUNITIES IN THE NEW SPACE CAPABILITIES

Synthetic Biology

We are on the verge of a revolution in our ability to develop and shape capabilities based on biology. The new approach is called "synthetic biology." The White House National Bioeconomy Blueprint 2012 describes it as "the design and wholesale construction of new biological parts and systems, and the re-design of existing, natural biological systems for tailored purposes."[2]

Lynn Rothschild is a brilliant biologist who originally specialized in extremophiles (organisms that thrive in incredibly hot, cold, acidic or otherwise extreme conditions). She has increasingly applied her knowledge to using biology to enhance our ability to function in space, other planets, and other places that do not have Earth-like conditions.

She describes nature's "genetic hardware store"[3]—the huge number of biological capabilities that have been developed over the last 3.5 billion years. As she explained in an e-mail to me, "Life is self-replicating and self-repairing and is modular and programmable. Using the tools of synthetic biology can greatly expand this hardware store and use it to enable space exploration in fields as diverse as human health, food and material production, and nanotechnology."

Up to now, we have manufactured on Earth and sent material into space. Synthetic biology will enable us to grow or manufacture things on spaceships, satellites, the moon, Mars, and asteroids. In fact, as we develop solutions for space, many of them will be used on Earth to enhance our capabilities here at home. Development in space will enable this because it has different constraints and no preexisting industries that would be displaced.

We need to put vastly more resources into the synthetic biology area, so we can develop the capacity to sustain life on long voyages to Mars and beyond. Furthermore, synthetic biology can begin preparing the moon and Mars for colonization by growing food and medicine while turning local assets into usable materials. The combination of robotics and synthetic biology will enable us to develop inhabitable sites on the moon and Mars. Some aspects of synthetic biology may accelerate and facilitate mining asteroids. Adaptable, engineered useful biology will be a surprisingly big part of how humans spread across the solar system and beyond.

The Moon-Mars Mission

Mars should be developed in parallel with the moon. The cost collapse and rapid launch capabilities of rockets—and the empowering impacts of artificial intelligence, robotics, synthetic biology, and entrepreneurial drive—should make it possible to go to the moon and Mars in parallel projects. Musk's proposal to start sending cargo ships to Mars by 2026 is the right approach. We still need a significant amount of robotic and synthetic biology development on Mars before we start landing large groups of people there. We should reject the moon-first philosophy. It is a reflection of past cost structures, NASA's historic bureaucratic timidity, and systemic inability to deliver on time and on budget.

Pay for What We Get

NASA and the Department of Defense should shift toward private sector–style pay for performance contracts. The current cumbersome contracting system is a major hindrance for startups–and a useless time, energy, and attention absorber for larger companies.

It brings together negotiators and lobbyists rather than engineers and scientists and hinders progress.

Asteroid Mining

Asteroid mining should be resurrected as a major project. Developments in robotics make it possible to profitably mine the enormous wealth on some asteroids long before manned missions can develop them. The potential value of asteroids is almost beyond imagining. One NASA expert suggested that one asteroid, Amun 3554, by itself is worth 200 times more than all the gold America mined in California during the gold rush.

The most famous asteroid, 16 Psyche, is the target of the NASA Psyche Mission. The Jet Propulsion Laboratory launched the mission on October 13, 2023. It will begin exploring the asteroid in 2027. The current estimate is that the asteroid has a monetary value of $10,000 quadrillion ($10,000,000,000,000,000,000,000) in platinum, palladium, and other valuable minerals.[4] While we send humans to the moon and Mars, we should send increasingly capable robots to the most valuable asteroids.

Going Nuclear

Chemical rockets get us off the planet. If we intend to run around the solar system for exploration, mining, tourism, and other purposes, we need a robust program in developing nuclear propulsion in space. Nuclear-powered vehicles can travel faster, farther, and with a lot more endurance than chemically powered vehicles. We would not want to use nuclear power to routinely get off the planet, but once in space it will be invaluable. The desirability of nuclear engines in space was so obvious that President Dwight Eisenhower began a program to develop them in 1958.

The continuous power generation of a nuclear rocket reduces the time to Mars from seven months by chemical rockets to 45 days with a continuously accelerating nuclear engine.

As NASA's budget is freed up by cancelling giant boondoggles and a dramatic decline in launch costs, there should be a substantial increase in the research and development of nuclear engines in space. The goal should be making it the norm for off-planet vehicles for interplanetary and asteroid travel.

Cutting Red Tape

To get things moving at the most rapid pace possible, every element of regulatory and paperwork interference must be reviewed and eliminated when possible. The complexity and time requirements of federal regulations—and the existence of multiple offices with the ability to slow progress—is an enormous burden, especially for startups. Even for long-established, reliable companies, the extra time and effort is a significant factor in slowing the development of space and keeping costs up. In some cases, a single bureaucrat can drag things out and make things more costly. If airlines had to go through all these steps before every flight, there would be no commercial air travel. Simplifying, speeding up, and eliminating unnecessary obstructions to space activities will attract more small entrepreneurial companies.

The Space Tax Break

There should be a 20-year tax moratorium on any profits made from manufacturing in space or any activity undertaken on the moon, Mars, or an asteroid. Making it more desirable to invest in space activities will draw a lot more investors and business activity. Communications should not be included in the tax-free zone. It is already profitable and established. We do not need to incentivize it. Manufacturing and tourism are pioneering ventures. Encouraging them will accelerate the development of the American economy in space.

In addition to a tax moratorium, there should be a 100 percent write-off of any investment in tourism and manufacturing in space. The transcontinental railroads were built with the incentive of a square mile of land for every mile of railroad. In the 1920s and 1930s, air mail was heavily subsidized by the government and a nationwide air traffic control system was built at public expense. There was a general agreement that America needed airlines. Similarly, we need an incentivized system for maximizing the rate at which America becomes a spacefaring nation.

Rights in Space
We need a federal law establishing property rights for investments in space, the moon, Mars, and asteroids. If people invest their lives and money, there should be a clear set of rules for private property and common space. It is impossible to get people to invest resources if investments can disappear at the stroke of a bureaucrat's pen. Only sound, proper, legal rules can make free enterprise possible.

Establishing Acceptable Risk
As more people seek to go into space, there will be accidents and losses. We need to look at mountain climbing, scuba diving, hang gliding, and other voluntary risky endeavors to establish parameters of acceptable safety. The ultra-cautious, ultra-safe mantra of the modern astronaut period must be replaced with a more practical approach that limits but accepts risks. Would-be travelers

should be thoroughly briefed on the potential dangers. But their rights to accept risk must be respected.

The Space Lottery

Finally, a little whimsically, Congress should consider establishing a national lottery in which anyone could buy a ticket who wanted to go into space. Once a year (or a quarter or month, depending on the volume of ticket sales), one person or group could be picked to go into space. Their entire space trip preparation and space visit should be filmed for the equivalent of a reality show. The lottery would allow every American to have a chance to get into space, so it would not just be a playground for the wealthy. This democratizing effect could help make space much more vital and supported by the American people and their elected representatives.

FOURTEEN

America's 250th Birthday

On July 4, 2026, the United States will celebrate the 250th anniversary of the signing of the Declaration of Independence. In a real sense, this will be America's birthday party—and it should be celebrated as such.

This extraordinary document asserted, "We hold these truths to be self-evident, that all men are created equal, that they are endowed by their Creator with certain unalienable Rights, that among these are Life, Liberty and the pursuit of Happiness. That to secure these rights, Governments are instituted among Men, deriving their just powers from the consent of the governed."

This leap into an unknowable future by a small group of men in Philadelphia unleashed a moral and intellectual revolution that continues to reach hearts and minds across the planet. It is easy to forget how truly revolutionary the Declaration of Independence was. In 1776, virtually the entire world was governed by kings, emperors, and strong dictators. The concept that our rights come from God and not the king was in itself a revolution.

The emphasis on equality before the law conflicted with the norm that the powerful and those with powerful parents were to be treated better than mere commoners. The idea that every person—by nature of being human—received their rights from God broke through the rules by which government and the powerful defined what commoners were allowed to do.

Now we have an opportunity to celebrate the Declaration of Independence. That celebration should include an opportunity for every American to immerse themselves in the immutable principles from which our freedom and our identity as Americans emerged. However, in the age of President Trump and the Make America Great Again movement, the 250th anniversary can be much more than just a retrospective look backward. This great occasion can also be an opportunity to look forward to the next 250 years of American life. This dual celebration is an important part of the Trump-led MAGA movement.

President Trump is a staunch patriot. He stands firmly with the classic interpretation of American history and the great lessons that can be learned from the past. He is also an enthusiastic advocate of an even better, more exciting future. President Trump's reelection presents an opportunity to create a remarkably more dynamic and exciting 250th birthday party for America. We have an opportunity to celebrate retrospectively back to 1776 and prospectively out to 2276.

We can reemphasize our patriotism by remembering how we became the most powerful, prosperous, and freest country in history. In that process, we can revitalize the importance of patriotic values such as service to country, the importance of family and faith, and volunteerism and voluntary charitable organizations. However, we can also reemphasize our commitment to improving life for everyone through constant scientific and technological progress.

We have an opportunity to encourage people to be more patriotic and to be more optimistic about the world they could create and their children and grandchildren. Think about how far we have come from 13 colonies along the Atlantic seaboard to a gigantic continent-wide nation of 235 million people. Then you ask yourself what we could achieve in the next 250 years. The answers become absolutely dazzling.

President Trump has consistently articulated this dual opportunity. In the first White House Conference on American History, held on Constitution Day, September 17, 2020, President Trump said, "To grow up in America is to live in a land where anything is possible, where anyone can rise, and where any dream can come true—all because of the immortal principles our nation's founders inscribed nearly two and a half centuries ago."

In November 2020, President Trump created the 1776 Commission to better understand the history of and principles of our nation's founding among America's rising generations. In its report, the commission asserted: "As we approach the 250th anniversary of our independence, we must resolve to teach future generations of Americans an accurate history of our country so that we all learn and cherish our founding principles once again."

Further, there is a clear faith-based component to the 250th birthday celebration of America. As President Trump pledged, "As we chart a course toward the next 250 years, let us come together and rededicate ourselves as one nation under God."

Looking forward with a prospective view is vital for the celebration—and inspiring new generations of Americans to love their country and work to make it better. The amazing technological and scientific progress of the last 250 years sets the stage for thinking about an even more amazing and exciting next 250 years.

Think back to the great breakthroughs since the signing of the Declaration of Independence: the first steamship, the first mass production assembly line, the railroad, the telegraph, the first plane in 1903, the first manned spacecraft in 1961, the electric light, phonograph record, radio, movies, television, the internet, and so on. The last 250 years have been as exciting in improving our lives as they have been in expanding freedom.

Now, look forward and project the same pace of entrepreneurship and scientific, technological, and engineering progress. The possibilities are amazing. Even in the next few years, we are on the verge of curing cancer, diabetes, sickle cell anemia, diabetes, Alzheimer's, and other diseases. We are on the verge of self-driving cars (there are already self-driving taxis carrying passengers in a few pioneering cities). We will have modular nuclear power providing electricity for the enormous computing power artificial intelligence will require. All that power will be carbon free. Many of today's problems and dilemmas will be eliminated by the vast range of new science and technology.

The potential advances make the more distant future almost unimaginable because we can barely conceive it. Elon Musk's involvement makes the focus on the prospective and retrospective aspects of American history even more exciting. As I wrote in a previous chapter, Musk founded SpaceX and has built the reusable Starship (the most powerful rocket ever built) specifically to colonize Mars. It's clear the future is going to be as exciting and dynamic as the past. Musk did not tell his first employees at SpaceX that they were going to reach, visit, or explore Mars. He said from the first day that the mission of SpaceX was to enable humanity to colonize Mars. He had a specific vision that we had to become an interplanetary species in case the earth becomes uninhabitable. He did not think humanity could afford to keep all its eggs in one basket. Therefore, he was determined to make Mars a new basket.

Musk's visionary sense of a better future has a long history in America. Remember that in 1853 Horace Greeley, the New York newspaper publisher, said to Josiah Grinnell, "Go west young man and grow up with the country." Grinnell took that advice, went west, and founded the town of Grinnell in Iowa. It is the home of Grinnell College. Today, a reasonable modernization of Greeley's advice would be, "Go into space young man or woman."

If you take up the symmetry of retrospect and prospect, extraordinary horizons reveal themselves. Consider how far we have come in the 250 years since the Declaration of Independence was signed in Philadelphia. Now imagine what the next 250 years could bring. We will be far beyond Musk's vision of colonizing. In space we will almost certainly have launched beyond the solar system. We will routinely be living on several planets and on large space-based communities. Asteroids will be providing most of our mining needs.

The future is not only about space. It will be about artificial intelligence and robotics on a scale we can scarcely imagine. It will include breakthroughs in biology that will lead to extraordinarily long lives. We may have 150-year-old Americans with the health and energy of a 45-year-old today. People will work under the sea as well as on its surface.

If we do our job right, that future will be a future of freedom under the rule of law and within the Constitution. This is truly where the retrospective part of the 250th anniversary comes into play. This 250th anniversary is a real opportunity to reacquaint millions of Americans with the facts of our founding. We can reintroduce the heroic people who worked, fought, and in some cases died to make us a great and free country. We can renew the principles at the heart of the American experience.

If it is organized with energy and enthusiasm, 2026 could become a major source of renewed American patriotism—and in understanding of the American system of freedom under the Constitution and within the rule of law.

When the future seems bleak, our lives become bleak. The left is busy telling young people they are going to die from climate change—and they should avoid having children because it is unfair to bring them into a dying world. The left rejects religious belief and leaves a spiritual vacuum that is all too often filled by fanatical politics, substance abuse, and/or deep isolation.

In an earlier time, a period of bleakness and hopelessness was replaced almost overnight by optimism and hope. Samuel Eliot Morison's biography of the impact of Christopher Columbus describes how an entire culture can be changed by a new spirit of hope. Morison wrote:

> At the end of 1492 most men in Western Europe felt exceedingly gloomy about the future. Christian civilization appeared to be shrinking in area and dividing into hostile units as its sphere contracted. For over a century there had been no important advance in natural science and registration in the universities dwindled as the instruction they offered became increasingly jejune and lifeless. Institutions were decaying, well-meaning people were growing cynical or desperate, and many intelligent men, for want of something better to do, were endeavoring to escape the present through studying the pagan past...

Yet, even as the chroniclers of Nuremberg were correcting their proofs from Koberger's press, a Spanish caravel named *Nina* scudded before a winter gale into Lisbon with news of a discovery that was to give old Europe another chance. In a few years we find the mental picture completely changed. Strong monarchs are stamping out privy conspiracy and rebellion; the Church, purged and chastened by the Protestant Reformation, puts her house in order; new ideas flare up throughout Italy, France, Germany and the northern nations; faith in God revives and the human spirit is renewed. The change is complete and startling: "A new envisagement of the world has begun, and men are no longer sighing after the imaginary golden age that lay in the distant past, but speculating as to the golden age that might possibly lie in the oncoming future."

Christopher Columbus belonged to an age that was past, yet he became the sign and symbol of this new age of hope, glory and accomplishment. His medieval faith impelled him to a modern solution: Expansion.

Musk is in many ways a Christopher Columbus of our time. The potential for the next generation of Americans to be a space-faring people could dramatically inspire young people. Today's 10-to-14-year-olds could be imparted with a sense of optimism that could lead them to study and learn enough to be part of a great adventure.

On almost every front, there are comparable breakthroughs coming. We have only touched the surface of creativity that will be unleashed by artificial intelligence. We have virtually no understanding of what the revolution in robotics is going to do to improve our lives. Everywhere we turn, there are new inventions, innovations, and knowledge waiting to be developed and used to make life more interesting and exciting. As President Ronald Reagan used to say, "You ain't even nothing yet." America's 250th birthday should be a time of renewed optimism and excitement that our future will be even better than our past.

However, we can also celebrate today. The Make America Great Again movement is a remarkable effort by millions of Americans to retake control of their country. It signals an end to elite establishment dominance, which has grown bigger and stronger virtually every year since 1933.

A Make America Great Again–led 250th birthday for America should have a deeply grassroots, decentralized, and participatory approach. We live in an age of social media, videos, podcasts, spontaneous crowd sourcing patterns, and a host of participatory activities. They reach Americans far more directly, effectively, and with more emotional power than the traditional establishment structures and systems of the past.

During 2025, there should be a widespread effort to recruit and encourage the history part of the birthday and the prospective part. Different people and organizations will provide different assets for different purposes. Places such as George Washington's Mount Vernon estate can host online and in-person events about American history throughout 2026. Meanwhile, cutting-edge companies such as SpaceX, Blue Origin, Sierra Nevada Corporation, and others can have a huge impact in communicating how amazing the future can be. The extraordinary breakthroughs in biology should be a vivid part of this new, more optimistic future.

Smaller towns and isolated areas should be encouraged to participate online and in local gatherings to celebrate historic patriotism and explore how the breakthroughs in telecommunications, robotics, artificial intelligence, and other amazing capabilities are going to bring people together and make distance irrelevant. Amazon is an early example of the ability of new technologies to eliminate the isolation of small-town and rural America. There will be breakthroughs in learning, health, recreation, and employment that will eliminate the disadvantage of distance and allow people to live where they want and still enjoy the fullest possible lives.

One of the goals should be to have every small town in America celebrating our 250th birthday. Wherever possible, people should be able to access things online. There should be as many participatory opportunities as possible so citizens can explore the past and speculate about the future. The most successful and pervasive systems of communication should be recruited and encouraged to cooperate with information providers about the past and the future to make knowledge available in entertaining, fun, and educational ways to all Americans. The goal is to have every American engaged in the patriotic past and in the extraordinarily exciting future.

This should be a birthday party in which everyone can participate.

The U.S. Semiquincentennial Commission has an opportunity to broaden and popularize its planning. It could start by dropping the word "semiquincentennial" (which I can barely pronounce) and replace it with "America's 250th Birthday Party." They could send electronic invitations to every registered voter with QR codes to share information on activities. They should focus on high school seniors and college students—particularly through civil service and military recruitment programs—to inspire them and educate them on their future potential careers. The commission should partner with private sector companies to make similar outreach efforts to students in apprenticeships, career training, and other fields. If we start now, 2026 can be a truly decisive year in renewing and relaunching the American saga.

The Challenge of the 2026 Election

D espite President Donald Trump's triumph—and it is a triumph—there is a challenge coming that could decisively change the prospects for making America great again.

The 2026 election for the House of Representatives will be one of those decisive moments that can change American history. On one hand, a Republican victory allowing a continuation of the Trump-MAGA agenda would sustain the momentum and set the stage for a successful Republican run for president in 2028.

On the other hand, a Democratic takeover of the House would be a disaster for the Trump-MAGA agenda. It would almost certainly lead to obstruction and investigations—and might lead to impeachment efforts like the Nancy Pelosi House in 2019–2020.

While the White House party historically loses ground in the off-year, in 1934, 1998, and 2002 that pattern was broken. The White House party gained seats. There is every reason to believe that with the right strategy and planning, the Trump team can match President Roosevelt's achievement and keep the House Republican.

Consider President Trump's political achievements up to now. President Trump's nine-year journey to win the White House a second time was an epic unlike any presidential effort in American history. The attacks on him, beginning with Russiagate and moving on through eight years of the establishment's war, were the longest assault on any president in American history.

Despite the establishment's all-out effort, the MAGA movement kept growing. People found themselves angrier at the establishment. The same establishment lied, cheated, and violated all the norms of the American Constitution, the rule of law, and the American political tradition. Americans came to interpret attacks on President Trump as attacks on them.

President Trump and his supporters drove President Joe Biden out of the race and then defeated Vice President Kamala Harris by a decisive margin. President Trump carried the popular vote by a 2.28 million vote margin and carried all seven swing states that experts thought were going to be close.

Since the election, there has been a substantial shift toward President Trump in popular support and in the rush of companies, executives, and wealthy investors to join the Trump bandwagon. President Trump's Inaugural Address was the most revolutionary inaugural in American history. He has been astonishingly effective at moving the system and interacting with leaders around the world.

If he and his team apply the same energy, deliberate planning, and methodical implementation to keeping the House that they applied to winning the presidency and transforming government, they will probably keep the House. However, the campaign to keep the House must begin in early 2026. The stage for victory must be set by the end of July 2026. Voters grow much harder to reach, convince, and shift the closer you get to the election. The earlier you reach them, the more likely they are to see issues as news rather than campaign noise.

Furthermore, the campaign must focus on growing a bigger majority—not defending the current small majority. If the Republicans focus on defending their narrow majority, they run a high risk of losing because there will be no margin for error. In the real world, errors are unavoidable. Therefore, the campaign must focus on keeping all the Republican seats while picking up a number of Democratic seats. Since there are 13 Democrats in districts President Trump carried in 2024—and another 21 Democrats in districts President Trump came within 5 percent of carrying—there is a pretty good target pool on which to focus. Of course, if the national mood turns strongly pro-Trump, then a lot of unexpected seats could become vulnerable. In 1994, we had no idea we would defeat Ways and Means chairman Danny Rostenkowski in downtown Chicago, but we had a good candidate and the national tide swept him in and the Democrats out.

There are three major components to keeping the House Republican majority:

First is making sure the national mood is positive and the issues that dominate help Republicans and hurt Democrats. This requirement follows the Abraham Lincoln rule that with popular sentiment nothing can fail and without popular sentiment nothing can succeed. If the national mood heavily favors us, we will keep the House. If the national mood heavily opposes us, we will lose the House.

Second is creating an effective defense for the three Republican incumbents in seats Vice President Harris carried—and for the 12 incumbents in districts where Trump won by 5 percent or less. Furthermore, there must be special attention paid to the districts that have retiring members—or members who left for other offices. Finally, there must be a big effort to win any special elections involving seats from either party (one of the keys to our long-term success after the 1994 Contract with America victory was an intense commitment to win special elections even in Democratic districts). We lost no incumbents in 1994, winning the first majority in 40 years.

Third, Republicans must develop a two-year-long effort to communicate the gap in values and votes between the Democratic incumbents and the people of their districts. There is an initial target group of the 13 Democrats in districts President Trump carried and the 21 districts that President Trump came within 5 percent or less of carrying. These districts all have enough MAGA-Trump supporters that with the right messaging and off-year turnout effort, they can be won. The NRCC must constantly look for additional districts in which a retirement, a scandal, or the emergence of an unusually good Republican candidate makes them possible GOP wins.

In 1994, when we picked up 53 Democratic seats, we had candidates in 433 of the 435 districts. We wanted to spread the Democrats resources, so they had more challenges than they could defend against. We also wanted to at least make it possible for a rising tide to bring in some candidates we would never have targeted on a short list. Defeating Speaker Tom Foley in Washington State, Rostenkowski in Chicago, and Chairman Jack Brooks (who had served 42 years and was the most senior incumbent ever defeated for reelection) would all have been considered unbeatable by professional consultants. Yet, they added to our new majority.

Each of these three components have clear requirements for success.

First, the key to a positive national mood in 2026 is simple but not easy. If we are in a "Trump boom," Republicans will have a real chance at growing a bigger House GOP majority. If we are still suffering in the hangover from the Biden-Harris economic policies, people will punish us. Inadequate growth in 1982 cost President Reagan 26 House seats. Inadequate growth in 2018 cost President Trump 42 House Republican seats.

Passing the largest possible tax cut, deregulation, energy, jobs, and affordability are the keys to a successful 2026 election. There is no substitute for economic growth in creating the right environment for a Republican victory in 2026.

Once the economy is booming, there are two other steps that will help create the right environment for a successful Republican off-year campaign. We must drive home every promise kept and convince people that voting Republican had paid off in real change in directions they wanted. All too often, Republicans think that winning on Capitol Hill is enough. Overwhelmingly, the American people do not focus on the things we think are vital. They have lives to live, jobs to do, vacations to take, and children to nurture. Congressional action is often a distant blur. It is our job to make sure that every success is communicated so clearly and thoroughly that our supporters feel they have made the right choice. Many people who either did not vote or voted against us in 2024 could decide that we are keeping our word and getting things done. This will especially help reelect endangered Republicans.

We also must drive home the importance of the cultural issues—and the degree to which the left would still turn the country back to wokeness and DEI if it could. The left-wing

Democrats have been defeated but not converted. Given a chance, they will return to the radical and divisive policies they tried to impose on the American people. The cultural issues do more to define the Democrats away from most Americans than any other topic. We must continue to make it a national dialogue.

Second, endangered Republicans have a series of simple but demanding steps to take. They must get back home as much as possible and communicate that they represent the people of their districts to Washington—not Washington to the district. There is going to be a lot of turmoil in an administration as active and aggressive as President Trump's. It will be important to listen to the folks back home and get a sense of what they are seeing and how they feel about it. Republicans then must raise as much money as possible as early as possible. Money raised in 2025 is worth five times as much as money raised in 2026. It can intimidate potential opponents and allow for early campaigning (which hits much harder and penetrates better than the same money spent in September and October). Campaign money must include candidates' own FEC campaign funds—but also every other avenue that can legally help win the election in their district.

Next, they must assess every form of communication, from Fox News to local radio to social media. They need an active and aggressive media effort, including podcasts, their own web pages, and a deliberate effort to build up the largest possible email and text lists for official and campaign use. Finally, they need to find three issues that really matter to their constituents—and talk and write about them so much that they become part of the incumbent's identity. If they take these steps, they should be safe.

Third, the key to defeating the Democrats in marginal districts is thoroughly communicating their voting records. Their records must permeate their districts and define them so thoroughly that they can't go home and lie about it. The Democrats survive by voting for radical left-wing ideas in Washington and then going home and claiming they are moderate. Since most of the propaganda media favors the same weird ideas as the woke left, they do not attack the Democrats. In many cases, they don't even report their votes. So, for most of the country, the Democratic member of Congress they see at home is pleasant, is a good listener, does good casework, and has not a hint of radicalism.

The traditional Republican strategy is to try to communicate how bad the Democratic incumbent's voting record is only during the actual campaign in September and October. This is the political season when people tend to ignore or shrug off partisan attacks. The key is to begin in the first year communicating every bad vote so intensely that most voters in the district know their incumbent Democrat has been voting against their values.

If reporting the bad votes is done consistently, it will work like a slow drip water torture. Gradually, people will move from disbelief to questioning their incumbent to rejecting their incumbent. A good example of how vulnerable the Democrats are to reporting their votes back home is the vote on the Protection of Women and Girls in Sports Act from January 14, 2025. The vote on that act, which blocked people who were born male from competing against women and girls in sports, passed 218-206 with 1 abstention. It received only two votes from Democrats while 206 Democrats voted "no."

The American people favor protecting women and girls from biological males in sports. In fact, in January, a *New York Times/* IPSOS poll reported that 79 percent of the American people opposed males competing in women's sports. According to the

Times, even 67 percent of Democrats opposed men participating in women's sports. So, all but two of the Democrats voted against the views of 79 percent of the American people. That is 206 Democrats who are out of step with their voters.

Similarly, 83 percent of the American people support requiring local law enforcement to retain an arrested person suspected of being in the country illegally and holding them for the immigration authorities. Only 11 percent oppose. Yet, when the Laken Riley Act proposing to do just that came to a vote in the House, 156 Democrats voted "no." That means they were in step with 11 percent of the American people—and opposed to more than eight-in-ten Americans. This gap between the American people and their elected Democratic representatives can only be survivable if the American people never learn how their members vote.

So, the second most important project, after having a booming economy, is developing a system for keeping every citizen in Democratic swing districts thoroughly informed of how often their member votes against their values. A system of information that penetrates the district and reaches most people should be up and running as early as possible. It should be monitored in polling to ensure that the messages about the radical votes are reaching people. This should be launched in the spring and summer of 2025. We cannot wait until 2026 for it to become a project.

The steady drumbeat of bad votes will lead to candidates in the primary and the general election. It will make the incumbents vulnerable to challenge. It will increase fundraising for the challengers and decrease fundraising for the Democrats. As the back home grassroots pressure builds, it will lead to a civil war in the Democratic Party between the true believers and the survivalists.

It is possible for Republicans to increase their majority in the House in 2026. It is possible for President Trump—with a renewed majority—to lead America through four solid years of reform and recovery, launching a new Golden Age for America. It is possible, building on that, to elect a new Republican president and a solidly Republican House and Senate in 2028.

Those victories will be the end of President Roosevelt's New Deal Coalition nearly a century after it was created in 1932.

If all that happens, President Trump will have been the most consequential president of modern times—and may rank just below George Washington and Abraham Lincoln as leaders who have created a new and better future for America and the world.

With the help of the American people, it is possible. It is up to us to help save our country.

ACKNOWLEDGMENTS

As someone who has spent a lifetime thinking about politics and government, *Trump's Triumph* was an exhilarating book to write. Authoring this book on the eve of Donald J. Trump's historic second inauguration and the year before America's 250th birthday got me thinking about our nation's exciting future. This book, filled with ideas for keeping America safe, prosperous, and free, would not have been possible without the contributions of many remarkable people.

My wife, Callista, has been essential to our success. Her leadership as president and chief executive officer of Gingrich 360 improves everything we do. Her experience as U.S. ambassador to the Holy See has been invaluable.

I am grateful for the support of my daughters, Kathy Lubbers and Jackie Cushman. Kathy has been a fantastic book agent, and Jackie is a skilled author who has provided insightful feedback.

Thanks to our team at Gingrich 360, whose work and collaboration brought this project over the finish line. I'd especially like to thank Louie Brogdon, whose cheerful editing, writing, and organizational capabilities kept me on track. Thank you to

Joe DeSantis, who lent his expertise on health care, and Claire Christensen, who shared her insight on foreign policy. I'd also like to thank Rachel Peterson and Shane O'Grady for their incredible research assistance. Additionally, Bess Kelly coordinated our team's efforts, Taylor Swindle managed our team's finances, and Woody Hales organized my many commitments. And thanks to Garnsey Sloan for producing *Newt's World* and Red Gamso for overseeing our website and social media. To the entire Gingrich 360 team, whose work supported and facilitated this book, thank you.

I am grateful for the contributions of the team at America's New Majority Project, an ongoing initiative that aims to understand the nation's demographics and prove that conservative values and priorities are supported by a majority of Americans. Many of our findings from this project influenced and shaped the ideas in *Trump's Triumph*. Specifically, I'd like to thank Joe Gaylord, who helped me design the Contract with America in 1994 and provided invaluable input on this project. Also, I'd like to thank John McLaughlin, Stuart Polk, and Brian Larkin at McLaughlin & Associates, who coordinated and executed polling for America's New Majority Project.

Finally, thanks to our publisher, Daisy Hutton, and editor, Alex Pappas, at Hachette Book Group for their assistance, feedback, and input.

I am grateful for this phenomenal team. Their big ideas, cheerful persistence, and love of our nation made this book possible.

2025 INAUGURAL ADDRESS BY PRESIDENT DONALD J. TRUMP

U.S. Capitol, Washington, D.C., 12:10 p.m. EST

Thank you. Thank you very much, everybody. [*applause*] Wow. Thank you very, very much.

Vice President Vance, Speaker Johnson, Senator Thune, Chief Justice Roberts, justices of the Supreme Court of the United States, President Clinton, President Bush, President Obama, President Biden, Vice President Harris, and my fellow citizens, the golden age of America begins right now. [*applause*]

From this day forward, our country will flourish and be respected again all over the world. We will be the envy of every nation, and we will not allow ourselves to be taken advantage of any longer. During every single day of the Trump administration, I will, very simply, put America first. [*applause*]

Our sovereignty will be reclaimed. Our safety will be restored. The scales of justice will be rebalanced. The vicious, violent, and unfair weaponization of the Justice Department and our government will end. [*applause*]

And our top priority will be to create a nation that is proud, prosperous, and free. [*applause*]

America will soon be greater, stronger, and far more exceptional than ever before. [*applause*]

I return to the presidency confident and optimistic that we are at the start of a thrilling new era of national success. A tide of change is sweeping the country, sunlight is pouring over the entire world, and America has the chance to seize this opportunity like never before.

But first, we must be honest about the challenges we face. While they are plentiful, they will be annihilated by this great momentum that the world is now witnessing in the United States of America.

As we gather today, our government confronts a crisis of trust. For many years, a radical and corrupt establishment has extracted power and wealth from our citizens while the pillars of our society lay broken and seemingly in complete disrepair.

We now have a government that cannot manage even a simple crisis at home while, at the same time, stumbling into a continuing catalogue of catastrophic events abroad.

It fails to protect our magnificent, law-abiding American citizens but provides sanctuary and protection for dangerous criminals, many from prisons and mental institutions, that have illegally entered our country from all over the world.

We have a government that has given unlimited funding to the defense of foreign borders but refuses to defend American borders or, more importantly, its own people.

Our country can no longer deliver basic services in times of emergency, as recently shown by the wonderful people of North Carolina—who have been treated so badly [*applause*]—and other states who are still suffering from a hurricane that took place many months ago or, more recently, Los Angeles, where we are watching fires still tragically burn from weeks ago without even a token of defense. They're raging through the houses and communities, even affecting some of the wealthiest and most powerful individuals in our country—some of whom are sitting here right now. They don't have a home any longer. That's interesting. But we can't let this happen. Everyone is unable to do anything about it. That's going to change.

We have a public health system that does not deliver in times of disaster, yet more money is spent on it than any country anywhere in the world.

And we have an education system that teaches our children to be ashamed of themselves—in many cases, to hate our country despite the love that we try so desperately to provide to them. All of this will change starting today, and it will change very quickly. [*applause*]

My recent election is a mandate to completely and totally reverse a horrible betrayal and all of these many betrayals that have taken place and to give the people back their faith, their wealth, their democracy, and, indeed, their freedom. From this moment on, America's decline is over. [*applause*]

Our liberties and our nation's glorious destiny will no longer be denied. And we will immediately restore the integrity, competency, and loyalty of America's government.

Over the past eight years, I have been tested and challenged more than any president in our 250-year history, and I've learned a lot along the way.

The journey to reclaim our republic has not been an easy one—that, I can tell you. Those who wish to stop our cause have tried to take my freedom and, indeed, to take my life.

Just a few months ago, in a beautiful Pennsylvania field, an assassin's bullet ripped through my ear. But I felt then and believe even more so now that my life was saved for a reason. I was saved by God to make America great again. [*applause*]

Thank you. Thank you. [*applause*]

Thank you very much. [*applause*]

That is why each day under our administration of American patriots, we will be working to meet every crisis with dignity and power and strength. We will move with purpose and speed to bring back hope, prosperity, safety, and peace for citizens of every race, religion, color, and creed.

For American citizens, January 20, 2025, is Liberation Day. [*applause*] It is my hope that our recent presidential election will be remembered as the greatest and most consequential election in the history of our country.

As our victory showed, the entire nation is rapidly unifying behind our agenda with dramatic increases in support from virtually every element of our society: young and old, men and women, African Americans, Hispanic Americans, Asian Americans, urban, suburban, rural. And very importantly, we had a powerful win in all seven swing states [*applause*] and the popular vote, we won by millions of people. [*applause*]

To the Black and Hispanic communities, I want to thank you for the tremendous outpouring of love and trust that you have shown me with your vote. We set records, and I will not forget it. I've heard your voices in the campaign, and I look forward to working with you in the years to come.

Today is Martin Luther King Day. And his honor—this will be a great honor. But in his honor, we will strive together to make his dream a reality. We will make his dream come true. [*applause*]

Thank you. Thank you. Thank you. [*applause*]

National unity is now returning to America, and confidence and pride is soaring like never before. In everything we do, my administration will be inspired by a strong pursuit of excellence and unrelenting success. We will not forget our country, we will not forget our Constitution, and we will not forget our God. Can't do that. [*applause*]

Today, I will sign a series of historic executive orders. With these actions, we will begin the complete restoration of America and the revolution of common sense. It's all about common sense. [*applause*]

First, I will declare a national emergency at our southern border. [*applause*]

All illegal entry will immediately be halted, and we will begin the process of returning millions and millions of criminal aliens back to the places from which they came. We will reinstate my Remain in Mexico policy. [*applause*]

I will end the practice of catch and release. [*applause*]

And I will send troops to the southern border to repel the disastrous invasion of our country. [*applause*]

Under the orders I sign today, we will also be designating the cartels as foreign terrorist organizations. [*applause*]

And by invoking the Alien Enemies Act of 1798, I will direct our government to use the full and immense power of federal and state law enforcement to eliminate the presence of all foreign gangs and criminal networks bringing devastating crime to U.S. soil, including our cities and inner cities. [*applause*]

As commander in chief, I have no higher responsibility than to defend our country from threats and invasions, and that is exactly what I am going to do. We will do it at a level that nobody has ever seen before.

Next, I will direct all members of my cabinet to marshal the vast powers at their disposal to defeat what was record inflation and rapidly bring down costs and prices. [*applause*]

The inflation crisis was caused by massive overspending and escalating energy prices, and that is why today I will also declare a national energy emergency. We will drill, baby, drill. [*applause*]

America will be a manufacturing nation once again, and we have something that no other manufacturing nation will ever have—the largest amount of oil and gas of any country on earth—and we are going to use it. We'll use it. [*applause*]

We will bring prices down, fill our strategic reserves up again right to the top, and export American energy all over the world. [*applause*]

We will be a rich nation again, and it is that liquid gold under our feet that will help to do it.

With my actions today, we will end the Green New Deal, and we will revoke the electric vehicle mandate, saving our auto industry and keeping my sacred pledge to our great American autoworkers. [*applause*]

In other words, you'll be able to buy the car of your choice.

We will build automobiles in America again at a rate that nobody could have dreamt possible just a few years ago. And thank you to the autoworkers of our nation for your inspiring vote of confidence. We did tremendously with their vote. [*applause*]

I will immediately begin the overhaul of our trade system to protect American workers and families. Instead of taxing our citizens to enrich other countries, we will tariff and tax foreign countries to enrich our citizens. [*applause*]

For this purpose, we are establishing the External Revenue Service to collect all tariffs, duties, and revenues. It will be massive amounts of money pouring into our Treasury, coming from foreign sources.

The American dream will soon be back and thriving like never before.

To restore competence and effectiveness to our federal government, my administration will establish the brand-new Department of Government Efficiency. [*applause*]

After years and years of illegal and unconstitutional federal efforts to restrict free expression, I also will sign an executive order to immediately stop all government censorship and bring back free speech to America. [*applause*]

Never again will the immense power of the state be weaponized to persecute political opponents—something I know something about. [*laughter*] We will not allow that to happen. It will not happen again.

Under my leadership, we will restore fair, equal, and impartial justice under the constitutional rule of law. [*applause*]

And we are going to bring law and order back to our cities. [*applause*]

This week, I will also end the government policy of trying to socially engineer race and gender into every aspect of public and private life. [*applause*] We will forge a society that is colorblind and merit-based. [*applause*]

As of today, it will henceforth be the official policy of the United States government that there are only two genders: male and female. [*applause*]

This week, I will reinstate any service members who were unjustly expelled from our military for objecting to the COVID vaccine mandate with full back pay. [*applause*]

And I will sign an order to stop our warriors from being subjected to radical political theories and social experiments while on duty. It's going to end immediately. [*applause*] Our armed forces will be freed to focus on their sole mission: defeating America's enemies. [*applause*]

Like in 2017, we will again build the strongest military the world has ever seen. We will measure our success not only by the battles we win but also by the wars that we end—and perhaps most importantly, the wars we never get into. [*applause*]

My proudest legacy will be that of a peacemaker and unifier. That's what I want to be: a peacemaker and a unifier.

I'm pleased to say that as of yesterday, one day before I assumed office, the hostages in the Middle East are coming back home to their families. [*applause*]

Thank you.

America will reclaim its rightful place as the greatest, most powerful, most respected nation on Earth, inspiring the awe and admiration of the entire world.

A short time from now, we are going to be changing the name of the Gulf of Mexico to the Gulf of America [*applause*] and we will restore the name of a great president, William McKinley, to Mount McKinley, where it should be and where it belongs. [*applause*]

President McKinley made our country very rich through tariffs and through talent—he was a natural businessman—and gave Teddy Roosevelt the money for many of the great things he did, including the Panama Canal, which has foolishly been given to the country of Panama after the United States—the United States—I mean, think of this—spent more money than ever spent on a project before and lost 38,000 lives in the building of the Panama Canal.

We have been treated very badly from this foolish gift that should have never been made, and Panama's promise to us has been broken.

The purpose of our deal and the spirit of our treaty has been totally violated. American ships are being severely overcharged and not treated fairly in any way, shape, or form. And that includes the United States Navy.

And above all, China is operating the Panama Canal. And we didn't give it to China. We gave it to Panama, and we're taking it back. [applause]

Above all, my message to Americans today is that it is time for us to once again act with courage, vigor, and the vitality of history's greatest civilization.

So, as we liberate our nation, we will lead it to new heights of victory and success. We will not be deterred. Together, we will end the chronic disease epidemic and keep our children safe, healthy, and disease-free.

The United States will once again consider itself a growing nation—one that increases our wealth, expands our territory, builds our cities, raises our expectations, and carries our flag into new and beautiful horizons.

And we will pursue our manifest destiny into the stars, launching American astronauts to plant the Stars and Stripes on the planet Mars. [applause]

Ambition is the lifeblood of a great nation, and, right now, our nation is more ambitious than any other. There's no nation like our nation.

Americans are explorers, builders, innovators, entrepreneurs, and pioneers. The spirit of the frontier is written into our hearts. The call of the next great adventure resounds from within our souls.

Our American ancestors turned a small group of colonies on the edge of a vast continent into a mighty republic of the most extraordinary citizens on Earth. No one comes close.

Americans pushed thousands of miles through a rugged land of untamed wilderness. They crossed deserts, scaled mountains, braved untold dangers, won the Wild West, ended slavery, rescued millions from tyranny, lifted billions from poverty, harnessed electricity, split the atom, launched mankind into the heavens, and put the universe of human knowledge into the palm of the human hand. If we work together, there is nothing we cannot do and no dream we cannot achieve.

Many people thought it was impossible for me to stage such a historic political comeback. But as you see today, here I am. The American people have spoken. [*applause*]

I stand before you now as proof that you should never believe that something is impossible to do. In America, the impossible is what we do best. [*applause*]

From New York to Los Angeles, from Philadelphia to Phoenix, from Chicago to Miami, from Houston to right here in Washington, D.C., our country was forged and built by the generations of patriots who gave everything they had for our rights and for our freedom.

They were farmers and soldiers, cowboys and factory workers, steelworkers and coal miners, police officers and pioneers who pushed onward, marched forward, and let no obstacle defeat their spirit or their pride.

Together, they laid down the railroads, raised up the skyscrapers, built great highways, won two world wars, defeated fascism and communism, and triumphed over every single challenge that they faced.

After all we have been through together, we stand on the verge of the four greatest years in American history. With your help, we will restore America's promise and we will rebuild the nation that we love—and we love it so much.

We are one people, one family, and one glorious nation under God. So, to every parent who dreams for their child and every child who dreams for their future, I am with you, I will fight for you, and I will win for you. We're going to win like never before. [*applause*]

Thank you. Thank you. [*applause*]

Thank you. Thank you. [*applause*]

In recent years, our nation has suffered greatly. But we are going to bring it back and make it great again, greater than ever before.

We will be a nation like no other, full of compassion, courage, and exceptionalism. Our power will stop all wars and bring a new spirit of unity to a world that has been angry, violent, and totally unpredictable.

America will be respected again and admired again, including by people of religion, faith, and goodwill. We will be prosperous, we will be proud, we will be strong, and we will win like never before.

We will not be conquered, we will not be intimidated, we will not be broken, and we will not fail. From this day on, the United States of America will be a free, sovereign, and independent nation.

We will stand bravely, we will live proudly, we will dream boldly, and nothing will stand in our way because we are Americans. The future is ours, and our golden age has just begun.

Thank you. God bless America. Thank you all. Thank you. [*applause*] Thank you very much. Thank you very much. Thank you. [*applause*]

Thank you. [*applause*]

END   *12:40 p.m. EST*

THE 2024 GOP PLATFORM

2024 GOP PLATFORM
MAKE AMERICA GREAT AGAIN!

Dedication: To the Forgotten Men and Women of America

PREAMBLE
AMERICA FIRST: A RETURN TO COMMON SENSE

Our Nation's History is filled with the stories of brave men and women who gave everything they had to build America into the Greatest Nation in the History of the World. Generations of American Patriots have summoned the American Spirit of Strength, Determination, and Love of Country to overcome seemingly insurmountable challenges. The American People have proven time and again that we can overcome any obstacle and any force pitted against us.

In the early days of our Republic, the Founding Generation defeated what was then the most powerful Empire the World had ever seen. In the 20th Century, America vanquished Nazism and Fascism, and then triumphed over Soviet Communism after forty-four years of the Cold War.

But now we are a Nation in SERIOUS DECLINE. Our future, our identity, and our very way of life are under threat like never before. Today we must once again call upon the same

American Spirit that led us to prevail through every challenge of the past if we are going to lead our Nation to a brighter future.

For decades, our politicians sold our jobs and livelihoods to the highest bidders overseas with unfair Trade Deals and a blind faith in the siren song of globalism. They insulated themselves from criticism and the consequences of their own bad actions, allowing our Borders to be overrun, our cities to be overtaken by crime, our System of Justice to be weaponized, and our young people to develop a sense of hopelessness and despair. They rejected our History and our Values. Quite simply, they did everything in their power to destroy our Country.

In 2016, President Donald J. Trump was elected as an unapologetic Champion of the American People. He reignited the American Spirit and called on us to renew our National Pride. His Policies spurred Historic Economic Growth, Job Creation, and a Resurgence of American Manufacturing. President Trump and the Republican Party led America out of the pessimism induced by decades of failed leadership, showing us that the American People want Greatness for our Country again.

Yet after nearly four years of the Biden administration, America is now rocked by Raging Inflation, Open Borders, Rampant Crime, Attacks on our Children, and Global Conflict, Chaos, and Instability.

Like the Heroes who built and defended this Nation before us, we will never give up. We will restore our Nation of, by, and for the People. We will Make America Great Again.

We will be a Nation based on Truth, Justice, and Common Sense.

Common Sense tells us clearly, in President Trump's words, that "If we don't have a Border, we don't have a Country." Restoring sensible Border Security and Immigration Policy requires many steps, all of which would have been and indeed were taken for granted by prior Generations as obviously necessary and good. We must secure our Southern Border by completing the Border Wall that President Trump started. Hundreds of miles have already been built and work magnificently. The remaining Wall construction can be completed quickly, effectively, and inexpensively. We must also vigilantly check those who enter our Country by other routes and ensure that no one can enter our Country who does not have the Legal Right to do so, and we must deport the millions of illegal Migrants who Joe Biden has deliberately encouraged to invade our Country. We will start by prioritizing the most dangerous criminals and working with local Police. We must not allow Biden's Migrant Invasion to alter our Country. It must not stand. Under the Trump Administration and a Republican Congress, it will be defeated immediately.

Common Sense tells us clearly that if we don't have Domestic Manufacturing with low Inflation, not only will our Economy—and even our Military Equipment and Supplies—be at the mercy of Foreign Nations, but our Towns, Communities, and People cannot thrive. The Republican Party must return to its roots as the Party of Industry, Manufacturing, Infrastructure, and Workers. President Trump's economic policy to end Inflation and return Manufacturing Jobs is not only what the American Economy and American Workers need right now, it is also what they want right now.

Common Sense tells us clearly that we must unleash American Energy if we want to destroy Inflation and rapidly bring down prices, build the Greatest Economy in History, revive our Defense Industrial Base, fuel Emerging Industries, and establish the United States as the Manufacturing Superpower of the World.

We will DRILL, BABY, DRILL and we will become Energy Independent, and even Dominant again. The United States has more liquid gold under our feet than any other Nation, and it's not even close. The Republican Party will harness that potential to power our future.

Common Sense tells us clearly that if we don't have a Strong Military, we won't be able to defend our interests and we will be at the mercy of Hostile Nations. The Policy of the Republican Party must be to ensure that America's Military is the strongest and best-equipped in the World—and that our Government uses that great strength sparingly, and only in clear instances where our National Interests are threatened.

Common Sense tells us clearly that the Republican Party must stand for Equal Treatment for All. Likewise, the Republican Party must ensure the equal application of law to all regardless of political affiliation or personal beliefs. Recent Democrat-led political persecutions threaten to destroy 250 years of American Principle and Practice and must be stopped.

America needs determined Republican Leadership at every level of Government to address the core threats to our very survival: Our disastrously Open Border, our weakened Economy, crippling restrictions on American Energy Production, our depleted Military, attacks on the American System of Justice, and much more.

To make clear our commitment, we offer to the American people the 2024 GOP Platform to Make America Great Again! It is a forward-looking Agenda that begins with the following twenty promises that we will accomplish very quickly when we win the White House and Republican Majorities in the House and Senate.

When America is united, confident, and committed to our principles, it will never fail.

Today and together, with Love for our Country, Faith in our People, and Trust in God's Good Grace, we will Make America Great Again!

CHAPTER ONE:
DEFEAT INFLATION AND QUICKLY
BRING DOWN ALL PRICES

Our Commitment:

The Republican Party will reverse the worst Inflation crisis in four decades that has crushed the middle class, devastated family budgets, and pushed the dream of homeownership out of reach for millions. We will defeat Inflation, tackle the cost-of-living crisis, improve fiscal sanity, restore price stability, and quickly bring down prices.

Inflation is a crushing tax on American families. History shows that Inflation will not magically disappear while policies remain the same. We commit to unleashing American Energy, reining in wasteful spending, cutting excessive Regulations, securing our Borders, and restoring Peace through Strength. Together, we will restore Prosperity, ensure Economic Security, and build a brighter future for American Workers and their families. Our dedication to these Policies will make America stronger, more resilient, and more prosperous than ever before.

1. *Unleash American Energy*

   Under President Trump, the U.S. became the Number One Producer of Oil and Natural Gas in the World—and we will soon be again by lifting restrictions on American Energy Production and terminating the Socialist Green New Deal. Republicans will unleash Energy Production from all sources, including nuclear, to immediately slash Inflation and power American homes, cars, and factories with reliable, abundant, and affordable Energy.

2. *Rein in Wasteful Federal Spending*
Republicans will immediately stabilize the Economy by slashing wasteful Government spending and promoting Economic Growth.

3. *Cut Costly and Burdensome Regulations*
Republicans will reinstate President Trump's Deregulation Policies, which saved Americans $11,000 per household, and end Democrats' regulatory onslaught that disproportionately harms low- and middle-income households.

4. *Stop Illegal Immigration*
Republicans will secure the Border, deport Illegal Aliens, and reverse the Democrats' Open Borders Policies that have driven up the cost of Housing, Education, and Healthcare for American families.

5. *Restore Peace through Strength*
War breeds Inflation while geopolitical stability brings price stability. Republicans will end the global chaos and restore Peace through Strength, reducing geopolitical risks and lowering commodity prices.

CHAPTER TWO:
SEAL THE BORDER, AND STOP THE MIGRANT INVASION

Our Commitment:

Republicans offer an aggressive plan to stop the open-border policies that have opened the floodgates to a tidal wave of illegal Aliens, deadly drugs, and Migrant Crime. We will end the Invasion at the

Southern Border, restore Law and Order, protect American Sovereignty, and deliver a Safe and Prosperous Future for all Americans.

1. *Secure the Border*

   Republicans will restore every Border Policy of the Trump administration and halt all releases of Illegal Aliens into the interior. We will complete the Border Wall, shift massive portions of Federal Law Enforcement to Immigration Enforcement, and use advanced technology to monitor and secure the Border. We will use all resources needed to stop the Invasion—including moving thousands of Troops currently stationed overseas to our own Southern Border. We will deploy the U.S. Navy to impose a full Fentanyl Blockade on the waters of our Region— boarding and inspecting ships to look for fentanyl and fentanyl precursors. Before we defend the Borders of Foreign Countries, we must first secure the Border of our Country.

2. *Enforce Immigration Laws*

   Republicans will strengthen ICE, increase penalties for illegal entry and overstaying Visas, and reinstate "Remain in Mexico" and other Policies that helped reduce Illegal Immigration by historic lows in President Trump's first term. We will also invoke the Alien Enemies Act to remove all known or suspected gang members, drug dealers, or cartel members from the United States, ending the scourge of Illegal Alien gang violence once and for all. We will bring back the Travel Ban, and use Title 42 to end the child trafficking crisis by returning all trafficked children to their families in their Home Countries immediately.

3. *Begin Largest Deportation Program in American History*

   President Trump and Republicans will reverse the Democrats' destructive Open Borders Policies that have allowed criminal gangs and Illegal Aliens from around the World to roam the United States without consequences. The Republican Party is committed to sending Illegal Aliens back home and removing those who have violated our Laws.

4. *Strict Vetting*

   Republicans will use existing Federal Law to keep foreign Christian-hating Communists, Marxists, and Socialists out of America. Those who join our Country must love our Country. We will use extreme vetting to ensure that jihadists and jihadist sympathizers are not admitted.

5. *Stop Sanctuary Cities*

   Republicans will cut federal Funding to sanctuary jurisdictions that release dangerous Illegal Alien criminals onto our streets, rather than handing them over to ICE. We will require local cooperation with Federal Immigration Enforcement.

6. *Ensure Our Legal Immigration System Puts American Workers First*

   Republicans will prioritize Merit-based immigration, ensuring those admitted to our Country contribute positively to our Society and Economy, and never become a drain on Public Resources. We will end Chain Migration, and put American Workers first!

CHAPTER THREE:
BUILD THE GREATEST ECONOMY IN HISTORY

Our Commitment:

American Workers are the most productive, talented, and innovative on Earth. The only thing holding them back is the suffocating policies of the Democrat Party. Our America First Economic Agenda rests on five pillars: Slashing Regulations, cutting Taxes, securing Fair Trade Deals, ensuring Reliable and

Abundant Low-Cost Energy, and championing Innovation. Together, we will restore Economic Prosperity and Opportunity for all Americans.

1. *Cut Regulations*
   Republicans will slash Regulations that stifle Jobs, Freedom, Innovation and make everything more expensive. We will implement Transparency and Common Sense in rulemaking.

2. *Make Trump Tax Cuts Permanent and No Tax on Tips*
   Republicans will make permanent the provisions of the Trump Tax Cuts and Jobs Act that doubled the standard deduction, expanded the Child Tax Credit, and spurred Economic Growth for all Americans. We will eliminate Taxes on Tips for millions of Restaurant and Hospitality Workers, and pursue additional Tax Cuts.

3. *Fair and Reciprocal Trade Deals*
   Republicans will continue forging an America First Trade Policy as set forth in Chapter 5, standing up to Countries that cheat and prioritizing American Producers over Foreign Outsourcers. We will bring our critical Supply Chains back home. President Trump turned American Trade Policy around, protecting U.S. Producers, and renegotiating failed agreements.

4. *Reliable and Abundant Low-Cost Energy*
   Republicans will increase Energy Production across the board, streamline permitting, and end market-distorting restrictions on Oil, Natural Gas, and Coal. The Republican Party will once again make America Energy Independent, and then Energy Dominant, lowering Energy prices even below the record lows achieved during President Trump's first term.

5. *Champion Innovation*

Republicans will pave the way for future Economic Greatness by leading the World in Emerging Industries.

Crypto: Republicans will end Democrats' unlawful and unAmerican Crypto crackdown and oppose the creation of a Central Bank Digital Currency. We will defend the right to mine Bitcoin, and ensure every American has the right to self-custody of their Digital Assets, and transact free from Government Surveillance and Control.

Artificial Intelligence (AI): We will repeal Joe Biden's dangerous Executive Order that hinders AI Innovation, and imposes Radical Leftwing ideas on the development of this technology. In its place, Republicans support AI Development rooted in Free Speech and Human Flourishing.

Expanding Freedom, Prosperity and Safety in Space: Under Republican Leadership, the United States will create a robust Manufacturing Industry in Near Earth Orbit, send American Astronauts back to the Moon, and onward to Mars, and enhance partnerships with the rapidly expanding Commercial Space sector to revolutionize our ability to access, live in, and develop assets in Space.

CHAPTER FOUR:
BRING BACK THE AMERICAN DREAM AND MAKE IT AFFORDABLE AGAIN FOR FAMILIES, YOUNG PEOPLE, AND EVERYONE

Our Commitment:

Republicans offer a plan to make the American Dream affordable again. We commit to reducing Housing, Education, and

Healthcare costs, while lowering everyday expenses, and increasing opportunities.

1. *Housing Affordability*

   To help new home buyers, Republicans will reduce mortgage rates by slashing Inflation, open limited portions of Federal Lands to allow for new home construction, promote homeownership through Tax Incentives and support for first-time buyers, and cut unnecessary Regulations that raise housing costs.

2. *Accessible Higher Education*

   To reduce the cost of Higher Education, Republicans will support the creation of additional, drastically more affordable alternatives to a traditional four-year College degree.

3. *Affordable Healthcare*

   Healthcare and prescription drug costs are out of control. Republicans will increase Transparency, promote Choice and Competition, and expand access to new Affordable Healthcare and prescription drug options. We will protect Medicare, and ensure Seniors receive the care they need without being burdened by excessive costs.

4. *Lower Everyday Costs*

   Republicans will reduce the Regulatory burden, lower Energy costs, and promote Economic Policies that drive down the cost of living and prices for everyday goods and services.

CHAPTER FIVE:
PROTECT AMERICAN WORKERS AND FARMERS FROM UNFAIR TRADE

Our Commitment:

The Republican Party stands for a patriotic "America First" Economic Policy. Republicans offer a robust plan to protect American Workers, Farmers, and Industries from unfair Foreign Competition. We commit to rebalancing Trade, securing Strategic Independence, and revitalizing Manufacturing. We will prioritize Domestic Production, and ensure National Independence in essential goods and services. Together, we will build a Strong, Self-reliant, and Prosperous America.

1. *Rebalance Trade*
   Our Trade deficit in goods has grown to over $1 Trillion Dollars a year. Republicans will support baseline Tariffs on Foreign-made goods, pass the Trump Reciprocal Trade Act, and respond to unfair Trading practices. As Tariffs on Foreign Producers go up, Taxes on American Workers, Families, and Businesses can come down.

2. *Secure Strategic Independence from China*
   Republicans will revoke China's Most Favored Nation status, phase out imports of essential goods, and stop China from buying American Real Estate and Industries.

3. *Save the American Auto Industry*
   Republicans will revive the U.S. Auto Industry by reversing harmful Regulations, canceling Biden's Electric Vehicle and other Mandates, and preventing the importation of Chinese vehicles.

4. *Bring Home Critical Supply Chains*
   Republicans will bring critical Supply Chains back to the U.S., ensuring National Security and Economic Stability, while also creating Jobs and raising Wages for American Workers.

5. *Buy American and Hire American*

Republicans will strengthen Buy American and Hire American Policies, banning companies that outsource jobs from doing business with the Federal Government.

6. *Become the Manufacturing Superpower*

By protecting American Workers from unfair Foreign Competition and unleashing American Energy, Republicans will restore American Manufacturing, creating Jobs, Wealth, and Investment.

CHAPTER SIX:
PROTECT SENIORS

Our Commitment:

President Trump has made absolutely clear that he will not cut one penny from Medicare or Social Security. American Citizens work hard their whole lives, contributing to Social Security and Medicare. These programs are promises to our Seniors, ensuring they can live their golden years with dignity. Republicans will protect these vital programs and ensure Economic Stability. We will work with our Great Seniors, in order to allow them to be active and healthy. We commit to safeguarding the future for our Seniors and all American families.

1. *Protect Social Security*

Social Security is a lifeline for millions of Retirees, yet corrupt politicians have robbed Social Security to fund their pet projects. Republicans will restore Economic Stability to ensure the long-term sustainability of Social Security.

2. *Strengthen Medicare*

Republicans will protect Medicare's finances from being financially crushed by the Democrat plan to add tens of millions of new illegal immigrants to the rolls of Medicare. We vow to strengthen Medicare for future generations.

3. *Support Active and Healthy Living*

Republicans will support increased focus on Chronic Disease prevention and management, Long-Term Care, and Benefit flexibility. We will expand access to Primary Care and support Policies that help Seniors remain in their homes and maintain Financial Security.

4. *Protect Care at Home for the Elderly*

Republicans will shift resources back to at-home Senior Care, overturn disincentives that lead to Care Worker shortages, and support unpaid Family Caregivers through Tax Credits and reduced red tape.

5. *Protect Economic Foundations for Supporting Seniors*

Republicans will tackle Inflation, unleash American Energy, restore Economic Growth, and secure our Borders to preserve Social Security and Medicare funding for the next Generation and beyond. We will ensure these programs remain solvent long into the future by reversing harmful Democrat policies and unleashing a new Economic Boom.

CHAPTER SEVEN:
CULTIVATE GREAT K–12 SCHOOLS LEADING TO GREAT JOBS AND GREAT LIVES FOR YOUNG PEOPLE

Our Commitment:

Republicans offer a plan to cultivate great K–12 schools, ensure safe learning environments free from political meddling, and restore Parental Rights. We commit to an Education System that empowers students, supports families, and promotes American Values. Our Education System must prepare students for successful lives and well-paying jobs.

1. *Great Principals and Great Teachers*
   Republicans will support schools that focus on Excellence and Parental Rights. We will support ending Teacher Tenure, adopting Merit pay, and allowing various publicly supported Educational models.

2. *Universal School Choice*
   Republicans believe families should be empowered to choose the best Education for their children. We support Universal School Choice in every State in America. We will expand 529 Education Savings Accounts and support Homeschooling Families equally.

3. *Prepare Students for Jobs and Careers*
   Republicans will emphasize Education to prepare students for great jobs and careers, supporting project-based learning and schools that offer meaningful work experience. We will expose politicized education models and fund proven career training programs.

4. *Safe, Secure, and Drug-Free Schools*
   Republicans will support overhauling standards on school discipline, advocate for immediate suspension of violent students, and support hardening schools to help keep violence away from our places of learning.

5. *Restore Parental Rights*
   Republicans will restore Parental Rights in Education, and enforce our Civil Rights Laws to stop schools from discriminating on the basis of Race. We trust Parents!

6. *Knowledge and Skills, Not CRT and Gender Indoctrination*
   Republicans will ensure children are taught fundamentals like Reading, History, Science, and Math, not Leftwing propaganda. We will defund schools that engage in inappropriate political indoctrination of our children using Federal Taxpayer Dollars.

7. *Promote Love of Country with Authentic Civics Education*
   Republicans will reinstate the 1776 Commission, promote Fair and Patriotic Civics Education, and veto efforts to nationalize Civics Education. We will support schools that teach America's Founding Principles and Western Civilization.

8. *Freedom to Pray*
   Republicans will champion the First Amendment Right to Pray and Read the Bible in school, and stand up to those who violate the Religious Freedoms of American students.

9. *Return Education to the States*
   The United States spends more money per pupil on Education than any other Country in the World, and yet we are at the bottom of every educational list in terms of results. We are going to close the Department of Education in Washington, D.C., and send it back to the States, where it belongs, and let the States run our educational system as it should be run. Our Great Teachers, who are so important to the future well-being of our Country, will be cherished and protected by the Republican Party so that they can do the job of educating our students that they so dearly want to do. It is our goal to bring Education in the United States to the highest level, one that it has never attained before!

CHAPTER EIGHT:
BRING COMMON SENSE TO GOVERNMENT AND RENEW THE PILLARS OF AMERICAN CIVILIZATION

Our Commitment:

Republicans offer a plan to renew American Civilization with Common Sense Policies that supports families, restores Law and Order, cares for Veterans, promotes beauty, and honors American History. We commit to strengthening the Foundations of our Society for a brighter future.

1. *Empower American Families*

   Republicans will promote a Culture that values the Sanctity of Marriage, the blessings of childhood, the foundational role of families, and supports working parents. We will end policies that punish families.

2. *Rebuild Our Cities and Restore Law and Order*

   Republicans will restore safety in our neighborhoods by replenishing Police Departments, restoring Common Sense Policing, and protecting Officers from frivolous lawsuits. We will stand up to Marxist Prosecutors, vigorously defend the Right of every American to live in peace, and we will compassionately address homelessness to restore order to our streets.

3. *Make Washington, D.C., the Safest and Most Beautiful Capital City*

   Republicans will reassert greater Federal Control over Washington, D.C., to restore Law and Order in our Capital City, and ensure Federal Buildings and Monuments are well-maintained.

4. *Take Care of Our Veterans*

   Republicans will end luxury housing and Taxpayer benefits for Illegal Immigrants and use those savings to shelter and treat homeless Veterans. We will restore Trump Administration reforms to expand Veterans' Healthcare Choices, protect Whistleblowers, and hold accountable poorly performing employees not giving our Veterans the care they deserve.

5. *Make Colleges and Universities Sane and Affordable*

   Republicans will fire Radical Left accreditors, drive down Tuition costs, restore Due Process protections, and pursue Civil Rights cases against Schools that discriminate.

6. *Combat Antisemitism*

   Republicans condemn antisemitism, and support revoking Visas of Foreign Nationals who support terrorism and jihadism. We will hold accountable those who perpetrate violence against Jewish people.

7. *Overcome the Crisis in Liberal Arts Education*

   Republicans support the restoration of Classic Liberal Arts Education.

8. *Restore American Beauty*

   Republicans will promote beauty in Public Architecture and preserve our Natural Treasures. We will build cherished symbols of our Nation, and restore genuine Conservation efforts.

9. *Honor American History*

   Republicans celebrate our Great American Heroes and are proud that the Story of America makes everyone free. We will organize a National Celebration to mark the 250th Anniversary of the Founding of the United States of America.

CHAPTER NINE:
GOVERNMENT OF, BY, AND FOR THE PEOPLE

Our Commitment:

Republicans will offer a clear, precise, and USA oriented plan to stop the Radical Left Democrats' Weaponization of Government and its Assault on American Liberty. We will restore Government of, by, and for the People, ensuring Accountability, protecting Individual Liberties, and fixing our once very corrupt Elections. We commit to upholding the Constitution of the United States, appointing judges who respect the rule of law, and defending the Rights of all Americans to Life, Liberty, and the Pursuit of Happiness. We will maintain the Supreme Court as it was always meant to be, at 9 Justices. We will not allow the Democrat Party to increase this number, as they would like to do, by 4, 6, 8, 10, and even 12 Justices. We will block them at every turn.

1. *Republicans Will Stop Woke and Weaponized Government*
   We will hold accountable those who have misused the power of Government to unjustly prosecute their Political Opponents. We will declassify Government records, root out wrongdoers, and fire corrupt employees.
2. *Republicans Will Dismantle Censorship & Protect Free Speech*
   We will ban the Federal Government from colluding with anyone to censor Lawful Speech, defund institutions engaged in censorship, and hold accountable all bureaucrats involved with illegal censoring. We will protect Free Speech online.
3. *Republicans Will Defend Religious Liberty*
   We are the defenders of the First Amendment Right to Religious Liberty. It protects the Right not only to Worship

according to the dictates of Conscience, but also to act in accordance with those Beliefs, not just in places of Worship, but in everyday life. Our ranks include men and women from every Faith and Tradition, and we respect the Right of every American to follow his or her deeply held Beliefs. To protect Religious Liberty, Republicans support a new Federal Task Force on Fighting Anti-Christian Bias that will investigate all forms of illegal discrimination, harassment, and persecution against Christians in America.

4. *Republicans Will Protect and Defend a Vote of the People, from within the States, on the Issue of Life*
We proudly stand for families and Life. We believe that the 14th Amendment to the Constitution of the United States guarantees that no person can be denied Life or Liberty without Due Process, and that the States are, therefore, free to pass Laws protecting those Rights. After 51 years, because of us, that power has been given to the States and to a vote of the People. We will oppose Late Term Abortion, while supporting mothers and policies that advance Prenatal Care, access to Birth Control, and IVF (fertility treatments).

5. *Republicans Will End Left-wing Gender Insanity*
We will keep men out of women's sports, ban Taxpayer funding for sex change surgeries, and stop Taxpayer-funded Schools from promoting gender transition, reverse Biden's radical rewrite of Title IX Education Regulations, and restore protections for women and girls.

6. *Republicans Will Ensure Election Integrity*
We will implement measures to secure our Elections, including Voter ID, highly sophisticated paper ballots, proof of

Citizenship, and same day Voting. We will not allow the Democrats to give Voting Rights to illegal Aliens.

7. *Republicans Will Protect Americans in the Territories*
The territories of Guam, the Commonwealth of the Northern Mariana Islands, American Samoa, the U.S. Virgin Islands, and Puerto Rico are of vital importance to our National Security, and we welcome their greater participation in all aspects of the political process.

CHAPTER TEN:
RETURN TO PEACE THROUGH STRENGTH

Our Commitment:

Keeping the American People safe requires a strong America. The Biden administration's weak Foreign Policy has made us less safe and a laughingstock all over the World. The Republican Plan is to return Peace through Strength, rebuilding our Military and Alliances, countering China, defeating terrorism, building an Iron Dome Missile Defense Shield, promoting American Values, securing our Homeland and Borders, and reviving our Defense Industrial Base. We will build a Military bigger, better, and stronger than ever before. Our full commitment is to protecting America and ensuring a safe and prosperous future for all.

1. *The National Interest*
Republicans will promote a Foreign Policy centered on the most essential American Interests, starting with protecting the American Homeland, our People, our Borders, our Great American Flag, and our Rights under God.

2. *Modernize the Military*

Republicans will ensure our Military is the most modern, lethal and powerful Force in the World. We will invest in cutting-edge research and advanced technologies, including an Iron Dome Missile Defense Shield, support our Troops with higher pay, and get woke Leftwing Democrats fired as soon as possible.

3. *Strengthen Alliances*

Republicans will strengthen Alliances by ensuring that our Allies must meet their obligations to invest in our Common Defense and by restoring Peace to Europe. We will stand with Israel, and seek peace in the Middle East. We will rebuild our Alliance Network in the Region to ensure a future of Peace, Stability, and Prosperity. Likewise, we will champion Strong, Sovereign, and Independent Nations in the Indo-Pacific, thriving in Peace and Commerce with others.

4. *Strengthen Economic, Military, and Diplomatic Capabilities*

Republicans will strengthen Economic, Military, and Diplomatic capabilities to protect the American way of life from the malign influences of Countries that stand against us around the World.

5. *Defend America's Borders*

Against all odds, President Trump has completed Hundreds of Miles of Wall, and he will quickly finish the job. Republicans will mobilize Military personnel and assets as necessary to crack down hard on the cartels that traffic drugs and people into our Country.

6. *Revive our Industrial Base*

Our Industrial Base is critical to ensuring good jobs for our people but also the reliable production of vital Defense platforms and supplies. Our Policy must be to revive our Industrial Base, with priority on Defense-critical industries. Equipment and parts critical to American Security must be MADE IN THE USA.

7. *Protect Critical Infrastructure*

Republicans will use all tools of National Power to protect our Nation's Critical Infrastructure and Industrial Base from malicious cyber actors. This will be a National Priority, and we will both raise the Security Standards for our Critical Systems and Networks and defend them against bad actors.

NOTES

CHAPTER 1: TRIUMPH

1. Associated Press. "Russia's War in Ukraine Overshadows Other Global Events at the G-20 Summit." AP News, November 15, 2022. https://apnews.com /article/russia-ukraine-2022-midterm-elections-business-elections-presidential -elections-5468774d18e8c46f81b55e9260b13e93/.

CHAPTER 2: KAMALA'S COLLAPSE

1. Yzola, Alana. "Black Sororities and Fraternities Are Mobilizing Online and in Secret Chats for Voter Turnout." *Wired*, August 13, 2024. https://www.wired .com/story/black-sororities-and-fraternities-mobilizing-online-voting/.

2. McDermott, Mara. "Minnesota's 'Tampon Law' Requires Free Period Products in Public Schools." NPR, August 7, 2024. https://www.npr.org/2024/08/07/nx -s1-5066878/tim-walz-tampon-law-minnesota/.

3. Associated Press. "Tim Walz Makes Misleading Claims Related to Tiananmen Massacre." AP News, October 6, 2024. https://apnews.com/article/walz-china -tiananmen-square-protests-8d433bf7184e8c430aa31d1f5460fe87/.

4. CBS News Minnesota. "Tim Walz Pressed About 2018 'Weapons of War' Statement in CNN Interview." CBS News, September 14, 2024. https:// www.cbsnews.com/minnesota/news/tim-walz-cnn-interview-military-service -weapons-of-war/.

5. Politico. "Walz Downplays Past False Statements in Rare Interview." October 6, 2024. https://www.politico.com/news/2024/10/06/tim-walz-fox-tv-interview -00182620/.

6. Svitek, Patrick. "On Differences with Biden, Harris Says 'Not a Thing That Comes to Mind.'" *The Washington Post*, October 8, 2024. https://www .washingtonpost.com/politics/2024/10/08/harris-biden-differences-view -howard-stern/.

7. Gilmour, David. "'I Find That Guy Very Funny': Jon Stewart Defends Trump Rally Roast Comedian Tony Hinchcliffe for 'Doing What He Does.'" Mediaite,

October 29, 2024. https://www.mediaite.com/tv/i-find-that-guy-very-funny
-jon-stewart-defends-trump-rally-roast-comedian-tony-hinchcliffe-for-doing
-what-he-does/.

CHAPTER 4: GOVERNING VS. CAMPAIGNING

1. Guelzo, Allen C., "'Public Sentiment Is Everything': Abraham Lincoln and the
    Power of Public Opinion," in Lucas E. Morel, ed., *Lincoln and Liberty: Wisdom
    for the Ages* (Lexington: University Press of Kentucky, 2014).

CHAPTER 5: MAKE AMERICA AFFORDABLE AGAIN

1. Kreil, Erik. "United States Produces More Crude Oil than Any Country,
    Ever—U.S. Energy Information Administration (EIA)." U.S. Energy
    Information Administration, March 11, 2024. https://www.eia.gov
    /todayinenergy/detail.php?id=61545.

2. Soraghan, Mike. "4 Things Trump Can—and Can't—Do to Boost Oil and
    Gas." E&E News by Politico, November 19, 2024. https://www.eenews.net
    /articles/4-things-trump-can-and-cant-do-to-boost-oil-and-gas/.

3. Storrow, Benjamin, and E&E News. "Coal Is Bad for the Environment. Is
    Liquified Natural Gas Any Better?" *Scientific American*, February 6, 2024.
    https://www.scientificamerican.com/article/coal-is-bad-for-the-environment-is
    -liquified-natural-gas-any-better/.

4. Statista. "U.S. Average Gas Prices by Year 1990-2018." Statista, 2018. https://
    www.statista.com/statistics/204740/retail-price-of-gasoline-in-the-united-states
    -since-1990/.

5. AAA. "Fuel Prices." 2022. https://gasprices.aaa.com/.

6. Musk, Elon. "Elon Musk and Vivek Ramaswamy: The DOGE Plan to Reform
    Government." *The Wall Street Journal*, November 20, 2024. https://www.wsj
    .com/opinion/musk-and-ramaswamy-the-doge-plan-to-reform-government
    -supreme-court-guidance-end-executive-power-grab-fa51c020.

7. Government Accountability Office. "Medicare and Medicaid: Additional
    Actions Needed to Enhance Program Integrity and Save Billions." April 16,
    2024. https://www.gao.gov/products/gao-24-107487.

8. Committee for a Responsible Federal Budget. "Reversing Biden Executive
    Actions Could Save up to $1.4 Trillion." November 26, 2024. https://www.crfb
    .org/blogs/reversing-biden-executive-actions-could-save-14-trillion.

9. Boehm, Eric. "The National Debt Just Hit $36 Trillion. Where Is Trump's
    Plan to Control It?" Reason, November 15, 2024. https://reason.com/2024/11
    /15/the-national-debt-just-hit-36-trillion-does-trump-have-a-plan-to-control-it/.

10. Heckman, Jory. "Agencies' Headquarters in DC Remained 'Nearly Empty' in 2023, Real-Estate Board Finds." Federal News Network, April 22, 2024. https://federalnewsnetwork.com/facilities-construction/2024/04/agencies -headquarters-in-dc-remained-nearly-empty-in-2023-real-estate-board-finds/.

11. Moore, Stephen. "No, Bill Clinton Didn't Balance the Budget." Cato Institute, October 8, 1998. https://www.cato.org/commentary/no-bill-clinton-didnt -balance-budget.

12. Foster, J. D. "Tax Cuts, Not the Clinton Tax Hike, Produced the 1990s Boom." The Heritage Foundation, March 8, 2008. https://www.heritage.org/taxes /report/tax-cuts-not-the-clinton-tax-hike-produced-the-1990s-boom.

13. House Budget Committee. "Smith on Five-Year Anniversary of Tax Cuts and Jobs Act: Republican Tax Relief Delivered for American Families." December 22, 2022. https://budget.house.gov/press-release/smith-on-five-year-anniversary -of-tax-cuts-and-jobs-act-republican-tax-relief-delivered-for-american-families/.

14. Greenberg, Scott. "Pass-through Businesses: Data and Policy." Tax Foundation, May 3, 2024. https://taxfoundation.org/research/all/federal/pass-through -businesses-data-and-policy/.

15. Committee for a Responsible Federal Budget. "Donald Trump's Suggestion to End Taxation of Social Security Benefits." July 31, 2024. https://www.crfb.org /blogs/donald-trumps-suggestion-end-taxation-social-security-benefits.

16. The White House. "The Child Tax Credit." 2021. https://www.whitehouse .gov/child-tax-credit/.

CHAPTER 6: AMERICANS AND IMMIGRATION

1. The White House. "Securing Our Borders." January 21, 2025. https://www .whitehouse.gov/presidential-actions/2025/01/securing-our-borders/.

2. The White House. "Declaring a National Emergency at the Southern Border of the United States." January 21, 2025. https://www.whitehouse.gov/presidential -actions/2025/01/declaring-a-national-emergency-at-the-southern-border-of-the -united-states/.

3. The White House. "Guaranteeing the States Protection Against Invasion." January 21, 2025. https://www.whitehouse.gov/presidential-actions/2025/01 /guaranteeing-the-states-protection-against-invasion/.

4. The White House. "Clarifying the Military's Role in Protecting the Territorial Integrity of the United States." January 21, 2025. https://www.whitehouse.gov /presidential-actions/2025/01/clarifying-the-militarys-role-in-protecting-the -territorial-integrity-of-the-united-states/.

5. The White House. "Protecting the American People Against Invasion." January 21, 2025. https://www.whitehouse.gov/presidential-actions/2025/01/protecting-the-american-people-against-invasion/.

6. The White House. "Protecting the United States from Foreign Terrorists and Other National Security and Public Safety Threats." January 21, 2025. https://www.whitehouse.gov/presidential-actions/2025/01/protecting-the-united-states-from-foreign-terrorists-and-othernational-security-and-public-safety-threats/.

7. The White House. "Designating Cartels and Other Organizations as Foreign Terrorist Organizations and Specially Designated Global Terrorists." January 21, 2025. https://www.whitehouse.gov/presidential-actions/2025/01/designating-cartels-and-other-organizations-as-foreign-terrorist-organizations-and-specially-designated-global-terrorists/.

8. FWD.us. "New Poll: Overwhelming Majority of U.S. Voters Across Political Spectrum Support Legislation for Dreamers Paired with Border Security." October 27, 2022. https://www.fwd.us/news/new-poll-overwhelming-majority-of-u-s-voters-across-political-spectrum-support-legislation-for-dreamers-paired-with-border-security/.

9. Tenser, Phil. "Majority Supports Path to Citizenship for Dreamers, Undocumented Migrants, UMass-Amherst/WCVB Poll Finds." WCVB, February 14, 2024. https://www.wcvb.com/article/immigration-policy-umass-amherst-wcvb-national-poll/46773078.

CHAPTER 7: ENTREPRENEURIAL GOVERNMENT

1. Papst, Chris. "At 13 Baltimore City High Schools, Zero Students Tested Proficient on 2023 State Math Exam." WBFF, 2023. https://foxbaltimore.com/news/project-baltimore/at-13-baltimore-city-high-schools-zero-students-tested-proficient-on-2023-state-math-exam.

CHAPTER 8: EDUCATION FOR SURVIVAL

1. Papst, Chris. "At 13 Baltimore City High Schools, Zero Students Tested Proficient on 2023 State Math Exam." WBFF, 2023. https://foxbaltimore.com/news/project-baltimore/at-13-baltimore-city-high-schools-zero-students-tested-proficient-on-2023-state-math-exam.

2. Gorman, Linda. "Education." Econlib, n.d. https://www.econlib.org/library/Enc/Education.html.

3. Monticello. "If We Are to Guard Against Ignorance... (Spurious Quotation)," n.d. https://www.monticello.org/research-education/thomas-jefferson-encyclopedia/if-we-are-guard-against-ignorance-spurious-quotation/.

4. Lucco, Joseph. "The Eisenhower Principle in Business Strategy Management." ClearPoint Strategy, August 19, 2024. https://www.clearpointstrategy.com/blog/eisenhower-principle-and-business-strategy-management.

5. National Literacy Institute. "Literacy Statistics 2022–2023." March 7, 2024. https://www.thenationalliteracyinstitute.com/post/literacy-statistics-2022 -2023.

6. PBS. "John Gardner: Uncommon American." 2024. https://www.pbs.org /johngardner/sections/writings.html.

CHAPTER 9: THE ENORMOUS CHALLENGE OF HEALTH AND HEALTH CARE IN AMERICA

1. Gingrich, Newt. "Newt Gingrich: Don't Let Lobbyists Raise Health Costs." *USA Today*, March 30, 2016. https://www.usatoday.com/story/opinion/2016/03 /30/newt-gingrich-telemedicine-technology-eye-tests-lobbying/82395420/.

2. HealthCare.gov. "Health Domains Are Now Available." 2020. https://www .healthcare.gov/preventive-care-adults/.

3. Ornish, D., and A. Ornish. *UnDo It.* New York, NY: Random House, 2019.

4. Silberman, Anna, Rajni Banthia, Ivette S. Estay, Colleen Kemp, Joli Studley, Dennis Hareras, and Dean Ornish. "The Effectiveness and Efficacy of an Intensive Cardiac Rehabilitation Program in 24 Sites." *American Journal of Health Promotion*, March 1, 2010: 260–66. https://pubmed.ncbi.nlm.nih.gov /20232608/.

5. Preventative Medicine Research Institute. "Lifestyle Changes Significantly Improve Cognition and Function in Early Alzheimer's Disease for the First Time in a Randomized Controlled Trial." PR Newswire, June 7, 2024. https:// www.prnewswire.com/news-releases/lifestyle-changes-significantly-improve -cognition-and-function-in-early-alzheimers-disease-for-the-first-time-in -a-randomized-controlled-trial-302166826.html.

6. Johnson, Kevin B., Wei-Qi Wei, Dilhan Weeraratne, Mark E. Frisse, Karl Misulis, Kyu Rhee, Juan Zhao, and Jane L. Snowdon. "Precision Medicine, AI, and the Future of Personalized Health Care." *Clinical and Translational Science*, October 12, 2020. https://pmc.ncbi.nlm.nih.gov/articles/PMC7877825/.

7. Association of Health Care Journalists. "Hospital Mergers and Health Care Price Increases: A Primer for Reporters." September 24, 2024. https:// healthjournalism.org/blog/2024/09/hospital-mergers-and-health-care-price -increases-a-primer-for-reporters/.

8. Wainer, David. "How American Health Insurance Got So Infuriating." *The Wall Street Journal*, December 20, 2024. https://www.wsj.com/health /healthcare/american-health-insurance-denials-4f09c751.

9. Tessier, Melissa. "Medicine Has Changed: 63% of Physicians Don't Want Their Children to Work in Medicine According to New Doximity Poll." Doximity, 2024. https://opmed.doximity.com/articles/medicine-has-changed-63-of -physicians-don-t-want-their-children-to-work-in-medicine-according-to-new -doximity-poll.

10. Weaver, Christopher. "How Health Insurers Racked Up Billions in Extra Payments from Medicare Advantage." *The Wall Street Journal*, January 2, 2025. https://www.wsj.com/health/healthcare/how-health-insurers-racked-up-billions -in-extra-payments-from-medicare-advantage-9d4c8a89.

11. Weaver. "How Health Insurers Racked Up Billions in Extra Payments from Medicare Advantage."

12. Tabarrok, Alex. "Are Health Administrators to Blame?" Marginal Revolution, August 17, 2019. https://marginalrevolution.com/marginalrevolution/2019/08 /are-health-administrators-to-blame.html.

13. Turquoise Health. "'Is Price Transparency Helping?' White Paper." 2021. https://hey.turquoise.health/is-price-transparency-helping-white-paper/.

14. Grogan, Joseph. "The Inflation Reduction Act Is Already Killing Potential Cures." USC Schaeffer, November 3, 2022. https://healthpolicy.usc.edu/article /the-inflation-reduction-act-is-already-killing-potential-cures/.

CHAPTER 10: SECURITY TO SURVIVAL

1. Kennan, George F. "The Sources of Soviet Conduct." Foreign Affairs, July 1, 1947. https://www.foreignaffairs.com/russian-federation/george-kennan-sources -soviet-conduct.

2. Kaplan, Robert D. "The Coming Anarchy." *The Atlantic*, February 1994. https://www.theatlantic.com/magazine/archive/1994/02/the-coming-anarchy /304670/.

CHAPTER 11: A DEFENSE SYSTEM THAT WORKS

1. Eisenhower, Dwight D. "Text of the Address by President Eisenhower, Broadcast and Televised from His Office in the White House, Tuesday Evening, January 17, 1961, 8:30 to 9:00 p.m., EST." January 17, 1961. https:// www.eisenhowerlibrary.gov/sites/default/files/research/online-documents /farewell-address/1961-01-17-press-release.pdf.

2. Smith, Adam. "Chapter X: On Wages and Profit in the Different Employments of Labour and Stock: Inequalities by the Policy of Europe." In *The Wealth of Nations*, 1776.

3. McHugh, Francis J. "Gaming at the Naval War College." U.S. Naval Institute, March 1964. https://www.usni.org/magazines/proceedings/1964/march /gaming-naval-war-college.

CHAPTER 13: AMERICANS IN SPACE

1. Bloomberg, Michael R. "NASA's $100 Bn Moon Mission: A Boondoggle or the Future of Space Exploration?" *The Economic Times*, October 17, 2024. https://economictimes.indiatimes.com/news/science/nasas-100-bn-moon-mission-a-boondoggle-or-the-future-of-space-exploration/articleshow/114312891.cms?from=mdr.

2. The White House. "National Bioeconomy Blueprint." April 2012. https://obamawhitehouse.archives.gov/sites/default/files/microsites/ostp/national_bioeconomy_blueprint_april_2012.pdf.

3. Vorobets, Mark V. "Interview with Lynn Rothschild from Planetary Systems Branch." NASA, April 30, 2020. https://www.nasa.gov/general/interview-with-lynn-rothschild-from-planetary-systems-branch/.

4. Carter, Jamie. "There May Be Water on Psyche, the Asteroid 'Worth $10,000 Quadrillion.'" *Forbes*, August 22, 2024. https://www.forbes.com/sites/jamiecartereurope/2024/08/22/there-may-be-water-on-psyche-the-asteroid-worth-10000-quadrillion/.

ABOUT THE AUTHOR

NEWT GINGRICH is a former Speaker of the U.S. House of Representatives and 2012 presidential candidate. He is chairman of Gingrich 360, a multimedia production and consulting company based in Arlington, Virginia. He is also a Fox News contributor and author of 44 books, including national bestsellers *March to the Majority, Defeating Big Government Socialism, Beyond Biden,* and *Trump and the American Future.* He lives in Naples, Florida, and McLean, Virginia, with his wife, Callista L. Gingrich, former U.S. ambassador to the Holy See.